PRAISE FOR ROY BLOUNT JR.

"[Blount] knows from rhythm and melody. His prose can sing in deft comic riffs."   —ROBERT PINSKY, *The New York Times Book Review*

"Reading . . . Roy Blount Jr. is like panning for gold at Tiffany's—you know the nuggets will be there, the only question is their brilliance."
—DAVID E. JONES, *Chicago Tribune*

"Roy Blount Jr. is smart and witty, no matter what subject he tackles."
—MARILYN DAHL, *Shelf Awareness*

"Pithy and cleverly entertaining . . . Blount revels in unabashed om-nivorism . . . Blount's southern upbringing takes center stage as he smacks his lips and his prose."   —MARK KNOBLAUCH, *Booklist*

"You'd be pulling off a major stunt / To hold in your laughter while read-ing Roy Blount."   —DENNIS DRABELLE, *The Washington Post*

"Roy Blount Jr. is one of the most clever (see sly, witty, cunning, nimble) wordsmiths cavorting in the English language, or what remains of it."
—CARL HIAASEN, author of *Bad Monkey*

"[Roy Blount Jr.'s] many columns celebrating food can cause a reader to salivate."   —MERRITT MOSELEY, *Sewanee Review*

"Roy Blount Jr. is so funny, and he sounds like he's just talking, and the next thing you know he has tossed off an essay as elegant and intri-cately structured as a birdsong. His ear for American speech is better than anybody's."   —IAN FRAZIER

"Danced in Blount's arms, English swings smartly."
—JACK SHAFER, *The New York Times Book Review*

Joan Griswold

ROY BLOUNT JR.

Save Room for Pie

Roy Blount Jr. is the author of twenty-four books, covering subjects from the Pittsburgh Steelers to what dogs are thinking to the ins and outs of etymology. He is a regular panelist on NPR's *Wait Wait . . . Don't Tell Me!*, a member of the American Heritage Dictionary Usage Panel, and a member of the Fellowship of Southern Writers. Born in Indianapolis and raised in Decatur, Georgia, he now divides his time between New Orleans and western Massachusetts with his wife, the painter Joan Griswold, and their cat, Jimmy.

Save Room
for Pie

Save Room for Pie

FOOD SONGS
AND CHEWY RUMINATIONS

ROY BLOUNT JR.

SARAH CRICHTON BOOKS

FARRAR, STRAUS AND GIROUX   NEW YORK

Sarah Crichton Books
Farrar, Straus and Giroux
18 West 18th Street, New York 10011

Grateful acknowledgment is made for permission to reprint the following material:
Excerpts from pages xii, xiii, ix, x, xi, xiv, and xv [1472 words] of *Am I Pig Enough for You Yet? Voices of the Barnyard* by Valerie Shaff and Roy Blount Jr. Copyright © 2001 by Valerie Shaff and Roy Blount Jr. Reprinted by permission of HarperCollins Publishers. Excerpts from the book *Camels Are Easy, Comedy's Hard* by Roy Blount Jr. Copyright © 1991 by Roy Blount Jr. Used with the permission of Open Road Integrated Media, Inc. Excerpts from the book *Crackers* by Roy Blount Jr. Copyright © 1977, 1979, 1980 by Roy Blount Jr. Used with the permission of Open Road Integrated Media, Inc. Excerpts from the book *Not Exactly What I Had in Mind* by Roy Blount Jr. Copyright © 1967, 1968, 1970, 1974, 1975, 1976, 1977, 1978, 1980, 1981, 1982 by Roy Blount Jr. Used with the permission of Open Road Integrated Media, Inc. Excerpts from the book *What Men Don't Tell Women* by Roy Blount Jr. Copyright © 1984 by Roy Blount Jr. Used with the permission of Open Road Integrated Media, Inc. Excerpts from the book *One Fell Soup* by Roy Blount Jr. Copyright © 1991 by Roy Blount Jr. Used with the permission of Open Road Integrated Media, Inc.

The Library of Congress has cataloged the hardcover edition as follows:
Blount, Roy, Jr., 1941 — author.
[Works. Selections]
Save room for pie : food songs and chewy ruminations / Roy Blount, Jr. — First edition.
    pages   cm
Includes bibliographical references.
ISBN 978-0-374-17520-7 (hardcover) — ISBN 978-0-374-71288-4 (e-book)
1. Food—Anecdotes.   2. Food in literature.   3. Blount, Roy, Jr., 1941—Anecdotes. I. Title.

TX355.5.B56 2016
641.3—dc23

2015036049

Paperback ISBN: 978-0-374-53688-6

Designed by Abby Kagan
Hand-lettering by Barry Blitt

www.fsgbooks.com
www.twitter.com/fsgbooks • www.facebook.com/fsgbooks

For Joan.

Mmmmm-*m*.

Good food is real, it's healthy, it's produced sustainably,
it's fair and it's affordable.
—MARK BITTMAN, *The New York Times*

He had heard the roots tearing as he eased
a carrot out of the ground.
—EDWARD ST. AUBYN, *Bad News*

If you're going to have fried chicken, have fried chicken.
—MICHELLE OBAMA'S MOM

TABLE D'CONTENTS

AUTHOR'S NOTE

The reader will find scattered through the text of this book, like lovely flecks of onion in the meat loaf, a number of inserts: tiny bits of verse, brief personal anecdotes, and what appear to be news items. Most of the news items are ones I composed, over the years, for the "Bluff the Listener" segment of National Public Radio's *Wait Wait . . . Don't Tell Me!*, on which I appear frequently as a panelist. Four of these are versions of items that actually appeared in the news. (*Want to guess? Then don't read the next sentence.*) These four involve pie throwing in Canada, the dairy herds of Cuba, copper wires up your nose, and Christ in jeans and T-shirt. If you were a caller on the show and picked one of those items to be real, you would have won Carl Kasell's voice on your answering machine. All the other items are fictional. If you picked any of those (*really?*), I apologize. The other parts of this book (with a few, I think, obvious exceptions) strive to be factual. Many of them started out as columns for *Garden & Gun* magazine. —RB

PART ONE

WHY I EAT

IT'S GOOD TO EAT

My wife, Joan, and I live partly in rural western Massachusetts, where one minute people are discussing the different tastes of bear (very strong) and woodchuck—I guess you don't ever want to try muskrat, though people do—and the next minute the topic turns to whether turmeric has to be organic. Just the other night in the midst of a hearty meal, we were Googling to see how much more nutritious sesame seeds are with the hulls on than with them off. Not a simple matter, because while the hulls do have food value they also contain—never mind. I try to keep things light by asking how *many* sesame seeds you should take daily. But these are, after all, matters of life and death.

Speaking of which, I heard the other day that Google has a task force working on an end to death. Not Google's death, people's. If eternal life is anything like teen sex (probably not, come to think of it), it will no doubt come along too late for me. But let's say I get the message, through Gmail: "Hooray, immortality is here! Click for two weeks free." And I don't reply right away. Google, again: "Grateful? No? What *else* do you want?"

"Everybody has their own ideas of paradise. Ours is very traditional," says Philo Merriday, resident manager of a motel and theme park outside Gatlinburg, Tennessee, known as Heaven on Earth. According to a review this week on FamilyDestinations.com (three stars out of five), Heaven on Earth strives to give guests a foretaste of glory divine. Instead of a pool, Heaven on Earth has a cloud—a gauzy expanse that the reviewer, after lying on it in a long white gown, found "relaxing." Harp music is piped in, and guests are encouraged to play along on instruments provided on a basis of first come, first served. Attendants passing out complimentary ambrosia and angel food cake are not winged but are otherwise celestially attired, and guests may experience sensations of flying by hooking up to cables on a loop around the complex. No religious services are held. "We're nondenominational," says Merriday. "Anyway, church in heaven would be gilding the lily. We want you to feel that you're *there*."

Here is my response: "Mashed potatoes with that. And gravy."

Because there will be a catch. To live forever, I'll have to give up food, except for Googruel or Gvittles or whatever they're going to call the only sustenance you can live on forever. Maybe something virtual, you don't even get to chew. And I'll have to think long and hard.

I grew up on food, among people who were devoted to the joy of getting plenty of it. Some years ago, I visited Mel Blount, the great Pittsburgh Steeler cornerback, on his family farm in Vidalia, Georgia, and wrote this:

> "Keep 'em fed," Mel's father used to say about his offspring. "Keep 'em fed and they'll work." They're still working—for instance, tossing a crop of fifty- or sixty-pound watermelons along a family bucket-brigade line ("And you can't stop") to load them into a truck. And every time I walked into Mel's mother's house, she, Alice Blount—at 9:00 a.m., 11:30 a.m., 4:30 p.m., or 9:30 p.m.—she was putting fried chicken, stewed chicken, butter beans, soupy white lima beans, grits, gravy, corn bread, rice, mashed potatoes, thick-sliced bacon, collard greens, biscuits, ham, black-eyed peas, sweet iced tea, and hot sauce onto the table and saying, "Y'all about let it get cold." When I start eating food like that, it takes me back to when I was fourteen, could eat steadily for hours with impunity, and figured I'd be a sports immortal myself. Inside every thin Southern person is a fat person signaling to get out. Mine has partially emerged, as has Mel's brother Bobby's. One night Bobby leaned back from the table, slapped his stomach proprietarily with both hands, and said, "Roy, this is all the savings I got." Mel has had the football glory, but Bobby (who some say was the best athlete in the family) may well have had more food, and he seems pleased with his end of the deal.

If Google can arrange something like that in perpetuity, farm to table, I'm in. Doesn't have to be soul food, as long as it's good. In a lifetime of eating, I have savored Madhur Jaffrey's home cooking, Donald Link's prizewinning hot tamales (I was a judge), and an eight-course banquet in the Palace of Versailles. And see "What We Ate in Japan."

As to *healthful* eating, I take a positive approach. When I hear that something I like is good for me or anyway better than something else (for instance, that Velveeta has more protein and fewer bad fats than many real cheeses, because it is largely whey), I say, "*Hey!* Let's see if we have some in the fridge." (To mix with RO*TEL. I wouldn't eat Velveeta without mixing it with something containing an asterisk.) When I hear that something I like is *not* so good (for instance, that Velveeta is rich in sodium), I say, "Let us not rush to judgment."

And there is room for positivity today. It may not last (remember when bread, *with gluten*, was the staff of life?), but lately I have heard good things, from authorities recognized by my wife, about watermelon, avocado, egg yolk, cane syrup, okra, lard, oysters, beef (if raised right), whiskey, hot peppers, coffee, (dark) chocolate, butter!

Butter! Not margarine, no, *p'tooey*, and none of your quasi-buttery "spreads," but actual, cow-given butter:

> Bananas are yellow in their season.
> Butter is always. And better on peas, on
> Toast, on corn bread, on corn on the cob.
> A baked potato begins to throb
> With life, with juice when butter melts
> Down, down into each crevice and . . .
> Oh! Nothing elts
> Melts the way butter melts.
> Truer words were never uttered:
> Anything good is better buttered.

But we can't be complacent about food. As we learn from the media that mice don't really like cheese, milk doesn't suit cats, elephants aren't partial to peanuts (I worked with one, though, who loved M&M's), dogs shouldn't be given bones (unless they're raw, and who keeps raw bones around?), and bananas (as we know them outside the rain forest) are bad for monkeys, we realize that our timeworn conceptions need to be shaken up. You know the expression "acquired taste"? It's a sneer, is what it is. I once heard George Will, on television, refer to Michael Jackson (his *music* I mean) as "an acquired taste." Michael Jackson? Moonwalking? ("Walking backwards forwards," as someone described it, or maybe the other way around.) Either you can't help deriving at least some fleeting enjoyment from that weird little dervish's work, or you can be determined not to: acquired distaste. In today's changing food environment, you're crazy not to acquire tastes. I have gone so far as to acquire one for kale.

Like many people, I got my back up against kale. I had been eating other greens regularly and naturally for years and years and years when, boom, kale was the new manna. So was kimchi, but kimchi was a discovery for me (I thought you had to find it where I had found it, in a Korean grocery in Queens, New York), and it was fermented (hey-hey!). The other night at a place in the Bywater neighborhood of New Orleans called Booty's, which serves street food from around the world, I had a kimchi pancake with pork-belly hash that made me want to shout.

Kale, though, had been around, lurking in the background, and in fact I had enjoyed it as the original green in a Portuguese soup that I went on to make myself: using red beans, canned tomatoes, chorizo sausage (which conspire, those three, in a cloudy liquor), chopped onions, and fresh collard greens. We grow collard greens (and in Massachusetts they don't get gritty, somehow). Some people look down on collard greens, so more collard greens for me. Who *needs* kale? was my feeling. But then the other night Joan fried some kale just long enough in a little olive oil with a sprinkling of parmesan, and bingo: a chew that I have to rank (see "Song to Ribs," "Song to a Nice Baked Potata") among the best chews in my experience. And it's healthy, which is fine with me.

I can also *eschew* with enthusiasm. I do have a weakness for frozen waffles and saltine crackers (oyster crackers even more) and the "mixed-fruit jelly" that you get in a diner (the tublets it comes in should be bigger, though, and more squeez-

In Salem, Oregon, police who stopped a car being driven erratically grew suspicious when they detected no smell of alcohol and the teenage driver volunteered to take a sobriety test yet seemed to be high on something. They noticed eight empty packets of nondairy creamer on the floor of the car. "Okay!" the driver said. "I was snorting it. It's legal. Everybody I know is doing it." Puzzled experts say nondairy creamer has no known narcotic effect, but, as one put it, "If you snort eight packets of anything, you have a problem."

able so you don't lose so much in the corners). But "nondairy creamer" will never pass my lips. Nor Hostess Twinkies, nor Hot Pockets.

Indeed we keep an organic garden, which last summer produced five small but delicious fresh-picked ears of corn, alone. (And a bumper crop, thanks to the Missus, of kale.) When Joan is out of town, and I'm tempted to slip away from the organic grocery section, I feel adulterous (see "Steak, Environmentally"), and not in a good way. But where I come from, the worst thing you can be toward food is persnickety. Eating *primarily* for health is too much like marrying for money. In other words, it's not completely crazy, but unless a meal or a relationship commences with *yum*, I don't see it going anywhere.

And how can anybody keep up with what we should and shouldn't eat? I notice that people who used to say, "They say," with regard to what they've heard is deadly or not, are now saying, "What they're saying is . . ." They used to say lots of fruits, things like groats, and scratchy bread:

> "People who eat
> Wonder bread
> Must be underbred.
> Did no one explain
> About whole grain?"
> —Say the elite.

> So *their* childhood
> Did not include
> Tomato slice red
> As a harlot's lip
> On Wonder bread
> With Miracle Whip?

At the moment, as I write this, I'm being advised that the only way to avoid eating yourself into an early grave (too late for me, *ha!*) is to eschew grains—and all other carbohydrates, including orange juice for God's sake—and get plenty of good healthy (not trans-) fat. Well, I'm not going to give up orange juice, but I hear the part about fat.

Breath is nice,
And some love vice,
And I'm a bear for reading,
But all of these,
Without some peas
Or onions, fall exceeding-
Ly short of feeding.

The human hand
And eye are grand
(Trained or amateurish),
But none of these,
Without some cheese
Or toast that's warm and *beurre*ish
Really nourish.

So much talk
Today of walk-
Ing, running, sweat, and sleekness!
Let me stress:
Some fat, unless
You're riding in the Preakness,
Is no weakness.

Suet in you,
Just like sinew,
Throbs with tonic value.
All the weight
From what you ate
That *tasted* great
Will resonate
Like turtledove timbale, you
Bet. So sing the food chorale (eu-
Peptic musicale), you
Hungry guy or gal, you.
Salut!

That's where I'm coming from. And am I a butterball? "For a man of your age," someone said to me the other day, "how do you manage not to be any more paunchy than you are?" He was a friend of mine, and was about to ask a favor, but the next day (in Felix's

Once my then girlfriend (now wife), Joan, and I shared a banquet dais with Mike Wallace of *60 Minutes*. He was a powerful presence, as may be imagined. At one point, he reached over and ate, without asking, the glaze off Joan's crème caramel.

I was not aware of this at the time. If I had been, I would have hurriedly eaten the glaze off mine.

But it must have been legal, *droit de TV*.

oyster bar in New Orleans) I heard something along the same lines from a complete stranger—whom I had asked for a favor. "Could you pass the horseradish?" I said.

"You going to eat all two dozen of them?" she asked. "You're like an uncle of mine. And he's dead. You're not even all that fat."

I may be too thick in the middle to be a TV personality (on the radio, people have told me, I sound more portly than I am) or to live in certain parts of California, but you accept all that, and life goes on. My height, I have been told, should be twice my waist measurement. At my point in life, I am in fact settling slightly. In a doctor's office, I have to stretch to reach my definitive height of six feet even. I can hardly be expected, at this stage, to grow four inches taller. If I thought I could learn to dance the Lindy Hop really well, I would consider going into training. But as a man in Clarksdale, Mississippi, once told me on the radio, "I'm seventy-three years old *already*." We were eating fried catfish at the time. I hope people in Clarksdale, Mississippi, still eat fried catfish on the radio.

When I met Satchel Paige, the immortal baseball pitcher, he was openly eating a piece of fried chicken. "But," I said to him, "I thought you said, 'Avoid fried foods, because they angry up the blood.'" That remark had, after all, been famously attributed to him. "I said avoid 'em," he said. "I didn't say *I* avoided 'em." With that in mind, here are some guidelines.

Guideline 1

Eat less gravy than you want. Wait—consider this: you *can't*, possibly, eat *as much* gravy as you want. A book titled *Favorite Recipes, Favorite Sayings* by Mary Howard Shelfer Morgan, of Tallahassee, Florida, quotes a wise saying by First Lieutenant William Howard Shelfer (1917–44), whom I infer to be her father or uncle who died in the war: "The only way to have enough gravy is to funnel it down from the attic through a hose." Eating *less* gravy than you want, therefore, is feasible on the face of it. It will also enable you to eat less mashed potatoes, or whatever you were going to put the gravy on, than you thought you wanted.

Codicil to Guideline 1
After five potato chips, you are just trying to reclaim the glory of the first two—*and you know it.*

Guideline 2
Never eat anything promoted as "amazing," because it might actually be: "Everyone loves Cheetos, the crunchy cheezy [*sic*] treat that you have to lick your fingers to savor every flavor, but this new amazing flavor infuses American Mountain Dew with the crunchy Cheetos snack. This combo version by Frito-Lay Japan . . . in cooperation with Pepsi, ensures an authentic taste experience."

Guideline 3
Hard liquor may be better for you, at some yet-to-be-determined ratio, say two fingers to eight ounces, than soft drinks. As a boy in Decatur, Georgia, I would ride my bike to the gas station, in front of which stood a big, rusting, red-metal box with a slide-open door at the top. I'd reach down into that well of ice gradually melting among variously shaped cold bottles randomly heaped, and I'd swush around heavily for a while and come up with a NuGrape. A Grapette. A Sun Drop. An Orange Crush, with its pebbly, thick-walled bottle the color of iodine. A Bireley's chocolate drink. Bireley's put out an orange, too. A Nehi black cherry. An RC Cola, a Dr Pepper, a Frostie Root Beer, a Squirt, a Canada Dry ginger ale. Ice water would run down my arm, and I would have myself a *very* cold, *highly* satisfactory drink. I don't think anything has ever struck me as prettier colored than NuGrape foam back then. I was a child, with little experience of the world. But in college English, when I came upon "the blushful Hippocrene, / With beaded bubbles winking at the brim, / And purple-stainèd mouth," it brought back NuGrape.

As I acquired other tastes, those sugar potions became too icky for me. But I would still enjoy an occasional Coke. I lived near Atlanta, the corporate and ancestral home of Coca-Cola. Coke was *the* cola, the one on the periodic table; Coke was It. But then It came out with that commercial showing people singing, "I'd like to buy [Oh, not sell?] the world a Coke / And keep it company." Uh-oh. Conceptually, It had gone Icky. Then It changed Its very essence. Transubstantiated Itself into New Coke, which tasted more like Pepsi! As if Louis Armstrong had decided to imitate Al Hirt! And then, when It saw the reaction to what It had done, It brought back Its old self—now called Coca-Cola Classic, which sounded like a golf tournament. After a while, It discontinued New Coke, which had become known officially as Coca-Cola II, and dropped the "Classic" from old Coke. Today, under Its Minute Maid brand, Coca-Cola sells a juice It calls Pomegranate Blueberry, which is 0.3 percent pomegranate, 0.2 percent blueberry, and nearly all the rest grape and apple juice, dyed dark purple. The picture on the label shows an apple and some grapes peeping from behind a pomegranate and some blueberries. "HELP NOURISH YOUR BRAIN," it says in big letters on the label. (*Some* research suggests that antioxidants in pomegranate juice *may* be good for your brain.) The other day I turned on the television and saw a cat, with a German accent, saying, "What if life tasted as good as Diet Coke?" Talk about icky. Diet icky. And of course people say you really ought to drink Mexican Coke, which is sweetened with cane sugar instead of icky corn syrup, so It tastes like It should. Would whiskey put you through all that?

Guideline 4

If it sounds like the name of a pool hustler (Natural Fats), it's probably good for you, within reason. If it smacks of sadomasochism (Whipped Spread), it's not.

Guideline 5

Save room for pie. Pie being the highest form of food. When we say "Sweet as an angel eating pie," we do not mean icky; we mean sublime. Eudora Welty, in her story "Kin," celebrates the perfect ending to a pleasant day: "wonderful black, bitter, moist chocolate pie under mountains

Quebec's premier Lucien Bouchard's government got a faceful of criticism this week. Members of the Liberal Party opposition demanded to know why $112,440 of taxpayers' money had gone to fund a symposium on comical activism, starring international slapstick terrorists who throw cream pies at public figures deemed to be taking themselves too seriously. One defensive minister provoked giggles by saying, "Never have we supported pie throwing." Imagine that in French! The finance minister, Bernard Landry, himself the target just last week of a pie that he managed to dodge, was less nimble in fending off criticism of the funding. "It is not the taxpayers who were pied," he spluttered, quickly adding—lest anyone interpret that remark as in any way exculpatory—that the pie throwers "have a sense of democracy as weak as their aim."

of meringue." Ralph Waldo Emerson, according to his friend James B. Thayer, loved pie so much he ate it regularly for breakfast. One morning, Emerson offered several gentleman guests, one after another, a piece of pie. Each gentleman declined. "'But . . . ,' Mr. Emerson remonstrated, . . . thrusting the knife under a piece of the pie, and putting the entire weight of his character into his manner, 'but . . . *what is pie for?*'" There. There you are. That rhetorical question, extended across a broad spectrum of *good food*, is the answer to Why I Eat. Was breakfast pie bad for Emerson? In only slightly premature old age, the author of "Self-Reliance" began losing his memory, but by all accounts he retained a nice smile. "He suffered very little," according to his son Edward Waldo, "took his nourishment well, went to his study and tried to work, accomplished less and less, but did not notice it." More and more, I think of this as my fallback ambition. But might Emerson's golden years have been even mellower if he had *saved room* for pie?

Unquestionably, too much pie will make you sluggish. And you cannot truly know, except by some rough principle such as "more than one piece" (but what *size* pieces?), how much is too much until you have had it. You can, however, know, or believe you know, how much *room* you have for pie. One's room for pie is like one's capacity for love, in this sense: few life-affirming people underestimate their own. So don't worry about that. But we don't want to fritter away, so to speak, our room for pie. As we eat our pre-pie courses, we should bear this in mind. Don't crowd pie out, is what I am saying. Room for pie is like energy reserves, good credit, an ace in the hole. If you're stuffing yourself with Cheez

Doodles, and you know this is wrong, you can try telling yourself, "Stop, you miserable swine." Which will make yourself say to you, "You're not the boss of me!" Or you can ask yourself, "What if, in the next moment, a piece of pie comes along? If we eat one more Cheez Doodle, will we have room for that pie?"

BUT NOTHING IS SIMPLE

As a lifelong eater, I know the following:

- We are what we eat. Venison puts hair on our chests, and if we eat food that has been reduced to foam, we are very, very silly.
- We are what we eat eats. Pork fed on garbage, good. Pork fed on germ killers, bad.
- And never forget all the little fellas that make what we eat possible: we are all part earthworm and part bee.

Fine. I'm on board. But food and I used to get along so simply. When Beethoven was composing, he didn't think; he composed. When I was eating, I ate.

Now . . . I join a save-the-planet march. Somebody's sign says, "Eat What's Good for the Earth's Digestion." If that were just a matter of my not giving heartburn to the graveyard, it would go down pretty easy with me. But you also have to factor in the global climate and the global economy and, on a personal note, chronic sinusitis. I *know* you don't want to hear about it! *I* don't want to hear about it! But if I don't make a clean breast of this, eventually somebody is going to pipe up and say, "What does he know about food? He's anosmic!"

Yes. As I wend my wondering way toward growing older than dirt, I still have all my original knees, hips, and heart valves, pretty fair semblances at least (knock on wood) of the old bodily functions, and only one good reason to curse my fate.

Recurrent anosmia. See, you never even heard of it. There's no common term for it. Unscented? Smell-less? Aroma-impaired?

I'm lucky. According to Gary Beauchamp of the Monell Chemical Senses Center in Philadelphia, six million Americans cannot smell *at all*. My olfactory sense isn't dead yet, but for twenty years I have been losing and regaining and again losing it. After three surgeries on my sinuses and many courses of antibiotics, I can breathe. But when the smell is gone, I'm tasting-impaired. I still get sweet, sour, bitter, salty, and umami; and spicy hot, which is essentially pain; and the basic textures, which to the tasting-impaired are as useful as the Seven Dwarfs: Crunchy, Slick, Crumbly, Crackly, Gooey, Juicy, and Chewy. But I miss so many subtler flavors it's a damn shame.

I don't . . . smell . . . well. *Stop*, I know what you're instinctively on the verge of saying; I've heard it over and over—little play on "well" and "good" there, right? My friend, *I have anosmia*. I will do what it takes to squash the "well/good" response, if I have to resort to a bad-taste umami joke:

Umami so fat, her ass looks like two pigs fighting over a Milk Dud.

To not smell well isn't funny. I'm *deprived*.

So why not try what is called a deprivation diet. I eliminated dairy and gluten. Do you realize what that means? No cheeseburgers, no pizza, no pasta (actually, there are some decent gluten-free versions, assuming you don't overcook them slightly and turn them into globs, and quinoa's not a bad gluten-free starchy thing), no ice cream, no macaroni and cheese, no *croutons*. No . . . butter. First science tells me, go ahead, love butter, glory in butter, and then science tells me, not so fast.

I went to have my blood tested for antibodies and proudly told the health professional involved that I had already given up dairy and gluten. No, no, she said. That skews the blood tests. So I went back on dairy (butter, I had butter) and gluten (croissant, I had croissant) for a while, came back in for the tests, and found that I had been needlessly eschewing gluten but should keep avoiding dairy (and even *goat* milk products), and also almonds, lemon, cauliflower (I love cauliflower— there's a clean watery aspect at the heart of it that I also find in good mozzarella and oysters), and *eggs*. In the hope that eggs, and those other delicacies, will regain their savor, I have to stop eating them. In their place, lots of herbal supplements.

Bulletin: It's working! Today I walked around the French Quarter of New Orleans hungrily inhaling the aromarama: gumbo, jasmine, street musicians. And I ate, and the whole righteous taste of Buffa's red beans and rice swam into my ken, and I smacked my lips in thanks.

Bulletin: That was yesterday. Today, I might as well be eating in Ohio.

Will I never have butter again? To be sure, Joan found me an olive-oil-based confection, every ingredient unimpeachable, which isn't bad; it resembles butter. But how do you write a poem about it?

That may not strike you as a pressing question. But consider this, one of the truest things I ever wrote:

I Like Meat

Cold meat or hot meat,
Sliced thick or thin.
I guess I've just got meat
Under my skin.

If I may paraphrase a Shakespeare sonnet: if that ain't so, and upon me proved, then no one ever wrote, and no one ever ate. Since writing "I Like Meat," however, I have become more eco-conscious. I still like meat, but I need to qualify that simple truth. And so I have backed, and filled, and fiddled and fussed, to carve out the following addendum:

But when I shop
For lamb, for example,
I'll choose no chop
That did not gambol—

So we can say
(You know my wife)
That our entrée
Has had a life.

> And though it cost
> A leg and an arm
> From New Post-Lost-
> Paradise Farm,
>
> That lamb chop must,
> If we're to buy it,
> Have enjoyed a just
> Organic diet.
>
> So we can bleat
> With every bite:
> "What we eat
> Has eaten right!"

Look at that. First, I cravenly blame my wife (and now I'm cravenly crawfishing away from doing so), when, in fact, I have come to share, by and large, her alimentary sentiments; maybe I feel, sometimes, that life would be simpler if I hadn't, but that's my problem.

Second, and more crucially, where did that "bleat" come from? Oh, sure, "bleat" popped things into focus—but not into the focus I had in mind. Did I want to imply that people who adhere to a healthy, sustainable, relatively merciful diet are sheep-like conformists? No, that "bleat," I feel certain, is not what I mean. I think it reflects the depth of my resistance to being picky about food.

High-mindedly picky, I mean. Knee-jerk pickiness, I must have a gift for, because one of the few things I have written that people tell me (with some accuracy) they remember word for word is "Song Against Broccoli":

> The neighborhood stores are all out of broccoli,
> Loccoli.

A version of those lines was quoted by *The New York Times* when the first president Bush took it upon himself to declare his regular-lad distaste ("It tastes like medicine") for broccoli. Fortunately, the *Times* did a follow-up story, and I was able to go on record: "Unwilling to join the Bush camp and fresh from a plate of broccoli with garlic sauce, Mr. Blount said this new couplet captured his from-the-heart feelings":

> While others are gorging on chocolate, I'm
> Gladsomely crying, "It's broccoli time."

That of course was a lie. But I have, over the years, eaten loads of broccoli—have even *chosen to cook broccoli for myself.* All in all, I am not unfond of broccoli. True, broccoli's top is too fuzzy and its stalk too stalky (you might say broccoli is all seeds and stems)—but these are the reactions of an infant child. Broccoli is *good* for us, and we need to—

I don't know. This book is no recipe for self-improvement, no *Maybe What You're Eating Is What's Been Eating You.* The only thing it proves is that food gets into nearly everything I write. Not literally. With computers, you have to be so dainty to avoid getting the least bit of sauerkraut, bean dip, or even peanut butter into their works. My old manual typewriter—pardon me while I be an old fart—was full of crumbs. Might be a raisin down in there. Grease stains on the platen. And by gum that machine sounded, when it and I were going good, like popcorn a-popping. But a tiny slosh of orange juice, which my old typewriter would have taken in stride, killed the first laptop I ever had. So I sublimate, and nearly everything gets into what I write about food. Certainly food pops up in most of my greatest hits—or so I assume, from the savage cries, during question-and-answer sessions, of "Hey, give us 'Song to Oysters'!" Which you will find on page 93, in the "Meat of the Waters" section. And "What's that thing where people are talking around the dinner table?" Which—oh, here it is, on the next page.

THE WAY FOLKS ARE MEANT TO EAT

When I was growing up in Georgia, we ate till we got *tired*. Then we went, "Whoo!" and leaned back and wholeheartedly expressed how much we regretted that we couldn't summon up the strength, right then, to eat some more.

When I moved to the Northeast, I met someone who said she liked to stop eating while she was still just a little bit hungry. I was taken aback. Intellectually, I could see it was a sound and even an admirable policy. It kept her in better shape than mine did me. I just thought it was crazy.

We have only so much appetite allotted to us in our time on this earth, was my feeling, and it's a shame to run the risk of wasting any of it. People I grew up with wanted to get on out beyond their appetite a ways, to make sure they used all of it. They wanted to get *full*. They *intended* to get full. If a meal left them feeling just a touch short of overstuffed, they were disappointed. I knew a man once who complained about little Spanish peanuts because they never added up to enough to give him any reason to stop eating them until they were all gone, and then he was still up to eating some more. "I can't get ahead of them," he said.

But eating right is not just a question of quantity. Primarily, it's quality. It's not letting any available *goodness* go unswallowed. The people I grew up eating with didn't just take a few of the most obvious bites out of a piece of chicken and decide abstractly, "Well, I have eaten this piece of chicken." They recognized that the institution of fried chicken demands a great deal of chickens, and my people felt bound to hold up their end. They ate down to the bones and pulled the bones apart and ate in between the bones and chewed on the bones themselves. And the bones that weren't too splintery they gave to the dogs, who were glad to have them. (Unless they're overbred, dogs generally are Southern.)

And people I grew up with *talked* while they ate, about what they were eating. When several sides and generations of a family of such folks sat down together around a table, with ten or twelve generous platters in front of them, they sounded something like this:

". . . and us to Thy service, amen."

"Pitch in."

"I don't know where to start first."

"Mmmmm-*m*."

"Big Mama has outdone herself tonight."

"Well, I just hope y'all can enjoy it."

"I BLEEVE I COULD EAT A HORSE!"

"Would you look at them tomaters?"

"Hoooo, don't they look good?"

"Now, Tatum, slow down."

"You let that child enjoy himself."

"You'd think we didn't feed him at home."

"He didn't get 'ny snap beans! Lord, pass that child some snap beans!"

"Lilah, how 'bout you over there? You need *something* more. Butter beans!"

"Ooo, land, naw, I'm workin' on this *corn*."

"Come on, just a dab."

"Well, you talked me into it."

"Mmmmmm."

"Awful early, to be gettin' this gooda corn."

"Eunice, would you send that okry back around?"

"Look at me, just a-puttin' it away."

"I'M EATIN' LIKE A FIELD HAND!"

"Little more tea, to wash it down?"

"Mm-m, these greens!"

"ANYBODY WANT ANYTHING?"

"I will have one more heppin' of that squash, if nobody minds."

"It's so gooooood."

"Little corn bread, to sop that juice?"

"*One* more moufful of ham, then I do have to stop, sure nuff."

"Look at all this chicken left! Have a little more there, Charles."

"Where would he put it?"

"And just a spoonful of that gravy, to put on my peas."

"Charles! We didn't raise you to mix your gravy with your peas!"

"Celia, now you let that child eat the way he likes it."

"Mm. Mmm. *Mm.*"

"More rolls, anybody?"

"I think this is all I can hold."

"You better eat some more of this good chicken!"

"No'm, I got to save room for pie."

"*Pie? There's pie? All this and pie?*"

"Now, Neetie, you know good and well we wouldn't let you go home and tell people we didn't serve you any *pie.*"

"*Look* at that *pie.*"

"What is *in* this pie?"

"This pie is so goooood."

"Ah-mm, *m.*"

"How do you get your crust to do like this, Big Mama? My crust won't *do* like this."

"Aw, your crust does fine."

"Mm, m, m."

"Mmmmmm-*m.*"

"Well, I have eat myself sick."

"Mm-*hm.* Wadn't 'at goooood?"

"I don't think I could . . . touch . . . another . . . bite."

"I'M 'BOUT TO POP!"

"*Mm.*"

"Yes, Lord."

"Them tomaters was specially good."

"Got plenny more now, I could slice right up."

"Noooo, noooo. I'd die."

PART TWO

ESSENTIALS

Man walks into the doctor's office; he's got a carrot in one ear, broccoli in the other ear, and a stalk of celery up his nose. "Doctor," he says, "I'm run-down, tired all the time, ache all over—what's the matter with me?"

"Well, to start with," the doctor says, "you're not eating right."

SONG TO THE APPLE

What about the apple hasn't been said?
Everybody knows it's red
Or green or yellow,
And Adam was a lukewarm fellow
Ere he and Eve took apple bites.
And then: Oh Lordy! Earthly delights.

And now when (*croarch*) your teeth sink through that
Skin and . . . *Nmmsh'crnch'l'mmn.* The truth: At
No time does it cross your thinking
That this is just as louche as drinking?

ANIMALS EAT

Imagine being a cow. I would fret:

I stand out here from dawn to dusk a-ruminating, yet
I haven't thought of anything illuminating yet.

I can't see a cow falling back, in effect, on some trendy rationale:

The reason why, I think, is that instead of gains and losses,
What I'm into, bottom line, is . . . whatchamacallit. Process.

She might have already concluded all a *milk* cow needs to about human exceptionalism:

"Moo"?
Excuse me?
I'm out here doing
What I'm meant to do:
Chew.
And someone moos me?

And repeating:
"Moo."
I'm *eating*.
Do I go "Blah-blah-blah"
To you?

I can see myself more readily as a pig, with issues. The dark, Dickensian *Babe: Pig in the City* is a much better movie—the orangutan deserved Oscar consideration—than the original, more popular *Babe*. But in both of those films, as in any honest appreciation of our friends the barnyard animals, the issue arises that many of them will, given the nature of things, end up on our friend the dinner table. A place in the Florida Panhandle claims it can convert hogs, walking around, to long-link sausages in twenty minutes. How much of this registers on a growing pig? A pig may just think this:

If I'm the center of the universe, start with that,
Wouldn't the universe want me fat?

On humanitarian and ecological grounds, future generations may revile those of us who derived protein from sentient beings. In movies, the new zombies may be beef eaters. But what will those generations know about livestock?

I've never had cows or pigs, but for quite a while in the 1980s I helped provide a home, in and around our garage, to an old horse named Ollie and three free-range chickens: two hens, Flo and Lois, and a rooster, Jack. When the chickens circulated as a group, Jack generally appeared to be in the lead—an impression he managed to convey by judging where the hens were headed and then scooting, in an odd hoisting-of-the-skirts posture that suggested a scrambling archbishop, around in front of them. Once situated, he would draw up all stately, extend one foot forward ver-r-r-y slowly while darting his head about in surveillance (mostly, I think, for the effect of the comb toss) and going *buuuuuuuuk* in a low voice implying an as-if-effortless-yet-by-no-means-facile assumption of the awful burden of command—and then, when the leading foot finally touched the ground, there was a moment when Jack appeared to have frozen into a monument to poultry masculinity. And *then* he would shift his weight dramatically forward, hold that stance for a beat, and begin the process again. Walk of the cock. The hens meanwhile would be muttering and scratching up sustenance. Sometimes when they drifted away from Jack's train, he would turn, go *brerrk?*, gather up his lower plumage, take a running jump, and briefly, inappropriately, mount one of them. Their response was always to squawk, ruffle up, shake, and get back to pecking in the dirt.

By way of apology for my gender, and also just experimentally, I would scatter a variety of tidbits. Cheez Doodles the chickens pecked at and tossed aside, but when I dumped in front of them a pile of croutons that had gone stale, chickens and croutons dissolved into a blur of dust, crouton crumbs, and feathers. When the air cleared, there were no croutons, just chickens, blinking and catching their breath. I think this is about as much as you will ever get out of chickens in the way of gratitude. I composed a jingle:

> *Les poulets sont dans les croûtons—*
> *Mais . . .*
> *Où sont les tous-les-deux maintenant?*
> *C'est . . .*
> *Merveilleux, n'est-ce pas? Voyez:*
> *Les croûtons sont dans les poulets.*

At first, Jack tolerated my presence around the place, but maybe he felt I crossed some line with his hens, or he might just have resented, as I might have in his place, being treated as a figure of whimsy. After he caught me doing an imitation of his walk for visitors, he began to lurk behind things and leap out at me like Inspector Clouseau's valet. In fact, he would make, deep in his throat, nearly the same karate noises. When I stepped out the back door, he would fly up almost as high as my face, brandishing his spurs at me. Not wanting to yield alpha-male status to a chicken, I kept a stick by the door to brandish at him. Sometimes I was in the mood for this, but not always. Once or twice, I had to whap him with the stick—not a pleasant sensation, in part because it so clearly confirmed his opinion of me. Eventually, he would sidle off a bit, muttering, "Let that be a lesson to you"—always at pains to maneuver in such a way that no one could accuse him of anything worse than accepting a standoff. A couple of times he got in a good lick of his own. You hate to tell people you're late arriving somewhere because you had to whack your rooster with a stick and then go back in the house and put antiseptic on the scratch he left on your arm and then come back out and fend him off again.

The hens earned their keep by laying eggs—sometimes clandestinely here and there in the garage, where the eggs would go very bad, but usually in their nests, where we could harvest them, and because Flo and Lois enjoyed a rich diet of bugs and scraps as well as standard feed, their eggs had character even when fresh. Aside from crowing at unpredictable hours, Jack didn't contribute anything so far as I could see. Perhaps because he put so much of his energy into status preservation, none of the hidden eggs produced chicks, and I felt that our dogs, who took a wary, familial interest in Flo and Lois that Jack affected to ignore, could protect the hens against predators. So I placed a candid classified ad in *The Shopper's Guide*: "Free. One aggressive rooster. Come get him someone please."

A soft-spoken lady showed up. Was I sure this rooster was good and aggressive, she asked. That was the kind of rooster she needed, to guard her flock. Don't worry about that, I said. I stepped out in front of Jack and braced myself. He took one look at me and fled as if terrified. I ran after him. He hightailed it into the woods. I thrashed about, diving at him. He zigzagged, squawking in unwonted tones of innocent astonishment. I tried several times to throw a blanket over him. He dodged it every time. I lost my hat and glasses. He ran around pleading for an explanation. Finally, my son brought him down with a flying tackle.

The lady, looking flushed, said she was sorry but Jack wasn't what she had in mind. No, no, no, I said, Jack is just choosing this moment to be *passive*-aggressive, because he is so determined to make me look bad. Her look said, "Oh, so everything is about you." Give him a chance, I pleaded, he gets along with women. Mainly, I think, because she felt obligated not to leave Jack in this abusive environment, she sighed and acquiesced. I wrangled him into a cardboard box to load into her backseat. As I was about to close the door, Jack stuck his head out through a hole in the box. For the first time ever, he looked me squarely in the eye.

His look was hurt. Incredulous. It said, clear as day, "You didn't *like* me?"

Ollie, the horse, was likability equinified. Though he got too old for riding, he let toddlers be placed on his back. I saw a cat on his back more than once. And at night when he entered his stall, which was built into the back of the garage, the chickens would hop onto one of his hay bales, then onto his back, then onto his head, then onto a rafter to roost. During the day, he would graze in our neighbor's meadow, muse, and amble. He produced manure for the garden, which I would gather in a wheelbarrow as he looked at me and clearly wondered, "Uh . . . you realize what that is?" His only bad habit was getting through the fence and going down to the town library, whose lawn was greener.

His eyesight was going. I would spice up his life, and mine, by throwing apples from a distance onto the slope uphill of him. If tossed just right, they would roll down and come to a stop close to his nose. He would sniff, peer around, consider, shrug, and munch.

BEAR NOTES

Around where we live, people get bears. A bear will sit there and stare at you while he or she tips your bird feeder up to his or her lips and sucks down all the sunflower seeds. Or the bear might tear open your garage to get at the garbage can you have locked in there, which means that you have to lock your garbage can inside your car inside your garage and hope the bear won't tear open your car.

A veterinarian says one reason so many wild animals are venturing onto humanly occupied property lately is the pervasiveness of leash laws. We travel too much to have dogs now, but the ones I used to have were free-range dogs, who weren't formidable but thought they were, and whose scent alone kept varmints away. These days, most dogs I know even in the country live primarily indoors and get such exercise as they do by yawning and being taken for walks. Coyotes, not to mention bears, might eat unsupervised dogs. Our cat, Jimmy, has already had at least one face-off with a fox. He is no pushover, but an owl could get him. We keep him in at night.

One bear in our area alienated a roadside produce seller by eating a whole row of corn, throwing it all up at the end of the row, eating the next row and throwing it up, and so on through the patch. The farmer sprayed his next corn crop with a mixture of pork gravy and ammonia. "Pork gravy is cheap," he told me, "though it will gum up your sprayer." When the bear ate and threw up that crop too, the farmer dispatched him with a bow and arrow.

HOW ABOUT SHEEP?

Sheep, I am told, will clean up your garden at the end of the summer; they'll even polish off all those gargantuan residual zucchinis if you'll chop them up. Raising sheep is unprofitable these days, with artificial "fleece" supplanting wool. So who will eat those zucchinis? And will people cease to understand the expression "The grass is always greener on the other side of the fence"?

Says Jill Jakes, a former judge who raises sheep for love, "They really do believe that the hay on the other side of any obstacle is better than what's on their side." Her sheep are frequently so attracted to one another's fodder that they get their heads stuck in the narrow spaces between the slats that separate their enclosures within the barn (they also graze widely), and they won't pull back; they'll just munch placidly at whatever their trapped heads can reach until someone saws them out. When, however, the person who is their food contact exhibits behavior that is outside the box, they unite in protest. "One time, I was playing music in the barn, and I started dancing—Oh! The sheep were scandalized! They all backed into the far corners. They didn't know what this might mean for their future, for their next feeding." Jill never slaughters her sheep—"Oh, I *couldn't*"—but she does shear them, which "is a traumatic event for them—they don't recognize each other afterward. The wool around their face gives them a lot of their character. They have to get used to each other all over again."

By the way, Jill says, "Rams love to be scratched on top of the buttocks. They go into a transport of bliss. And—my dog Clothilde is crazy about certain sheep. She licks their ears. I saw her doing this, and—no,

I don't lick their ears—but now I do stroke the inside of their ears gently, and I whisper into their ears. Their eyes close instantly."

What does she whisper?

"Oh, 'Such a sweet good smart fellow'—same thing I whisper to guys."

HOLD THE FOAM

I remember reading, with a jolt, this headline in *The New York Times*: "American Cuisine Is Back."

I was eating a chicken potpie. "Where are you back from?" I asked it. No response. A chicken potpie is not a fun food.

And I mean that as a compliment. You know that expression on a dog's face, as he watches you plop food into his bowl? *Everything that's happened in my life so far has led up to this moment.* That is how I feel, at bottom, about something good to eat.

It's hard to turn me away from food. "Trust me," confided a wait-person once, "don't eat the garnish." And yet I had a hard time laying off that carrot curl. I don't eat a lot of carrots, but an occasional carrot shaving . . . Maybe management made her say that so they wouldn't have to keep buying new carrots. Now on the Internet you can find Rachel Maddow, the MSNBC news host, saying "Don't eat the garnish" with regard to cocktail olives and maraschino cherries. Honeybees, she says, have been turning a fluorescent red from sipping out of maraschino cherry vats. I'll cut out the cherries when I start getting rosy cheeks. Cocktail olives, she says, have "conceivably been lying out festering in their own juices in a warm room all night, with fingers on them." But isn't gin a disinfectant?

Silliness, alone, needn't put me off food. Someone told me she had recently enjoyed celery sorbet. Celery Sorbet sounds like the name of an exotic dancer. If served it, however, I would try it. If it tasted okay, I would say so.

What I will not eat is foam. Certain restaurants in recent years have been serving bacon foam. Ham froth. Mushroom fizz. Culinary foam is made of thoroughly strained (I'll say) juice from the food in question (mushroom juice? Don't ask me) mixed with gelatin and foo-foo'd up with nitrous oxide. You know that stuff you see on leaves in the woods, called cuckoo spit? That's what culinary foam looks like. You can tell it's not mildew because if you don't eat it right away, it turns into a gooey spot. It's like the belch of someone who ate bacon, captured atop your entrée. It was invented by a Spanish chef named Ferran Adrià, whose restaurant, El Bulli, was five times voted the best in the world. "Molecular gastronomy," Adrià's work was called. Breaking ingredients down to their quarks and neutrinos. In a documentary about his restaurant, according to *The New York Times*, "Mr. Adrià's bleary-eyed minions painstakingly purchase five grapes and three beans" on a shopping trip, and he is seen "sucking on a bizarre fluorescent fish ice pop or musing on the various tortures to which he can subject a defenseless sweet potato." Now El Bulli has closed, and reopened not as a restaurant but as a think tank, "a creativity center."

A creativity center is to an eatery as a credit default swap is to a roll of fifties, and as bacon foam is to bacon. I don't say cuisine *must* cater to people with teeth. I will eat (if "eat" is the word) crystal-clear consommé. I do get wistful, knowing at a glance there will be no chewing here. Oyster crackers, I'm thinking, would sure go good with this. Dipping into pure clear soup is even a little spooky, like being the first one off the high dive in the morning, when the water's so unruffled you can't see how far down in the air it starts. (I once saw a lunch-counter sign, "Today's Soup: Calm Chowder." You'd feel bad about stirring it.) Don Kelly of the Miami Marlins, primarily an infielder, has said this about playing a few innings at catcher: "The strangest thing is when you go to catch the ball and they hit it, and there's nothing there." Biting into foam must be like that.

"I like grits," Chet Atkins used to say, "because they have no bones."

I take his point. But *instant* grits—no. Too close to grit foam. You don't want grits to grate, but however near fluffy they've been cooked down to, they should retain a gritty gist.

On one of his comedy records back in the 1970s, Jerry Clower came down hard on those biscuits made from dough in refrigerated tubes. All over town, every morning, *Whop, Whop*, you could hear those tubes being broken open, he said—even though "them biscuits," as Jerry put it so well, "ain't fit to eat." Like trying to chew on a toothpick made of composition board: no grain. More recently, certain brands have discovered how to package patties of refrigerated dough that, when baked, actually come out a lot like biscuits. I say gastronomical science should trend in that direction. Not toward breaking food down further and further. That's my job.

It's springtime in Williamstown, Massachusetts, and what does that mean on the Williams College campus? Extreme Frisbee time! We're not talking about two people dreamily floating a harmless plastic dish back and forth in an open grassy area. Extreme Frisbee may take place in a dining hall or from one classroom window to another, and the Frisbee may be a dinner plate or a disk so huge that it takes two people to throw it, or it may be on fire. Too many people have been hit and classes disrupted by various flying saucers, but nobody wants to be stuffy about Frisbees, so Williams's dean of students, Franklin Waring, announced last week that anyone "throwing a flat round object on University property in an inappropriate manner, as deemed by the office of the dean, will be offered a choice: either eat said object, or be suspended for the rest of the term." The next day, an extra-crispy pizza sailed into the office of the dean.

SONG TO DECENT PIZZA

Yes, pepperoni, tomato,
  cheese,
Onions, peppers. But over
  all these
(And yes, oregano, yes, and
  'shrooms)
An underlying factor
  looms:
Pizza's founded on its
  crust.
Don't you foist upon me
  just

Some slack, doughy, gummy basis
For my sauce and all. There are no cases
Of edible pizzas—and I've had a lottom—
That aren't al dente on the bottom.

I COULD SEE JUST OVERALLS

Dismiss, if you will, the Garden of Eden as outmoded metaphor, but the Adam and Eve story was the first spicy one to which I was exposed. When I was a boy, there was not a lot of nudity around, especially in Georgia. And by the time nudity became the height of fashion (rendering obsolete, at least for a while, Mark Twain's observation "Clothes make the man. Naked people have little or no influence on society"), I was well into my first marriage, with children, cats, and dogs. I have noticed that children and household animals would prefer the nominal head of household to have clothes on.

Then I got divorced, and a nice-looking woman told me she had left a farm commune in the 1960s because she got tired, after some months, of "hoeing naked." In my mind's eye, I could see her gardening that way, among the little cabbages reeking of potential. But just

Since the fall of the Soviet Union, the no-longer-subsidized dairy herd of Cuba has fallen off drastically, creating a severe shortage of milk. But Cuban scientists may have a solution. They say they are "very, very close" to cloning a cow. And not just any cow, but the late Ubre Blanca, whose prodigious mammary glands made her a revolutionary heroine. After producing a Guinness-world-record 241 pounds of milk in a single day, Ubre Blanca frequently appeared on Cuban television being petted fondly by Castro himself. The great cow died in 1985, and her natural offspring turned out disappointingly ordinary. But some of her tissue was preserved, and the hope is that from these cells a line of super-cows can be produced. Nothing has come, however, of an earlier project proposed by Castro: the breeding of cows the size of dogs—small enough to be kept in Cuban family apartments and fed on grass grown in drawers under fluorescent lights.

thinking about the posture and the stroke of hoeing makes the small of my back hurt.

Why bring all this up now? Everything seems to be regressing rapidly back toward the dawn of humanity, doesn't it? And people are talking once again about having to live off the land. They're not talking about doing it in the nude, though. That's good.

A couple I knew in the 1970s informed me that they regarded themselves not as Americans but as forest animals. Involuntarily, I snorted. Not that I wanted this couple to be more patriotic; I just doubted they could subsist for long in the woods, barefooted.

By the way, people of the North have tried to tell me that the word "barefooted" is Southern; that "barefoot" is standard. But "barefooted as a yard dog" is a fuller-bodied expression than John Greenleaf Whittier's "barefoot boy, with cheek of tan." The feet involved are not only more pronounced but more grounded. That -ed at the end might stand for the toes. If you prefer "barefooted" over "barefoot," you are less likely to get romantic about living as a woodland creature or tilling the earth au naturel.

These days, I know wedded bliss finally, so far. But part of me is, I don't know, wistful that I never gardened naked, even for a couple of days, with that nice-looking woman.

In Eden, nobody needed to hoe. Adam and Eve coexisted mellowly with weeds, because trees bearing accessible fruits abounded. The first couple had dominion over the beasts and the fish, so hunting and fishing, and milking, and getting past the rooster to gather the eggs, must have been a snap. Until the serpent induced Eve to take a bite from the one forbidden fruit, the apple of knowledge, she and Adam, I gather, also coexisted mellowly with each other—lacking any sense of either *ooh-la-la*, on the one hand, or "Is that *all* you care about?" on the other. When Adam woke up in the morning for the first time, what did he think?

"Well, here I am. There's some fruit. That's good."

Then, when Eve arrived, what did the two of them think?

"Oh, hello. We have fruit here."

"Yes, so I see."

No story there. The real moment—even as a child, I got this—is when it hits them that they're naked. Then we know what they're thinking.

I have lived through two periods of American innocence, neither of which I felt right about. The first was the age of Aquarius, when all we needed was love. The second was the age of leverage, when all we needed was "market forces." Each of those ages had its charms. But there's something tangy in the air when a bubble bursts, and we feel divested and foresee a long row to hoe.

THE FALL: A ONE-ACT

NARRATOR
One day, Eve was walking through paradise, chewing a sprig of kale.

BIRD, *arriving on foot*
Hello, Eve. Whatcha eatin'?

EVE
Nice green crunchy food. We're *supposed* to eat it.

BIRD
No disputing tastes. Seen any worms?

EVE
Worms? Why?

BIRD
You don't *know*? About me and worms?

BUTTERFLY, *arriving*
Hello, Eve. Whatcha eatin'?

EVE
Nice green—

BUTTERFLY
Nectar in it? Any sweetness?

EVE
What's sweetness?

BUTTERFLY
You don't *know*? Never mind, more nectar for me.

EVE
Hello, Worm. Oh, a bird was looking for you!

WORM
Eve! Please! Don't you *know* . . .

EVE
What?

WORM
The *food chain*, girl. Just watch yourself.

EVE
That's silly. I like to watch the *other* animals.

WORM
You'd better watch some of 'em—for instance—

SNAKE, *sauntering in*
De-doot-de-doot. Hey!

EVE

Hello, sn——sn——sn——

SNAKE

Hot-cha.

EVE

I'm sorry, I can't quite call
your name. What did
you say?

SNAKE

Never mind names. I said,
"*Hot-cha.*"

EVE

I don't know that word.

SNAKE

You don't know . . . much.

Say you are walking along minding your own business when a runaway tour bus comes over the hill and knocks you flying through the air and you land, unconscious, on top of a taco truck that heedlessly carries you to Toledo, Ohio, where you know no one. Every third person who comes to visit you in the hospital will take your hand, give you a meaningful look, and say, "Things happen for a reason." Well, they don't. Dr. Charles Offenlocher, MIT professor of phenomenological statistics, has released a study titled "Things That Don't Happen for a Reason." His team of researchers researched over a thousand news stories that were inexplicable enough to appear on a Web site called *WTF News*. Diners injured by exploding catfish and the like. In not one of those cases, he reports, did anybody ever come up with a reason. "Well," asked an interviewer, "but isn't it possible that something seemingly inexplicable happened to you, Dr. Offenlocher, perhaps as a child, and now we see the reason: so you would undertake this study? Hmm?" "No," replied Offenlocher. "What makes you say that?"

EVE

That's what everybody keeps saying! What don't I know?

SNAKE

For instance, why you have to do the cleaning and cooking and
canning and all Adam has to do is go out and (*heavy sarcasm*) pick . . .
fruit.

EVE

I . . . just never thought about it.

SNAKE

Haven't you been raised above all the animals? Don't you have a
responsibility to stay on top of things?

EVE

Well, Adam usually . . .

SNAKE

Mm-hmmm. Here.

EVE

Why, that's an a——a——a—— . . .

SNAKE

Apple. I picked it for you. Just for you.

EVE

But . . .

SNAKE

I bet Adam never picks anything just for you.

EVE

He picks things.

SNAKE

Mm-hmm.

EVE

He brings them home.

SNAKE

Mm-hmm.

EVE

He says, "I'm starved!"

SNAKE

Mm-hm. And don't *you* ever feel starved? For . . . sweetness? Here, have a bite.

EVE

No. Not supposed to.

SNAKE

Who says?

EVE

Well! Our Father, that's who!

SNAKE

You ever *see* this "F——F——F——"

EVE

Father. No.

SNAKE

And who told you about him?

EVE

Well, Adam of course.

SNAKE

Mm . . . hmm. What if I told you Adam ate an apple? Before you even
got here. And that's why he's on top of things. Why he just picks,
and you have to clean, can, and cook?

EVE

Are you telling the truth?

SNAKE

Watch. (*Gulp.*) Remind you of anybody?

EVE

Adam . . . has that lump. But he's—

SNAKE

Of course, *I'm* just a reptile. I guess you wouldn't want to eat what *I* eat. You wouldn't even want to take a bite of this *other* apple here. And how do you think that makes me feel? I guess you think I don't have feelings. That's all right. I'll just go away forever. You wouldn't care.

EVE

Yes I would, I think. I feel . . . I've never felt this way before.

SNAKE

It's a beautiful feeling! It's *guilt*. Have a bite of apple.

EVE

I guess . . . (*Crunch.*)

WORM, *sticking his head out of the apple*
Well, if it isn't Miss Innocence.

BUTTERFLY, *fluttering by*
Swee-ee-eetnessss . . .

SNAKE

Heh-heh. How do you like them apples? And *look* at *you. Hot-cha.*

EVE

Eek! I'm snakèd!

SNAKE, *sauntering off*
Close enough. I'll be *seeing* you . . .

EVE

I don't have a thing to wear!

ADAM, *sauntering in*
Hi, Eve! Look what I picked. I think I'll call it . . . figs. I'm starved.

EVE

Give me the leaves!

ADAM

The *leaves*? What is it with you and leaves? And why are you all
hunched over like that?

EVE, *improvising a skirt*

As if you didn't know.

ADAM

Huh? Know what? How would I know?

EVE

You don't know . . . much. And the worst thing is, you don't care.

ADAM

Sure I do. I mean . . . what do you mean, "care"?

EVE

You know perfectly well "what I mean, 'care.'"

NARRATOR

Okay, stop it right there. This is not working. Adam, take a bite of the
apple.

WORM

Hey!

NARRATOR

Don't eat the worm.

WORM

Thanks for that, at least, but it's my apple!

NARRATOR

You're a worm! No talking! Forevermore!
(Worm looks crushed.)

BIRD

I'll take the worm!

NARRATOR

Go away, Bird.

BIRD

Why?

NARRATOR

What *is* it with everybody today? Here: feathers. Now you can fly.

BIRD

Cool! I still have dibs on the worm.

NARRATOR

"Dibs," is it? You speak to me of "dibs"? You just lost the power of
speech.

BIRD

Aww . . . Tweet.

NARRATOR

Bite the apple, Adam! I thought it would be easier all around if people
knew nothing. I should have known.

EVE

Are you Our Father? You don't sound fatherly to me.

NARRATOR

Father, Granny Smith, what does it matter?

EVE

What does it *matter*? Adam, you sat right there and told me we were created by Our Father.

ADAM

No, not exactly. I said—

EVE

Adam, will you *eat the apple*?

ADAM

Not supposed to.

> Beyond the missing link, beyond the apes and chimpanzees, beyond even the platypus and the possum, the human family tree goes back to the reptiles. Yet we feel little kinship with these cold-blooded creatures. Now, from scientists at the University of New Mexico, comes research suggesting that one of our nicest and most essential parts is prefigured in . . . a lizard. The skink is a lizard whose skin is mostly smooth, except for several scaly little bumps called papillae. Now these scientists report that the cellular structure of these papillae is remarkably like that of . . . nipples. A "nucleic dead end" kept the papillae from evolving into anything irresistible or milk-producing. But some of us humans have nipples *identical* in structure to the papillae of skinks. That would be those of us humans who are male.

EVE

But you *have* to. Doesn't he?

NARRATOR

Never mind, go ahead, Adam, I've got things to do.

EVE

Things? What *things* could possibly be more important than family?

NARRATOR

I didn't say "more important." *You* said "more important." I said "to do."

EVE

You know what you said, and so do I, and so does Adam. Don't you, Adam?

ADAM

Hunh?

NARRATOR

Adam, eat the f***ing apple!

ADAM

Okay, okay. (*Crunch. A beat.*)

EVE

Adam! My eyes are up here!

ADAM

Uhh . . . What's "f***ing"?

EVE

You know perfectly well. What we do at night. Hope-a-baby.

ADAM

Oh! I'm going to call it f***ing.

EVE

You think you can name everything. Well, you can't. Not anything
that already has a *pretty* name.

ADAM

Aww . . . It gets harder and harder to be a man.

EVE AND NARRATOR, *almost in unison, Narrator maybe half a beat
behind*
Are you *kidding*?

ADAM

Come on, Worm, let's go fishing.
(*Worm looks dubious.*)

EVE

You're going *fishing*? Like *that*?

SONG TO HOT DOGS

Rinnie? Lassie? Tell me what dog
Stirs such warmth up as the hot dog.
"*Hot dog!*" we say, to mean "Oh boy,"
Or "Wow," or "Yum." And we employ
The term in sports—as, hotdog skiing
And ballpark hot dogs, one type being
What Babe Ruth ate by the tens and twenties,
Another a player like Tito Fuentes,
Who's flashy as to his
   demeanor:
A showboat type: an
   overwiener.
Hot dogs are cool.
   And highly
   available.
And handy. But—not
   unassailable.
In fact—and I regret
   this greatly—
They're hard to greet
   with "Hot dog!"
   lately.
Critics say those red
   skins tend to
Hide exactly what
   we're into:

> In Harrisburg, Pennsylvania, media circles, the biggest mystery over the past year was what the beautiful TV newscaster Annalicia Bell could possibly see in her steady date, Linus Prosch. Linus was a head shorter and infinitely dumpier than the willowy Annalicia, and his most striking feature was peculiar hair. On top it was sandy and flat, but his ample facial plumage was fluffy and ash-blond, with a greenish tinge. Some observers suspected Linus dyed his whiskers, to promote what was his only topic of conversation, his business: an environmentally progressive hot dog stand called the Greener Wiener. Then, this week, scandal: it seems Linus's visibility was a cover for Annalicia's torrid affair with a very married local megachurch pastor—who also happened to be the Greener Wiener's principal investor. A local blogger came up with the best line: "It turns out Linus not only *had* a funny-looking beard; he also was one."

Mealdog, tripedog, snoutdog, snotdog?
Who can be quite sure what notdog?

Even though there be not in one
Mineral or vitamin one,
Hot dogs are an institution.
So's pollution.

BUT AIN'T NOTHING WRONG WITH A
VARSITY DOG

No, you can't go home again, but you can eat a Varsity chili dog in the Fox Theatre on national radio.

See, I am from Decatur, Georgia. I moved away from there in 1968, in search of some place more sophisticated, more in keeping with my own cutting-edge potential. Since then, Decatur has out-evolved me. According to Wikitravel, Decatur "has become a hot destination for college students and young professionals who want hip bars, great restaurants, and walkable neighborhoods," with "a substantial African-American population, a lesbian community and recent Ethiopian immigrants." In my childhood there, a bar would have had a hard time being hip, because it could not legally have served alcoholic beverages, and there weren't any restaurants either. There was some diversity: Methodists believed a tasteful sprinkle was quite sufficient, but God only knew what the *white* Baptists did, let alone the colored ones. (To use the ethnic adjective then considered natural in white conversation. We wouldn't have said "Negro Baptist" any more than "Negro water fountain." Many years later we would come round to "black Baptist," though it sounds a bit stark. No one would ever have said "colored power.")

Wikitravel goes on to note that "Decatur is one of the few parts of the sprawling Atlanta area that blends a small-town feel with an open-minded, freewheeling, artsy sensibility." That's me all over, I like to think—but only by the standards of yesterday's Decatur. Today's Decatur is so freewheeling it has produced a rap duo, Da BackWudz, which before disbanding was on MTV with, like, Young Jeezy, Lil Scrappy, and Slim Thug. The lyrics of Da BackWudz include shout-outs to Decatur. Rhyming with, for instance, "inhaler." These shout-outs never mention me.

Okay, no, I *don't* know the work of Young Jeezy, Lil Scrappy, or Slim Thug. But I checked out Da BackWudz on YouTube, and here and there I could relate—for instance, in "Mama Always Told Me" when Mama lays down some blessed assurance by phone. Then in "The World Could Be Yours": "Carryin on, this love jones heatin my soul / Like a pot of auntie collard greens on top of the stove."

But anyway, "the sprawling Atlanta area." Decatur used to be right next to Atlanta, whose downtown was about fifteen minutes west on twisty, dogwood-lined Ponce de Leon Avenue. Decatur is still right next to Atlanta, but now that's like being right next to a burst dam. Today, Atlanta is right next to Decatur on all sides. And just about everything in Atlanta that I could feel nostalgic about is gone.

Except that you can still take that same Ponce de Leon route to Peachtree Street and the Fox Theatre, with its onion domes and trompe l'oeil nighttime-sky ceiling (lit-up stars, moving clouds). And right around the corner is the Varsity drive-in, whose chili dogs and onion rings are just as fabulous.

I go way back with both these institutions. Once, watching a movie at the Fox with my parents, I dropped my gum on the floor, and before my mother could stop me, I picked it up and recommenced chewing it. She was appalled at first, but then she said, "Oh well, it *is* the Fox."

The chili, alone, on Varsity chili dogs is better than any other chili-dog chili, and you know how sloppy most chili dogs are? These are *neat* chili dogs, even when you add the chopped onions, which are handed to you wrapped up in wax paper so you can add as many of them as you like (there are always more than you need). The bun on the chili dog is so fresh and yeasty that when sliced (on the premises, bun by bun as called for), it embraces the fresh-cooked wienie cozily. Back in the Great

> A great cheap date is Renee,
> In the most positive way:
> "Each bite of these fries
> Is a total surprise—
> I don't know what to say."

Depression, Louis Bryan, who would marry my mother after my father died, delivered buns to the Varsity. They were unacceptable if they couldn't be wrapped around the finger of the Varsity's founder, Frank Gordy, without cracking. That is still true with regard to the finger of his successor, his granddaughter, Nancy Gordy Simms.

So, when I learned we'd be doing *Wait Wait . . . Don't Tell Me!*, the National Public Radio show on which I am a frequent panelist, at the Fox, you can see why I resolved to bring a Varsity chili dog. I wasn't sure it was even legal to eat a Varsity chili dog in the Fox, but how could it not be auld lang syne? And the experience was good. Near sellout crowd, and though the chili dog was cold, and I'd already had two for lunch, it went down well. But then our host, Peter Sagal, asked our distinguished guest, Dr. Thomas R. Frieden, the director of the Centers for Disease Control, whether since moving to Atlanta (Decatur, actually) he had developed a taste for Southern food. He confessed to a fondness for pie.

So. Hospitality. I still had a fried peach pie from the Varsity. So I tossed it to Dr. Frieden. Fed him perfectly. And he caught it. And then, when his segment was over, he walked off without it, and I thought, *What's wrong, cooties on it? Well, he would know.* But I also thought, *Whew.* Then he came back, and to roaring applause from forty-five-hundred-and-some-odd souls there in the fabulous Fox, he got that pie and left.

Rats. I don't care where you eat it, a Varsity chili dog isn't complete without a fried-pie chaser.

SONG TO HAMBURGERS

Whether you're a dean or miner,
Sommelier or turpentiner,
Critic or construction wurger,
You no doubt enjoy a burger.

You can get into its juices;
You appreciate its uses.
You can feel the steady pull of one.
You would like your right hand full of one.

And all the way! With everything!
Do bleu cheese, bacon, pickles spring
To mind? Okay, there's plenty room.
A burger can so much subsume.
An even tan enhues
    the bun,
And crunchy is the
    oni-on,
And dressed in
    yellow, flat
But not, ideally,
    thin: the pat.

Oh bun on patty on
    patty on bun,
From Florida to
    Washington,

From the W. Bush era: The Raiders are bogged down at midfield, going nowhere, and so is the game. Just as untold millions are about to switch over to a *Fear Factor* re-run, the ball is snapped—and Tampa Bay's Warren Sapp grows (digitally) to three times his size, swallows the ballcarrier, flies to Baghdad, eats up Saddam Hussein, is borne back to midfield by throngs of cheering Iraqis, spits out the ball (into the hands of a bemused official), turns to the camera, winks, and delivers a message from Burger King. We've moved on beyond the time-honored commercial time-out to the commercial change of possession.

Burgers line the thoroughfares,
Luring us into their lairs.

And a burger, in contrast to a bear,
Won't eat us. No. *Au contraire.*

THE LOWDOWN ON SOUTHERN HOSPITALITY

Come on in! Busy? *Me?* No! Sit right down here in my favorite chair and keep me up all night and drink all my liquor. Can I run out and kill our last chicken and fry her up for you? No? Wouldn't take a minute. Are you *sure?* Oh, don't let the chicken hear you, she'll be so disappointed.

What *can* I do to make you comfortable?

You want me to tell you about Southern hospitality?

Well.

It is true that I have long lived largely in the North but am Southern. So I have a certain perspective. For one thing, living in the North enables me to retain the belief that there still is a South, as such.

In the past, to be sure, I have accepted invitations to speak in a Bogalusa, Louisiana, home on Southern hospitality—"Is It All It's Cracked Up to Be?"—and at an inn in Millinocket, Maine, on Northern hospitality: "Why Isn't It Cracked Up to Be Anything?" I have engaged a descendant of General William Tecumseh Sherman in a widely reported debate, staged in a model Southern kitchen at the world's fair, on the issue "Resolved: That to Be a Host in the North and a Guest in the South Is the Best of Both Worlds."

And yet I have a certain resistance to comparisons between Northern and Southern anything. I am often asked, "What are Southern women like?" That is a question to which many people feel entitled to an answer. But I cannot speak with authority—not with authority as it is known in the South—about Southern women. I am acquainted with no more than 30, 35 percent of them, and several of those I haven't seen in years.

By the same token (it was Heraclitus, I believe, who said that we can enter the subway a thousand times, but never by the same token), I have not stayed in the great majority of homes and hotels, or patronized a majority of the stores and restaurants, in the South. Nor in the North, thank God. I have never gotten over the sight of whatever it was that was served to me as fried chicken one night in Akron.

"This is *fried* chicken?" I asked the waiter.

He looked at it. "I think so," he said.

I rest my case.

But that doesn't mean there is no such thing as Northern hospitality.

True, it is possible to meet with a less than heartwarming reception up north. I remember one Sunday morning in Cambridge, Massachusetts, I went to a cafeteria to get coffee and a donut before meeting a friend at the business school. I was greeted by a little machine that gave out tickets. I took a ticket and ordered coffee and a donut from the woman behind the steam table, who was gazing with angst down into a vat of scrambled eggs. I was tempted to tell her I agreed that scrambled eggs should never be assembled in vat-sized proportions, but she seemed to be thinking about something even worse. Without speaking or even looking up, she served me and punched my ticket to show how much I owed. I found a table, and after drinking my coffee and eating my donut and not bothering a soul, I presented the ticket to the woman at the cash register.

Everything seemed to be in order. I wasn't expecting anything more than a smooth transaction, but I was expecting that, a smooth transaction.

The woman at the cash register looked at my ticket, then raised her eyes as though in supplication. "Jaysus Murray and Jeosuph," she cried, pursing her lips unevenly like Humphrey Bogart. "Why do all you people come in on weekends?"

That was fifty years ago. To this day, I don't know what was wrong. I was too shaken to visit the business school, where they probably teach courses in putting the customer on the defensive.

But I wouldn't call that an example of Northern hospitality, exclusively.

WHAT MEN DON'T TELL WOMEN: HASKELL

"One thing I emphasize when speaking to groups of men is that so-called performance anxiety is a myth. Over the years, a man might tell a woman he had 'performance anxiety' so she would regard him as a challenge. Sometimes it worked. If not, he said he was just kidding and asked if she'd like another glass of wine.

"A normal man can do anything. If he wants to. Simple as that. And normal men have traditionally taken this for granted. Today, ironically, women psychiatrists on whom the 'performance-anxiety' gambit has worked may diagnose 'performance anxiety' in male patients. And these patients may believe them. That's why it is so crucial that we as normal men retain all-male venues where we can refresh ourselves as to basic principles. Such as that a normal man can do anything he wants to do. And he always wants to. Unless he is tired.

"When I speak to men's groups, I illustrate my point by singing Blind Sweet Papa Dewey Tatum's 'If Only All the Rest of Y'all Was Not Having Such a Fine Time Blues.'

"Now, I am a product of Old Greenwich, Connecticut. And Choate, Princeton, Harvard Law. My specialty was strikebreaking law until my firm began to represent the Teamsters. I own beautiful vacation homes in four different military dictatorships. Furthermore, I have this rather fluty voice and can't be bothered to keep time.

"If I can get up before people and sing the blues, then how can there be such a thing as 'performance anxiety'? In a normal man.

"We define a normal man as one who can eat two hamburgers."

In Nashville, Tennessee, I cultivated a hamburger joint for weeks, ordering, with an iron will, the same thing every time. Finally, I came in and said, "The usual."

"You mean 'the regular,'" the counter person, named Opaline, said.

I thought I meant "the usual." I thought I was the regular. But I didn't argue. "The regular, then," I said.

"In your case," she said, "what's that?"

Once, I was driving through Kentucky, a border state. I stopped at a truck stop, at about 2:00 a.m., for some coffee. "Where's that kid sister of yours?" a skinny trucker was saying to one of the waitresses.

"Oh, gone off. We don't know where," she said. "She's a wild kid, for nine."

"Hee-a-hee, I get a kick out of her," the skinny man said. "I'd say something and she'd come right back with something."

"She don't let you get nothing on her," the waitress said. "She's that much like Elizabeth."

Then a second waitress came over and said, perhaps in reference to Elizabeth, "You know she says she cleans out 'em sills evuh day, and Miz Clarkson come in here and said when 'em sills been cleaned out, and she said I done 'em this afternoon. And you know they was roaches in there that had died and was rotted. I said they sure do rot quick around here."

Though put off a bit by such forthrightness about infestation, I wanted to fall in with the camaraderie. Also, nobody had looked at me yet, and I needed coffee.

"No roaches in the coffee, are there?" I put in genially.

Immediately the second waitress went sullen. "No, at's just over'ere in 'em sills," she said. "You want some coffee?"

But I could tell she didn't care. There I was, at 2:00 a.m., somewhere near a town called something like Sopping Gorge, in a diner where I wasn't wanted.

Still, Southern hospitality is an institution. Before air-conditioning, climate was a factor. In the South, people were more likely to be sitting out on the porch when folks showed up. You couldn't pretend not to be home when there you were, sitting on the porch. You could pretend to be dead, but then you couldn't fan yourself.

Even today, rhetoric is a factor. The salesperson in Atlanta may give you just as glazed a look as the one in Boston. But the former is more likely to say, "These overalls are going to make your young one look cute as a doodlebug's butt." Southerners still derive energy from figures of speech, as plants do from photosynthesis.

I'll tell you something about Northerners, as a class: They don't think they are typical. A Southerner is too polite to tell them they are. So they don't go out of their way to be. That is what's so typical about them.

Southerners get a charge out of being typical. If a Northern visitor makes it clear to Southerners that he thinks it would be typical of them to rustle up a big, piping-hot meal of hush puppies and blackstrap, Southerners will do that, even if they were planning just to have a little salad that night.

Then the visitor will ask how to eat hush puppies and blackstrap. If a Southerner were to go up north and ask how, or why, he was supposed to eat sushi, Northerners would snicker. *Rightly.* But a Southerner won't even let on to Northerners that they are being typical when they ask how you eat hush puppies and blackstrap.

The strictly accurate answer is that nobody in his or her right mind eats these two things together, in any way at all. But that isn't a sociable answer. So a Southerner may say, "First you pour your plate full of the molasses, and then you crumble your hush puppies up in it, and then you take the *back* of your spoon, and . . ." A Southerner will say a thing like that just to see whether it is true that Northerners will believe anything. About the South.

Northerners, too, will explain things to visitors. It is a misconception that nobody in New York City, for instance, will offer you any guidance on the street. If you allow your pace to flag for a moment, longtime residents will assume you're from out of town (which as far as they are concerned could be Delaware or Namibia) and will come running up to you asking, triumphantly, "Are you lost?" Then they will start giving you directions. These directions are usually wrong (though you can't count on it), but they enable longtime residents to feel that they are *not* lost.

That is one kind of Northern hospitality. Another kind is when you walk into a dry cleaner's for the thirtieth time and the proprietor, recognizing you at last, says, "You again!" If you are willing to accept that he is never going to welcome you, then you're welcome. The advantage of this form of Northern hospitality is that it works irritation right into the equation, up front. Let's face it, people irritate each other. Especially hosts and guests.

Irritation is a part of Southern hospitality too. Say you run into a Southerner where you live in the North. And you take a thorn out of his paw or something, and he declares, "I want you to come visit us! And sleep in my bed! Me and Mama will take the cot! And bring your whole family!"

"Yes, do come," says the Southern wife. "We would *love* it."

"And I want you to hold my little baby daughter on your lap!" her husband cries. "And Mama will cook up a whole lot of groceries, and we'll all eat ourselves half to death!"

And sure enough, you show up. And the Southerners swing wide the portal, blink a little, and then recognize you and start hollering, "You came! Hallelujah! Sit down here! How long can you stay? Oh, no, you got to stay longer than a week; it'll take that long just to eat the old milk cow. Junior, run out back and kill Louisa. Milk her first.

"Here, let us carry all your bags—oh, isn't this a nice trunk—upstairs and . . ."

You are a little disappointed to note that there is no veranda.

"Oh, we lost our veranda in the Waw. Which Waw? Why, the Waw with *you* all. But that's all right."

And you are prevailed upon to stay a *couple* of weeks, and you yield to the Southerners' insistence that you eat three huge meals a day and several snacks to "tide you over"—and finally you override the Southerners' pleas that you stay around till the scuppernongs get ripe, and they say, "Well, I guess if you got your heart set on running off and leaving us," in a put-out tone of voice, and they pack up a big lunch of pecan pie and collard greens for you to eat on the way home, and after you go through about an hour and a half of waving, and repeating that you really do have to go, and promising to come back, soon, and to bring more relatives next time, you go back north.

And the Southerners close their door. And they slump back up against it. And they look at each other wide-eyed. And they say, shaking their heads over the simplemindedness of Yankees, *"They came!"*

"And like to never left!"

"And ate us out of house and home!"

Nothing—not even the sight of people eating hush puppies mushed up in blackstrap molasses—is sweeter than mounting irritation prolongedly held close to the bosom.

SONG TO GREASE

I feel that I will never cease
To hold in admiration grease.
It's grease makes frying things so crackly,
During and after. Think how slackly
Bacon lies before its grease
Effusively secures release.
Then that same grease protects the eggs
From hard burnt ruin. Grease! It begs
Comparison to that old stone
That turned base metals gold. The on-
Ly thing that grease won't do with food

Is make it evanesce once chewed.
In fact grease lends a certain weight
That makes it clear that you just ate
Something solid. Something thick.
Something like *das Ding an sich.*
This firm substantiation is al-
Lied directly with the sizzle.

Oh when our joints refuse to function,
When we stand in need of unction,
Bring us two pork chops apiece
A skillet, lots of room, and grease.

Though Batter's great and Fire is too,
And so, if you can Fry, are You,
What lubricates and crisps at once—
That's Grease—makes all the difference.

SONG TO EGGS

Forget our low-cholesterol diet.
Let's scramble an egg or fry it.

And by "an egg" I mean, say, three
Or four or five for you and me.

All that yellow that could've been chicks
With the white will nicely mix—

Doesn't bear thinking about too much,
But you and I know eggs are such

A soft essential course, or chorus,
They *must* be good both to and for us.

Or why else would a chicken lay them?
She had her hopes. Let's not betray them.

Let's embrace these eggs, let's tuck
Them in and brood upon our luck
And set here, going, *"Booo-uk, buk buk."*

Our best-laid plans will yield to fate.
And we will say, "We lived. We ate."

IRONIC BISCUITS?

Here it is, torn from the pages of the *New York Post*: Empire Biscuit! New eatery on Manhattan's Lower East Side! Packed with hip-or-hipsterish young adults grooving on a wide range of "biscuit-centric" (the term is the *Post*'s) bites to eat! From 8:00 a.m. until the wee, wee hours! The biscuits: Southern style! "It's a food that works for everything," says one of the owners, "breakfast, lunch, dinner, drunk."

Ah, biscuits. Is there anything that says "bosomy eats" more than hot homemade biscuits? You may recall, from the 1970s, Kinky Friedman's counter-women's-liberation song, "Get Your Biscuits in the Oven and Your Buns in the Bed." Let's try a more contemporary spin:

Say someday your sweetie's kiss gets
Stale, you still can crave her biscuits—
Or his, of course.

But who of either gender's baking biscuits
Nowadays? Hence statistics
Of divorce.

Can the biscuit gap be filled on Avenue A? Here I am at Empire Biscuit. Noon. I am the only customer. The vague young man behind the counter says the crowds come on the weekends and at 4:00 a.m., when the bars let out (and when he, thank God, he says, is not on duty). Hmm.

I order two of the basic biscuit sandwiches—an Edwards Country Ham and Egg and a House Made Pork Sausage Patty and Egg, $6.25 apiece—and one of the special combination biscuit sandwiches (which have names), "The You Oughta Know," pimento cheese and red pepper jelly. Sides: cheese grits and "sweet and sour" collards.

The grits are of the large-unit (whole kernel?) variety, cooked way soft, with some cheese sprinkled on top. Heritage, maybe, but this is not how I like my cheese grits. The collards are too sweet for me. I mean, you put a pinch of sugar in a pot of collards to bring out the flavor, but—am I right?—you don't want your collards to *taste* even halfway sweet. As to the sandwiches: the ham and the sausage and the pimento cheese are fine, and so is the pepper jelly, but a *lot* of pepper jelly *on top* of pimento cheese, all squeezed together between halves of a biscuit, overwhelms the pimento cheese. (Heaven only knows which elements prevail in "The First-Timer," Gorgonzola and nutmeg butter with candied mango jam; or "The You-So-Nasty," grilled pineapple, dried cherry, and jalapeño jam with house-made cream cheese.)

As to the biscuits. They don't *register*. They are not by any means *trashy* biscuits. I daresay they are from scratch, White Lily, no doubt, and lard. But these biscuits are flat. Uniform. Apparently designed to be readily sliced and filled with stuff (for instance, in "The Vacación," spiced rum butter and *banana pudding*), in such a way that the stuff will not ooze out.

Now, I might dismiss biscuit-centrism as a flawed concept on the grounds that in a biscuit sandwich the biscuit is not in the middle. But that would be playing with words. Nor will I flat-out accuse these biscuits of being ironic. I am quite aware that a common criticism (I guess it's meant to be a criticism) of people called hipsters is that they wear ironic mustaches. But that, as I understand it, is because these mustaches tend to be so pointed. The biscuits of Empire Biscuit—*here's* your irony—tend to get lost in the shuffle.

Biscuits, my friends, are a side. But not because they are subsidiary. Because they have a kind of musty (in a good sense), heavyish-but-fragile value unto themselves. Sure, put stuff in them, but not, in God's name, *banana pudding*, and not until you put in a big pat of butter and watch it melt down into all the crags and interstices of the biscuit itself. And glory in the crumble, and glory in the ooze.

Enough with the biscuit criticism (bis-crit to be short), you may be thinking. What you don't know is this: Empire Biscuit set me off on a biscuit bender. Over four days, in New York, the Atlanta airport, and Decatur, Georgia (my high-school reunion), I found biscuits in eleven restaurants. None quite hit the spot.

In a Thumbs Up Diner (an Atlanta-area chain) in Decatur, the biscuits were whole grain. Plus not crusty enough. And get this: the servers wore T-shirts saying, "Relax . . . it's just eggs."

What? That sounds like something you'd say to someone who's just been pelted with them. Irony, maybe, that I don't get. But tell me this: Did you ever hear anybody say, "It's just biscuits"?

SONG TO GUMBO

What you get when you simmer with feeling
Okra, ham, chicken, crab in the peeling,
Bell pepper, onion, sausages, shrimp, a l-
Ittle filé powder. Fraught yet simple,
Variegated yet unified through
Because its heart is laden with roux—
Oil stirred in a skillet with flour
Wisely over low heat for an hour.
What a brown you get from that!
And how profound a tone of fat,
What a deep amphibian jumbo,
Grows on those who cherish gumbo.

BOILING THE F-THING DOWN

This fancy high-tech conference, MiND (Musing in New Dimensions), invited me to give its keynote holiday-season lecture, on fruitcake. Well, when MiND calls, you don't stop to think. I said sure. And to myself: *Hot diggity, I'm gonna be the guy that put the IT in fruitcake.* Potential topics started popping:

Postmodern fruitcake. Virtual fruitcake. Fruitcake for our time, with the Bluetooth and GPS—no, "our time" is too retro. We need to get visionary about fruitcake. Maybe I could do the whole lecture in verse:

> *The fruitcake said*
> *To the date-nut bread,*
> *"Just . . . dates and nuts?"*
>
> *"That's right," that bread*
> *To the fruitcake said,*
> *"Nor ifs nor ands nor buts."*

But that goes less to the character of fruitcake than to that of date-nut bread. So how do we get to the essence of a thing? Go meta on its ass. Fruitcake that knows it's "fruitcake." Fruitcake that eats itself, or reminisces about itself—or a stand-up fruitcake, makes jokes about itself:

Fruitcake and a meat loaf sit down at a bar. Bartender says to the fruitcake, "Sorry, you can't bring your cat in here."

Turns out Elliott Arends, who is credited with developing Microsoft's spell-check utility, was also an engaging—now an embarrassing—diarist. When Arends died last fall, co-workers found the diary on his laptop and sent it around. Far from trashing anyone, the diary describes one co-worker as "a Mediterranean beauty whom I savor from, alas, the emotional-distance equivalent of Puget Sound." Another, as "the squash player I would hope to be, had I been born with the boasting gene." A vetting by Microsoft established that no proprietary information was revealed. What no one noticed, until a copy of the diary reached the *Seattle Times* columnist Vern Bergey, were at least 197 words that, though spelled right, were the wrong words. One entry begins, "Deer [spelled d-e-e-r] Dairy." Which, as Bergey noted, "may remind us of W. C. Fields: 'I'm going out to milk the elk.'" At another point, Arends writes, "Too few people care about correct *smelling*." But the capper comes in an emotional tribute to his employer: "I have labored long for Microsoft, but my reward has been *apple*." Presumably, writes Bergey, "Arends meant to write 'ample.' But he's not around to confirm this. And neither is Dr. Freud."

Hmm.

Watermelon says to a fruitcake: "*I* can reproduce myself. Because *I* have seeds. Whatcha got to say to that, pal?"

Fruitcake to watermelon: "Nuts."

Hmmm.

When is a fruitcake not a fruitcake? When it's . . .

Afire? People sometimes might set fire to a fruitcake, mightn't they? When they've soaked it in hooch? But it wouldn't stay burning long enough to qualify as a fire.

Alit? But there's no such thing as a lit. Could it be—*whoa*—that there are no new fruitcake jokes? Can something in fruitcake render all further jokes about fruitcake unfunny? Those little hard lemon-tasting things? Certainly there is nothing funny about those little things themselves; everyone hates those little things. But could I sell the notion that those little things emanate some . . . I don't even know what you call those little things.

Forget jokes. MiND wants to hear theories. What is the classic theory about fruitcake? That there is only one fruitcake, which gets passed around, and around, by the magic of regifting. Fortunately, the theorist in question was a friend of mine, Calvin "Bud" Trillin, the writer. But when I Googled "fruitcake theory," the Internet tended to ascribe the theory to Johnny Carson. I Googled harder. According to deeper in the Internet, the theory was popularized by Carson, who often repeated it around holiday time; but the original proposer of that theory on that show was Trillin; but Trillin has denied

In New Orleans many years ago, I met a wizened woman of the French Quarter who made and sold fruitcakes and also played the horses. A socially prominent lady ordered several hundred dollars' worth of fruitcakes for a lavish tea party she was giving and made the mistake of paying in advance. On the day of the party, the hostess put in a frantic call to the fruitcake lady: "My guests are all here, and the liquor is here—where are the fruitcakes?"

"Drink up, Doilin'," said the fruitcake lady. "The fruitcakes come in third."

that he came up with the theory, asserting instead that he heard it from someone in Denver.

Denver? And if the original theorist was someone in Denver, why had he or she not come forward? Perhaps that person heard the theory while watching Carson. Who might have been quoting Trillin. The person in Denver might even have been repeating to Trillin a theory that he heard Trillin put forward on Carson.

There was my topic for MiND: "Resolved, That Fruitcake Is the Only Thing About Which There Is Only One *Theory,* Which Gets Passed Around and Around."

Unfortunately, I e-mailed Trillin for clarification. He replied that in fact the theory was something that he heard from someone in Denver, but he did claim authorship of a *second* theory about fruitcake. (That no one ever bought a fruitcake for himself.)

There went that topic.

It was the day before the lecture date, and I had nothing. Nada. Oh, I guess I could have disproved both theories about fruitcake with one stroke, by going out and buying two of them for myself. But I don't like fruitcake that much.

So I lectured about meat loaf instead.

And nobody noticed.

A GRAPEFRUIT MOMENT

When my ball-of-fire granddaughter, Elsie, was two, I offered her a bite of very crisp bacon crumbled up in some soft scrambled egg. Her response reminded me how dramatic things taste to a child. Elsie is not finicky, but as an adult would say, she was not herself. The doctor had diagnosed "a viral syndrome, probably." Something, at any rate, was causing her to reject foods she usually loves. She was hungry, and welcomed the bacon-and-egg at sight and smell, but when it hit her palate, she looked so pained. As far as *she* knew, she was still herself, but bacon-and-egg, perhaps willfully, had lost its savor. Maybe it would never taste good again, maybe life would be yucky from now on.

I remembered, distantly, how much more I used to register, and relish, a bite of bacon, egg, toast, all together. Unless of course I had detected in the egg the least bit of underdone white. In that case, I would display such revulsion that my mother would sigh, with a pathos strong enough to counter nearly anything I could muster, and say, "Don't pick at your eggs, son. They're *good* eggs." And I would acknowledge, intellectually, and not without a back draft of guilt, that they were good, to her. But nothing could make me sense that they were good to me, and therefore my position, though I wouldn't dare put it into words, was the hell with them. And as far as I knew, I was right. I knew it was crucial not to lose touch with gut reaction.

I had not yet developed a liberal cast of mind. In the South of the late 1940s, where injustice was hard—but certainly possible—to overlook, I had not begun to awaken politically. Eventually, I did, but not because any disadvantaged person touched my soul. I have thought about this a lot. I believe it was because of grapefruit at David's house.

There have been times in my adulthood—hungover times, for instance—when grapefruit was the only thing that tasted right. But not in my early childhood.

My parents loved grapefruit. My father put salt on it, which struck me as exactly the wrong way to go. He salted watermelon, too. Cantaloupe he salted and peppered. Today I can recommend those seasonings, without finding them at all necessary, but back then they heightened my suspicion that grown-ups were often pretending or being perverse. My mother would put sugar on my grapefruit, to get me to eat it, but nope. She gave up on me and grapefruit.

My mother and I had some history with regard to eating. To hear her tell it, I refused all nourishment for several years. In desperation, she would tell me that the spoon full of baby food was an airplane coming in to land. My lips were sealed. As I advanced beyond toddling stage, she would go so far as to cut a boxwood switch and lay it next to my plate. I would eat what was put before me, or else. The threat of corporal punishment didn't work. In some ways, I was a tough kid.

"I couldn't make you eat to save my life," she would tell me later. Invocation of, yes, "the starving Armenians" did not move me. What did they have to do with my prerogatives?

Finally, heeding our family doctor's advice, she made herself stop worrying about wasted food or the possibility that I was starving myself to spite her. She backed off, and in due time I became a trencherman. Today, with pretty much the sole exception of Japanese red-bean desserts, I say yes to the comestible universe. I even kind of like fruitcake. Is anything, aside from the little hard yellow things, intrinsically bad about fruitcake? I suspect that fruitcake hatred is something that broad-minded people can feel all right about sharing. Everybody needs a guilt-free aversion. But a free society is one in which you can't make people do what makes sense, even if it's demonstrably good for them, until they are ready. Ideally, at least. And as a boy, I had a good deal of idealism with regard to myself.

What I remember of that early mealtime duress is probably from being told about it. What I richly recall is the free and ready enjoyment of my mother's good cooking. As a result, I lack colorful memories of horrid-food avoidance. My wife, Joan, so hated lima beans—they still make her shudder—that she would convey them by sleight of hand to the underside of the drop-leaf table and leave them on the little ledge there, where she would see their desiccated remains when she looked up during games of hide-and-seek and feel no remorse.

But I do remember going over to someone else's house when I was a kid. How different the smells could be, and how strange the food. I remember supper at my friend Jack's house. "Yum," he said, "riced potatoes." This was a concept new to me, but, hey, I liked potatoes, baked, boiled, fried, mashed, or au gratin. (My childhood friend Sally once mortified her parents at a nice restaurant by robustly telling the waiter, "I'll have some kernup greems and some *bo*-taters.")

But the riced potatoes of Jack's mother, in all due respect, were way too salty. I toyed with them, couldn't dig in. And even though I could see the faces of Jack and Jack's mother fall, I knew I was right.

It was different at David's house. I spent the night there. At breakfast, there was grapefruit.

"*Eww*," I said. "I can't stand grapefruit!"

There followed, as well there should have, an awkward pause. My mother would have killed me, figuratively, for being so rude. But there was something else in the air.

I looked over at David. "I mean," I said, one boy to another, "have you ever tasted grapefruit right after milk?"

"Don't taste it right after milk, then," he said.

It hit me that I was wrong. Not only had I hurt David's and his parents' feelings, which carried a different weight with me than my mother's did, because theirs did not assert the force of fiat. I had also caught myself nursing a repugnance, with unjustifiable pride. A more enlightened gut response began to dawn. I could ride with difference, with strangeness even, into a more bountiful life.

That little experience may not strike you as dramatic enough to be seminal. For that matter, you may doubt the sensitivity of my granddaughter's taste buds when I tell you that two days after her betrayal by bacon and eggs, I caught her licking the screen door. She didn't go yuck; she didn't go yum. She appeared to be filing a sensation away, without fear or favor. Attagirl, said the grapefruit.

LET THE LAST WORD IN "APPETITE"
NOT BE "PETITE"

I intend to eat the bear
That you see over there.

My dog would like to eat it, but
I have too well trained the mutt.

The bear is mine.
First, red wine,

Then I mean to eat the bear.
Broiled, mostly, medium rare.

Eat it all, from zotch to goozle,
Small bits fried in lard, as usual.

May well eat it all tonight.
And owe it all to *Appetite*.

Appetite! Every bite

I take I owe to you, for being there.
And now I'll be off with my bear.

PART THREE

MEAT OF THE LAND

STEAK, GENERALLY

I've been off my feed lately. Sluggish and easily peeved. I need—I *deserve*—
to be a more radiant, more effervescent me. A couple of people have
told me recently they feel much better after giving up hard liquor and red
meat. But I'm trying to feel good enough to take up hard liquor again.
This could be a country song: "Too Unraveled to Tie One On."

And give up steak? Steak is muscle, steak is blood, steak is why the
Lord made cowboys. Joe McCarthy, the old Yankee manager, walked
up to a rookie in a restaurant and asked him what he was eating. Duck,
the rookie said.

"Forget a *duck*," exclaimed the grizzled skipper. "Eat a big steak, shit
a big turd, and you'll always hit."

A steak needs to be big. At the Canyon Ranch health spa, I was
served a steak that brought tears to my eyes because I felt so sorry for it.
It was literally the size of my thumb. Seeing that steak on my plate was
like having a blind date open her door, and she's nice looking, but she
stands no taller than a partridge. A serious steak-house sirloin is sixteen
ounces. Eating a steak should be like wrestling a worthy opponent.

There's an essay by Alice Walker in which she ends up spitting out a
bite of steak because it amounts to "eating misery." She gets to that
point by feeling sorry for a horse who seemed brokenhearted because
he'd had a mare put in with him for breeding and then taken away. To
me, that's apples and oranges. I wouldn't want to eat sexually frustrated
horse, myself, but cattle . . .

Many years ago, I herded them a little bit, on my first wife's grandfather's ranch near Waco. I even gelded calves, with a pocketknife, so
the Great Cattle Spirit is never going to forgive me anyway. And if you
have ever tried to herd a cow from behind a tree and have concluded

> Sean Sparks and Sally Revere of Mesa, Arizona, will move next month into what they describe as the world's first modern house that is entirely organic. Constructed primarily of animal-dung brick, lit by lamps burning essential oils and bovine gas, decorated with plant dyes, and heated by solar power accumulated in water stored in tanks cast from ground cartilage and feathers, the house even looks organic. "Sort of like several big cows huddled together, don't you think?" boasts Revere. "But cheerful cows, with cellulose windows." The couple's only concession to the nonorganic will be a toolshed containing a few metal implements and a single outlet for recharging their electronic devices. "One of our neighbors accused us of being 'greener-than-thou,'" says Sparks, "but he's the one who's green—with envy."

that it would be easier to convey the drift of the thing to the tree than to the cow, I'll bet you are tempted to feel, as I do, that a cow is a lower form of life than a steak. What was it Frankie Laine sang in "Rawhide": "Don't try to understand 'em. / Just rope, throw, and brand 'em."

I know, I know, Frankie Laine was a terrible singer whose sensitivities are undoubtedly less to be emulated than Alice Walker's. In another essay, she admits to eating an occasional chicken leg or some crab or "even . . . shrimp," but she tries to avoid it, and "perhaps if they knew or cared (and somehow I know they know and care), my chicken and fish sister/fellow travelers on the planet might give me credit for effort."

Now, I can't see a chicken as my sister. But hens at least are nice to be around. And cows do look at you and moo.

There *is* such a thing as too much steak. I know this from the time some friends and I ate at Peter Luger's Steak House in Brooklyn. We devoured our porterhouses, but I noticed that many other patrons were overmatched by their steaks. I told the waiter that my dogs sure would enjoy some of those huge scraps. So along with our check he brought a garbage bag full of rejected steak chunks. It weighed more than the dogs. With a bone or two and a pair of leather chaps you could have assembled a sizable calf. The tiny apartment I was using in the city at that time lacked a refrigerator, so I dragged the bag to my friends' hotel room and stored it for the night in their minibar; we had to take out all the shelves and snacks and drinks to get it in.

The next day I schlepped the bag to the bus station and transported it 115 miles north to my house in the country. Along the way, it burst slightly. I had to wrap my shirt around it. But the whole time I kept thinking: Molly and Pie are *so* going to relish this. They are never going to forget this beautiful token of my love.

I got home, and the dogs were jumping all over me the way they always did when I returned after an absence of more than ten minutes, and I said to them, "Just wait. Just wait till I unwrap what I brought you."

I dumped all those enormous hunks of prime meat out before them. I stepped back.

And so did they. They looked at the meat. They looked away from it. They looked back at it and sighed, and each of them picked up a big gobbet of the finest steak and chewed on it briefly. Then they went off looking, I suppose, for burial sites.

I stopped them. "What's the matter?" I demanded. "The last time I saw you, you were snacking out of the cat box. Now I bring you this wonderful meat, all the way from Brooklyn, New York . . ."

They gave me hangdog looks. I had overwhelmed them. Exceeded their capacity for desire. It was as if you'd brought your teenage son the entire Rockettes in shorty nightgowns.

Could I get over steak if I overindulged in it? I decided to try. I had a skirt steak at a place called Frank's that hung over the sides of the platter and dripped scarlet/brown juice onto the tablecloth. I had a T-bone at Keens Steakhouse that was not so much red inside as magenta. At the Palm, I had a steak covered with melted butter, and at the next table one loud fat man in an expensive suit was confiding to another one, "This woman divorces me? I might as well change my name to Torres and drive a cab in Miami." And then he took in a big hunk of steak and went on, greasily: "When she was sixteen I said to her father, 'You say

Yes, nouvelle cuisine is over and French restaurants serve lots of rich food again, but fashionable Parisians have long known how to partake of every scrumptious course, from the snails all the way through the gruyère, and yet stay slim: they feed every other bite to the little dog. This practice, however, has sent many a little French dog to an early grave. Or maybe this was just a little joke among the French, as when a wife would look at a husband's waistline and say, "Il faut donner plus de morceaux au petit chien, n'est-ce pas?" Recently in Paris, however, trendy restaurants have gone literal with this joke and installed a new feature at every table: *le petit chien fou*, a crockery dog with a mechanized head that not only can handle all you can dish out but responds to every morsel by rolling its eyes and going, "Oooo-lahhh."

one word about me getting her in late and I'll go to the car and come back and kill you with a baseball bat.'"

That did not put me off steak.

Kobe steaks are from Japanese cows that are given regular sake massages and are fattened on beer. Kobe beef has a remarkably rich flavor, worth savoring carefully. It has to be cooked very rare, barely heated up, or the flavor is lost, in which case your entrée has eaten better than you are eating. While I was giving that flavor all the slow, meditative attention it deserved, I kept trying to think what this beef's texture was like. I had read reviews that compared it to butter, but it wasn't *that* tender.

Then I happened to bite myself. And it hit me: chewing on Kobe beef, as to texture, was like chewing on the inside of my mouth.

That did not put me off steak.

Then, one evening when I had a reservation at Gallaghers, I cut myself badly on the upper lip while shaving. I put a Band-Aid on it. I looked like a settler who'd been relieved of his mustache by a whimsical scalper and had it replaced by an ill-matching nineteenth-century skin graft.

Ordinarily, I wouldn't go out looking like that. But that's how determined I was to have another steak. While I was eating my sirloin, I dabbed my mouth with my napkin and realized that my own blood—not lots of it, but not just tiny speckles either—was mingling with the animal's.

That did not put me off steak.

SONG TO BEEF

Beef.
Good grief.

So firm, so red—
I know it's dead

Cow, and yet,
How can I get

Over beef?
It's my belief

That anything that
goes so well
With potatoes and
gravy—*How can
you tell*

*Me beef is bad when
beef gives gravy?*
Call out the army!
Call out the navy!

We know that a major pollutant of the atmosphere is methane gas emitted by livestock. We also know that methane is the major constituent of natural gas, widely used for heating and cooking. Well, finally someone has put poot and use together. Agronomists at the University of South Carolina have designed a fixture that can be humanely strapped onto a cow or sheep, which allows for solid waste elimination and yet captures most of the gas arising from the animals. Methane is absorbed in highly concentrated form by cells composed of a material developed by NASA for recycling air in space capsules. The agronomy department's experimental kitchen recently produced a dinner for eight cooked with gas produced in one twenty-four-hour period by a single cow. The entrée was chicken.

Ask them. And also ask the cow-
Boy. And tell me how
And also why
It is that I

Should get along
Without some beef behind my song.

STEAK, ENVIRONMENTALLY

Recently Joan went away for two weeks, to see about her mother. "Oh well," I thought, "at least I can go nonorganic." Don't get me wrong; we have a robust gustatory marriage. But she is determined to shop and cook and eat in such a way as not to destroy the planet. I've done a thing or two along those lines myself. You know nutria? Red-toothed beavers with long skinny tails? I ate two big servings of nutria once. It tasted sort of like pork, if a pig were a rodent. I did it on TV, as part of a campaign by the state of Louisiana to encourage the eating of these rodents because they are doing their best to consume that state's wetlands. I enjoyed the nutria, cooked by a French chef, but the campaign did not catch on, perhaps because I come off as being too much like the character in the Harry Crews novel *All We Need of Hell* whose mother says of him, "He'll eat anything he can chew up."

A friend of mine had an aunt who was into health food way before anybody else in Mississippi even considered it. She would send away for special beans and powders and nuts. And sure enough, she kept trim and lively and never got sick. But her family did not approve: it wasn't how the Lord meant folks to eat. At a ripe old age, this aunt went into a coma. And stayed that way for years and years. "See," said her family, "when her natural time came, her mind passed, but her body was too healthy to go." For everyone's sake, I'd prefer for my mind and body to go out together, ideally over a bowl of chili.

But when after Joan left I got to the grocery store and went straight over to the produce that cost two-thirds as much because it wasn't stamped "organic" and began to squeeze it openly—I felt, I don't know, it wasn't as if I were seeing other women. But I was seeing other vegetables. And speaking of other women, what if Joan's friend Merrilee walked by? If you ever need to know that something you want to eat will kill you, check with Merrilee.

No cure for the common cold? How about copper wires up your nose? It worked for Alexander Loschke of Frankfurt, Germany, who believes it can work for you. The businessman Loschke, a home gardener, noticed that when he put copper rings on his tomato stakes, his tomatoes flourished while others' rotted.

So? So—the next time he had a cold, Loschke put a ring of copper wire up each nostril. Thirty-six hours later, no cold. Theory is, the rings get more air into the nostrils (as, presumably, they do into growing tomatoes), and the air combats microorganisms. Loschke is selling the rings for twenty euros a pair. A jingle for him, to the tune of "May the Bird of Paradise Fly up Your Nose":

> Hey, put some copper wires right up your nose!
> Why not try it out, see how it goes?
> Went out without your sweater, and you froze—
> So put some copper wires right up your nose!

Soy products? *Haven't you heard?* Pasteurized milk? *Do you think calves drink that?* Pineapple? *Not unless you grew it yourself.*

So I had lunch at a Mexican place. Frijoles! They may not be holy, but they're damn near free! And made my way home. Where our cat, Jimmy, insisted that he be let out to take his chances in the food chain. (I did let him go, with a little prayer, because the fox and her litter that had been lurking on the land next door were reliably reported to have moved on.) And I found that Joan had e-mailed me a video. It showed a man named Allan Savory telling a TED conference that more and more of the earth is turning to desert.

Well, I didn't need convincing that the world is running out of water. And tempting as it may be to conclude, based on other YouTube videos, that this is caused by cats who have learned to flush the toilet (I know if Jimmy ever got the knack, he'd be at it nine hours a day), it's more likely people's doing.

But the aptly named Savory says all is not lost. Clever cattle growers around the world are reversing desertification by rotating their herds at thoughtful intervals so that bovine pee and poop, worked down into the soil by bovine footwork and given time to foster with hopeful seedlings, are turning virtually barren, all-but-grazed-out land into green pasture, which absorbs carbon rather than sending it up into the ozone layer. We can go on abusing the planet otherwise, and the cows (who, yes, can continue to fart) will save us.

And how can we help? By eating the right beef! Nothing fussy in that! First I went out and urinated on the lawn and walked around on it— mostly as a symbolic gesture, but we *might* want to get a cow. Then I went back to the store and bought a big juicy all-grass-fed steak. Which, to be sure, coast *nine dollars a pound* more than the feedlot-finished steaks, but it sure was tasty. And I felt involved in responsible husbandry.

P.S. Even more enlightening than Savory's speech was a visit to Joel Salatin's Polyface farm, in the Shenandoah Valley of Virginia. Salatin produces beef, pork, chicken, eggs, rabbits, and turkeys so sustainably (working together—chickens eating the fly larvae out of cows' manure while dropping their own manure and so on) that he creates more natural resources and energy than he uses. Michael Pollan describes the farm at length in *The Omnivore's Dilemma*, but to appreciate Salatin's "Pigaerator" in action, you have to see it. It's a shed where cows are munching hay from bins along the wall and peeing and dropping manure (I don't usually resort to exclamation points, but: fifty pounds per cow per day!) on a deep bed of wood chips, spoiled hay, and peanut hulls underfoot. And buried in all that are fermented whole grains of corn, and rooting in and out of it all in search of those treats are some of the most buoyant-looking pigs you ever saw. Aerating pigs, who love their jobs: stirring all that stuff into rich but unstinky compost. In time they'll be pork, but Salatin carries conviction when he says that his operation "honors the pigness of the pigs. And when you do that you begin viewing people that way, and other cultures—honoring the Tomness of Tom and the Maryness of Mary."

CHICKEN MEDLEY

How sweet it is to kiss the hand which
Holds a chicken salad sandwich.

Wonder product, chicken skin!
Tans while holding moistness in.

So often, here's the taste report of
Epicures: "Like chicken, sort of."

Ever wonder who the dickens
Joined the comic and schmaltz in chickens?

Nothing cuts a broader swath
Through the blues than chicken broth.

MORE TO A CHICKEN

We hear much about the dignity, mystery, and vulnerability of more alien, not to say less up-front, animals and aspects of nature. Chickens we chew on or chuckle over. Either a chicken sandwich or a rubber chicken may strike us as more essentially representative of what it is to be a chicken than a living chicken is.

Yet the chicken when granted a free-range life is as close to man and as savory as the apple, as full of itself as the lynx or the rose. A hen's feathers feel downy but organized when you lift her up. She has a peck like a catcher's snap throw to first. A chicken *never* makes eye contact with a person. Who is to say why it crosses the road?

Or which came first, chicken or egg? This is one of those questions like

- Do the same tastes really taste the same to different people, and if so, in what sense?
- If you watched an area of your skin steadily for several hours while coming down with chicken pox, could you discern the moment when a given pock appeared? And if not, why not?
- If you could get inside another person's head, would you know it, or would you think you were that person?

One of those questions, I mean, that people have, with mounting irritation, been wanting the *answer* to since early childhood.

So. I say, the chicken. If an egg had been first, the chances are that Adam, Eve, one of the beasts of the field, even one of the beasts of the air, whatever was around then, would have at least broken and probably eaten it. We have no way of knowing how many projected species were nipped off because they made the mistake of starting as eggs. I assume that the chicken came first, and evaded ingestion long enough to lay several dozen eggs. Also, if the egg came first, then what fertilized it? In fact, the egg must have come third.

"How come a chicken," asked Roger Miller, "can eat all the time and never get fat in the face?" I don't know. I do know that of all the great fried chicken I have eaten, my mother's (rolled in flour and dropped in *hot* shortening in a *hot, heavy* iron skillet, at *just* the right time, for just the right *length* of time) was the best. It was crisp without being encrusted. In her fried chicken, you couldn't tell where the crust left off and the chicken began.

In the comic books, they talked about caviar and pheasant under glass. I accepted these things as literary conventions. But in my thoughts they did not crunch, give, tear, bloom brownly. The richest brown—or *auburn*—in the synesthesial spectrum is well-fried chicken.

Once in Baltimore I heard Blaze Starr ask an audience whether they would like her to uncover entirely her (larger than life) bosoms. When the audience cried out yes, yes, ma'am, they certainly would, she froze; rolled her eyes; replied, with great, pungent reserve, "I reckon you *would* like some friiiied chicken."

The leg and the thigh (which we used to call with no *conscious* prudery the drumstick and second joint) are juicier, however, than the breast (which, interestingly, has never been known, I believe, by a dinner-table euphemism). And the sweetest pieces may not be the fleshiest. The wishbone—destroyed in most commercial cutting—and the "little drumstick," as we called the meatiest part of the wing, are both delicacies. So is the heart, which tastes a little like blood and a little like cardboard. But when chicken is fried right, the tastiest meat of all—delicate, chewy, elusive—is between the small bones of the breast: chicken rib meat. I am the only person I have ever known to mention this meat. Fried chicken is a personal experience, like the woods outside your house. But look for the rib meat. It's worth the trouble.

When I was about twelve, I got for Easter a baby chick that had been dyed pink. I now deplore the practice of dyeing chicks and ducklings, but this chick thrived and made a good pet. Some people don't believe this, but before all the pink had grown out of it, this chicken was already running around in the yard after me like a puppy. I used to carry it around in my shirt or my bicycle basket. (I am not going to say what its name was. You can't win, telling what you named a chicken. The reader's reaction will be either "That's not a funny name for a chicken" or "He had a chicken with a funny name, for a chicken. Big deal.") I didn't really love it the way you love a dog or a cat, but I really liked it, and it liked me. "I would think that would be embarrassing, being followed by a chicken," my then brother-in-law Gerald said once. "No," said my sister Susan. "That chicken liked him."

But the chick grew into a pullet. It didn't look right, and might have been illegal, to have a chicken in our neighborhood, and we didn't have the facilities for it. We didn't want the facilities for it, because at our previous house we had kept chickens in quantity (six), in and around a chicken house, and my father was softhearted about wringing their necks; that is, he would try to wring their necks in a softhearted way. When I asked my mother for details, she wrote:

> The chicken house was there complete with rather sad-looking and unproductive chickens when we bought the house. There was a rooster and five supposedly hens.
>
> The people we bought the house from had them because of the war and food shortage. I was sorry they were there, Daddy was glad. You were delighted with them. It also smelled bad and I hated cleaning it—so did Daddy and we tried to outwait each other. You can guess who won most often. We finally decided two eggs a week were not worth it. The chickens didn't look too healthy, then too they were all named and after one try we decided we couldn't eat them and gave them to a colored man.
>
> The one try was by Daddy. He assured me he could kill a chicken. His mother always wrung their necks etc. and he had watched. He violently wrung the neck (you were not told)—real hard, and threw the chicken to the ground. It lay stunned and then wobbled drunkenly off to the chicken house. We spent the rest of the week nursing it back to health.

When those chickens were gone, the chicken house remained. It was made of scrap lumber and tar paper. I used it as a fort, a left-center-field pavilion, and a clubhouse for a while, but by the time I was twelve, I had gotten off into other things, was playing Little League, and had peroxided the front of my hair, something that boys did in that place and time, believe or not, when trying to be cool or at least mainstream. And my mother hated the chicken house. She said it ruined our backyard.

She said she burned it down by accident. One afternoon she was raking leaves and burning them, and the fire spread to the chicken house. When Mrs. Hamright, out watering her bushes across the street, smelled smoke and heard the sirens coming, her reflex was to yell "Oh dear Lord" and squirt the hose through the window of her house onto her husband, Gordy, who was inside reading the paper. We eventually had to give him our copy of that evening's paper.

Mr. Lovejohn, the old man who lived with his middle-aged daughter next door to the Hamrights, and whom we ordinarily never saw except when he was sitting in his daughter's DeSoto early on Sunday morning waiting for her to get dressed and drive him to Sunday school and church, came over in his dark-brown suit at about the same time the firemen started thrashing around with the hoses. He said he wanted to "counsel with" us. He said fire was the wages of smoking in bed.

"Now, Mr. Lovejohn," my mother said, "no one in our family smokes, anywhere. And there aren't any beds in the chicken house."

"That don't excuse it," he said.

By the time the firemen got there, the chicken house was about gone, but they stretched hoses all over the back and side yards, trampled a young dogwood tree, and eyed our house as if they would love a chance to break some windows. We didn't have many fires in our area at that time, for some reason, and the fire department was accustomed to igniting abandoned structures—often chicken coops, in fact—on purpose and putting them out for practice, playing them along for maximum exercise.

Mrs. Hamright kept trying to get one of the firemen to tell her whether the fire was under control. I think he hated to admit that it was. Finally, he turned around and asked her, "Whud they have in there?"

"Chickens," she said.

"Yeah. Hit *them* rascals with a hose, they'd *take off.*"

My parents didn't want to go through all that again, so we gave my pet chicken to Louisiana, who came every Wednesday to iron and clean and yell, "You better not *bleev* that man, child," at the female characters in the soap operas and who received a lot of things we didn't know what to do with. The chicken was getting too big. I could see that. Having a grown chicken as a pet would have been strange.

"How is the chicken?" Susan and I would ask Louisiana on subsequent Wednesdays.

"Oh, fine," Louisiana would say. But when we said we wanted to visit it, she said she had let it go see her granddaughter, who lived eighty miles away.

"Does she play with it lots?" we asked.

She said she did.

SONG TO RIBS

Of meat there are but drabs and dribs
On ribs.
    But what do I think I will never be sated from?
    What may the time when you ate last be dated from?
    What was the first woman ever created from?

    Ribs.
    Your ribs.
    A rib.

The meat on ribs is *chewy:* you i-
Ntuitively do it to it.

I like the way the meat adheres
Close to the bone.

I think rib meat will stick for years
Close to my own.

I don't care who it is! "Your nibs,"
I'll say. "You may have dibs
On anything else. I have it on ribs."

If those are nice shirts, better get on your bibs.
Here comes Mama with a big plate of ribs.

SONG TO BACON

Consumer groups have gone and taken
Some of the savor out of bacon.
Protein per penny in bacon, they say,
Equals needles per square inch of hay.
Well, I know, after cooking all
That's left to eat is mighty small
(You also get a lot of lossage
In life, romance, and country sausage),
And I will vote for making it cheaper,
Wider, longer, leaner, deeper,
But let's not throw the baby, please,
Out with the (visual rhyme here) grease.
There's nothing crumbles like bacon still,
And I don't think there ever will
Be anything, whate'er you use
For meat, that chews like bacon chews.
Then too, I'd like these groups to tell
Us whether they factored in the smell.

The smell of it
  cooking's worth
two bucks a
  pound,
And how about the
  sound?

Whatever it might take to pass oneself off as Donald Trump, there's a man in Ardmore, Oklahoma, who doesn't have it. He did dine last week with two striking women at the International House of Pancakes in Ardmore, where he told his waitress, Autumn Trundle, that he'd left his wallet in New York but was obviously good for the eighty-seven-dollar check, because he was the Donald. "Not to be catty," says Trundle, "but they didn't seem like the, like, level of girls who Trump would take out. And isn't he married or something? This guy's hair did look sort of right, but not exactly, and he had a nose stud, so I said I'd have to see some ID. That's when he told me I was fired." The trumped-up Trump stuck to his story until police arrived and took him to jail.

HYMN TO HAM

Though Ham was one of Noah's sons
(Like Japheth), I can't see
That Ham meant any more to him
Than ham has meant to me.

On Christmas Eve
I said, "Yes, ma'am,
I do believe
I'll have more ham."

I said, "Yes, ma'am,
I do believe
I'll have more ham."

I said, "Yes, ma'am,
I do believe I'll have more ham."

And then after dinner my uncle said he
Was predominantly English but part Cherokee.
"As near as I can figure," I said, "I am
An eighth Scotch-Irish and seven-eighths ham."

Food fight in western Pennsylvania: Lillian Pernell, restaurant critic of the *Harrisburg Post*, has accused Dexter Fossey, her counterpart on the rival *Harrisburg Times*, of being a "crypto-vegan." Pernell cites Fossey's repeated negative references to meat dishes, for instance:

"The saddle of beef might be all right to sit in, but eat it? No."

"Happy clams are all alike, in one respect: none of them are in the Merry Mariner's chowder."

"The menu called it pork shoulder, but it tasted like the pits."

"Fossey never has a good word for meat," writes Pernell. "He is not just criticizing meat, he's trying to destroy it."

Fossey's response was to call Pernell "a carni-bore."

Ham.
My soul.
I took a big hot roll,
I put in some jam,
And butter that melted
　down in with the jam,
Which was blackberry jam,
And a big old folded-over
　oozy slice of HAM . . .
And my head swam.

Ham!
Hit me with a hammah,
Wham bam bam!
What good ammah
Without mah ham?

Ham's substantial, ham is fat,
Ham is firm and sound.
Ham's what God was getting at
When he made pigs so round.

Aunt Fay's as big as she can be—
She weighs one hundred, she must weigh three.
But Fay says, "Ham? Oh Lord, praise be,
Ham has never hampered me."

So let's program
A hymn to ham,
To appetizing, filling ham.
(I knew a Mona Willingham.)
And after that we'll all go cram
Ourselves from teeth to diaphragm
Full of ham.

SONG TO PIG KNUCKLES

Sweet though be the pig that suckles,
Give me one with ample knuckles.
Doctor, broker, teacher, lawyer
All say, "Knucks, it's good to gnawyer."
When your fighting spirit buckles,
Buck it up with meat of knuckles.

YES TO GIZZARDS

You will never hear anybody say this: "That thing grabbed my chicken by the tenders and held him underwater till, I'm telling you, we like to lost him."

You know why? Two reasons.

One, because nobody would ever volunteer that his fighting rooster was nearly drowned by a duck.

Two, because "chicken tenders" are not parts of a chicken. And yet pretty nearly everywhere fried chicken is sold, at least one way it comes is in these boneless, gristle-less, unrelated-to-anatomy "tenders." Like so many other things today, tenders are 10 percent chicken and 90 percent marketing.

I was reflecting on this fact in a Popeyes in Greenville, Mississippi,

> If a waiter said to you, "The special is the andouille," you might order that spicy sausage, or not. But when Etienne Picot was so informed—perhaps impatiently, and indistinctly—by the server Julio Valdez of Phinizy's Bistro in Manhattan, Picot's reaction, according to court testimony last week, was to bounce a ceramic butter pot off Valdez's forehead, knocking him cold and leaving a dent in his skull requiring surgery. Picot's defense? He is French. And he thought Valdez had said, "Espèce d'andouille!" Which is French slang for "You idiot!" The *New York Post* headline the next day: "The *Hinky Dinky Parlez-Vous* Defense!"

recently, when my eyes strayed over to the buffet. Not every fried-chicken outlet has a buffet, but this one did, perhaps because it was the Deep South. And on that buffet was a big pan of things that are very much actual working parts of actual birds known as chickens:

Chicken gizzards.

And I bought me some.

And I chewed. And chewed.

The gizzard is what a chicken has instead of teeth. When you are chewing a gizzard, you are having the rare experience of chewing what chews. Where else in the food chain are you going to get an experience like that? If eating pig's feet puts a spring in your step, you might in effect be trotting on the trotters, but that's a big "if."

Here's how chicken digestion operates. When a chicken pecks up a bug, say, it swallows it down to the crop, also known as the craw, as in "This whole concept of chicken tenders just sticks—figuratively speaking—in my craw." The crop holds the bug and marinates it in digestive juices until the gizzard says, raspily, "Okay, gimme what you got." And the gizzard's wrenchy slaunchwise muscles and its "horny callosities" (to quote one technical description), and the bits of grit and gravel that the chicken swallows in order to assist the gizzard, all go to work on that bug until it turns into . . .

What would you say it turns into? I'd say it turns into proto-chicken. Let's set aside the old conundrum of which came first, chicken or egg. The chicken gizzard is where chicken begins.

Here, from *The Birder's Handbook: A Field Guide to the Natural History of North American Birds*, is a tribute to the gizzard: "Objects that require more than 400 pounds of pressure per square inch to crush have been flattened within 24 hours when experimentally fed to a turkey."

Aside from Molly Bloom saying yes and yes and yes so expansively at the end, what does any reader of *Ulysses*, by James Joyce, remember? "Mr. Leopold Bloom ate with relish the inner organs of beasts and fowls. He liked thick giblet soup, nutty gizzards," and so on. Joyce himself obviously relished that passage, because further along in the book he's still tasting it: "As said before he ate with relish the inner organs, nutty gizzards," and so on. What a comedown it would be if *Ulysses* were written today, and Mr. Bloom ate without effort odd notional figments of fowl.

> Bruxism. Nocturnal dental gritting and grinding. For two out of five Americans today, it's a chronic complaint. Dentists and psychotherapists do what they can to treat it. But for a growing number of communicants, bruxism is a fulfillment of the biblical prophecy "There shall be weeping and wailing and gnashing of teeth." In California alone, there are now more than a dozen Bruxist congregations. "We are not, quote, 'Holy Grinders,'" says a spokesman for the sect. "We do not, quote, 'speak in teeth.' We do take widespread nighttime gnashing as a sign. That the last days are at hand."

There's an Uncle Remus story, "Brother Rabbit and the Gizzard-Eater," which ends (spoiler alert) in Br'er Rabbit's cackling,

> "You po' ol' Gater, ef you know'd A fum Izzard,
> You'd know mighty well dat I'd keep my Gizzard."

But gizzards are not always cherished things, in literature. For a serious person to concern himself with conventional politics, wrote Henry David Thoreau in his essay "Life Without Principle," would be "as if a thinker submitted himself to be rasped by the great gizzard of creation. Politics is, as it were, the gizzard of society, full of grit and gravel, and the two political parties are its two opposite halves . . . which grind on each other."

I hear that, all right. And maybe a chicken would rather have some slicker method of digestion. Peel the outer layer off an uncleaned gizzard and you are likely to find all manner of

> The school librarian Cynthia McArdle of Racine, Wisconsin, has won the North American Organ Meat Institute's NAOMI award for the best short love poem involving an organ meat. The judge, Billy Collins, called her submission "refreshingly unrhymed, except for the nice touch with the title—no 'liver aquiver' or 'kidney didn't he'—yet there's a formal coherence." Here, in its entirety, is "For Gus": "What liver and onions / Do for each other / We do, my love, for us."

inorganic detritus. Human heartburn must be a piece of cake compared with chicken gizzardburn.

But that's the chicken's problem. The toughness that the bird requires in this vital organ translates into this indubitable virtue for whoever undertakes to eat one: the harder it is to chew, the longer you get to taste it.

The same may be said for sustainable grass-fed, grass-finished beef.

PART FOUR

MEAT OF THE WATERS

SONG TO OYSTERS

I like to eat an uncooked oyster.
Nothing's slicker, nothing's moister.
Nothing's easier on your gorge,
Or when the time comes, to dischorge.
But not to let it too long rest
Within your mouth is always best.
For if your mind dwells on an oyster,
Nothing's slicker, nothing's moister.

I prefer my oyster fried.
Then I'm sure my oyster died.

BORN FOR THE PAN

I am sitting in my Massachusetts kitchen looking out at a trout stream, thinking I should go catch some fish. Not in the trout stream. I have in the past caught trout out there, in the Konkapot River, which borders my backyard, and I have cooked it in here. But when people start talking about freshwater trout, they use expressions like "the wily rainbow."

First of all: Does that sound like good eating to you? Trout are a delicate fish. Flimsy, I almost want to say. I tend not to sauté them

> The British prime minister Tony Blair would never have been born had it not been for a deep-fat fryer. So says his father, Leo, this week in the *Daily Mail*. "Some of me mates and I'd been fishing and caught a few and drunk a few pints and my friend Charley said come round to my flat, where I have a new American cooker, and we'll fry 'em up right fresh. Fires up this cooker so it's full of bubbling melted fat, and—right fresh, I'll say—we were fryin' 'em alive. Kindest way, really. And one of the fellows says, here, let's throw in the eel. We'd caught an eel. And when the eel hit the oil, the cooker was thrown over, and we're slidin', going thump against the wall and shoutin' and steppin' on hot fish all in pursuit of that eel, and there's a banging on the door and I'm closest—I open up and there's the young lady from next door, to complain of the hubbub, you see, and that's when I first saw my life's love and mother of the future PM. And her first words to me, she looked at that lightly fried, thoroughly agitated eel, of which I had ahold of for the nonce, and she says, 'Bloody hell.'"

quite right, and their thin skin and little fishfleshflakes are so fine . . . I grew up in Georgia, among people who lived to eat, and fished to eat. Here is what I would like to eat right now:

Four or five little fried panfish. Bream, bluegills, crappie. Fish made for a pan. Scale him (which roughs up his coloring, but his flesh can take it) and clean him (you can bury his head and innards in your garden plot, deep enough that the varmints won't dig them up, and he'll feed your collards) and dredge him in cornmeal and salt and pepper and drop him into hot grease, and you've got something that is sort of like . . . I'm going to say . . .

Sort of like pie. Pecan pie maybe. In this sense: it's crunchy—in a chewy, not a crudité, way—and it's juicy, salty, sweet. All in one bite.

Second of all: I realize that I am not looking at this from the viewpoint of the panfish. He no more regards himself as a panfish than I regard myself as a Massachusettsian just because I find myself more or less fitting into this place. But here's what I like to believe: that a panfish does not regard himself, or herself, at all. Nobody ever says "the wily bream." Whereas trout probably have a professional association.

What people I grew up among would say about panfish was, "We caught a mess of nice crappie, some of them big as your hand. But most of them a little smaller—"

"Which is the best eating," would be the response.

I say, let trout prove their wiliness on somebody more wily than I. Life is too short for getting into mind games with fish, especially fish that are my neighbors. I used to have a neighbor across the river who was wily, in his way. When the people next to him complained about the noise his kids were making, he set those kids to running around and around the complaining people's house screaming their heads off all afternoon. If the trout out back are as sly as trout in general are cracked up to be, I'd be wise not to mess with them. They might scheme with the beavers who live upstream, who chewed down one of my crab apple trees overnight and took a chunk out of another one before I wrapped chicken wire around it.

Why don't I undertake to catch trout and release them, you may ask.

To me, that would be like going to the meat counter and pointing to a nice steak and feeling it up and wheeling it around in your cart for a while and then taking it back.

A little bit like that, and a little bit like going to the pound and picking out a lively puppy and petting him and saying ain't he the cutest thing and driving him home and showing him the crate he could sleep in and then putting him back in the car and returning him to the pound.

Catch and release leaves me with an empty feeling. And think about it: if any animal is easy to visualize in a food chain, it is a fish. Snorkeling or scuba diving—swimming around looking at fish in their element— now that is interesting. And respectful. Catch and release, to me, is playing with your food.

I am not an insensitive person. For instance, I don't have the heart to use the worms from my compost heap for bait. They're working for me—I should thread them on a hook? But you take a cricket. When you stick a hook through a cricket, he just looks a little startled. Throw a cricket out there on the right-sized hook and *pop*, your bobber goes down and so does the deal. Panfish take to fishing naturally. You don't have to cadge and wheedle, nor heave and groan: you've got a *connection*, flippety-flippety.

As far as I am aware, there is no opening day of panfishing season. It's when I can get around to it. I don't know of any panfishing derivatives—products, marketing, jamborees—so I don't have to feel like I need a bumper sticker that says "Panfishermen Do It Up Brown" or a cork endorsed by somebody on TV. I can just go to a pond I know and catch supper.

HAVE A LITTLE RIVER

If you have a pond or a little lake or something in your backyard, that's nice. But you really ought to get yourself a river. Of course we're talking about a lot of water. Every time I look at the river that I happen to have running along my backyard up here in western Massachusetts, it's a good deal of water streaming briskly on by. I don't know how you'd come up with that much water, and then you'd have to make it go. My river runs itself. It's called the Konkapot.

> I live upon the Konkapot,
> I am a Konkapotian.
> My river doesn't hold a lot
> Of water, like an ocean—
>
> But oceans just slosh back and forth,
> Frothing up and down.
> The Konkapot runs south from north,
> In and out of town.

The town is Mill River. It's named for the mills—cider, saw, and paper—that operated up and down the Konkapot in the eighteenth and nineteenth centuries. The river is named for a Mohican Indian chief who was converted to Christianity and screwed out of vast amounts of property around here by English people in the eighteenth century. In 1763, a Stockbridge, Massachusetts, selectman named Ephraim Williams leased 140 acres of land from Konkapot's son, Robert (who by some accounts drank), for five hundred years at an annual rent of one peppercorn, according to *A Life of John Konkapot*, by Lion G. Miles.

It passes through Mill River village
(Helping make it scenic),
Enriches my small garden tillage,
Becomes part Umpachenic,

Then takes off for the Nutmeg border
To join the Housatonic.
Its virtues, in ascending order,
Are visual and sonic.

The Umpachene is another small river, which flows into the Konkapot just below my place. The Nutmeg State is Connecticut. The Housatonic is the bigger river that the Konkapot gives itself up to. My wife and grandchildren like to go tubing on the river—sitting on old tractor-trailer-tire tubes and floating along. When the river's low enough for tubing to be unthrilling enough for my taste, I bump on the bottom too much. My prostate has held up this long, no sense leaving it on a pointy rock.

It's lovely to behold in ways
    I cannot render verbal—
Nor can I adequately praise
    The tenor of its burble.

However, since I tend to value
    Sound more than sight,
Let's just see if I can tell you
    How it sounds at night.

It sounds restful, I'll tell you that. Once from a sudden downpour of rain it flooded all the way up to the edge of the house and swept away most of the lawn and garden, but how can you hold a grudge against a river?

> Like water running—not from taps
>> But running like a line
> Of verse—a line by Keats, perhaps.
>> Not like one of mine.

> Convey the sound? I can't begin.
>> But maybe I'll be able
> To characterize the river in
>> Relation to the table.

Sometime when the river is low, we might actually put a table in it and have a cooling meal. As it is, we put chairs in it and have cooling drinks. And I have eaten trout I've caught from it. But . . . I hate to tell you this, you'll think I'm a wuss. But it's the truth: I don't feel right about taking fish from the Konkapot anymore. They're my neighbors. They may think my attitude toward them is crazy, though. Maybe you remember, as I do, old *Pogo* comics in which Albert and Churchy, say, have lines in the water but are ignoring them because they're arguing, and a fish sticks his head out of the water and says, "Are you going to fish, or are you going to talk?"

> Whether it trickles green and slow,
>> Like drizzled olive oil,
> Or, replete with sunbaked snow,
>> The Konkapot's aboil,

> It's most like wine that always flows
>> And yet does not run out,
> Is always chilled and always goes
>> Very well with trout.

SONG TO CATFISH

To look at a living catfish,
Which is gray, which is whiskered and slick,
You may say, "Nunh-*unh*, none of that fish,"
And look away quick.

But fried,
That's the sweetest fish you ever tried.
Put a little dough on your hook and throw it out thayor
And *pop* you got a fish that cooked'll be fit for a mayor.

Close white fishfleshflakes, wrapped in crunch . . .
I couldn't eat all the catfish I could eat for dinner if I started
    at lunch.

JUST PUT THE HAIRDO OUT OF YOUR MIND

Frankly, I have never attended a mullet festival, and cannot know what
passions such an event might engender. Still, I am willing to call an idiot
whoever it was at the 2014 Boggy Bayou Mullet Festival in Niceville,
Florida, who threw a full beer can that hit, while he was performing, the
country singer Dustin Lynch in the face. On YouTube, you can watch

Lynch, undaunted, peering into the crowd and saying, "I want to come to your workplace and throw [stuff] at you, man."

You can see where that could lead. "Mommy, Mommy, why is the man in the big hat throwing [stuff] at the Jiffy Lube man? Can I throw [stuff] at the Jiffy Lube man?"

And here's what people will be thinking: *That's about the kind of trend you'd expect to arise from a celebration of the mullet.* The "lowly" mullet, as it is so often called, the "humble," the "much maligned" mullet. Time for a reassessment.

Famously, what people throw during a mullet festival is mullet, and not at anyone, but for distance, charity, and a reason to *drink* beer. The Flora-Bama Lounge and Oyster Bar, on the Florida-Alabama line, draws some thirty-five thousand people annually to its Interstate Mullet Toss. The all-time record, 179 feet, could be seen as a tribute to mullet aerodynamics.

Yeah, but—mullets are indeed noted jumpers. Sometimes they boil up above the surface en masse, and that is quite a sight, but what you want to do then is throw out in there amongst them because there might be some real nice drum or snook up underneath there making them jump. Other times mullet jump individually, for reasons unclear to science—*bing*, all of a sudden a mullet jumps right over your boat. Which is cool, but then the mullet characteristically lands flat, with a splat. The preferred way to toss a mullet is to fold it over and throw it like a softball.

Do people toss trout? No. It wouldn't be respectful. Or tilapia, even. In recent years, tilapia has become the fourth most popular fish course in America, although it is no less a bottom-feeder than mullet. Indeed many tilapia imported from China have been fattened up on pig and chicken doody. Yet when I mention that I am writing about mullet, so many people's response is, "Does anybody ever *eat* one?"

I should think so. Mullet, the saying goes, is a fish for people who like the taste of fish. A specialty of the very nice Spring Creek Restaurant in Crawfordville, Florida, is a real nice dinner of fried mullet, caught in local waters from the establishment's own boat. In St. Petersburg, Florida, Ted Peters Famous Smoked Fish has been largely mullet-based since 1951. At Balise, in New Orleans, the chef Justin Devillier serves tender green beans tossed in buttermilk dressing and topped with mullet *bottarga*, which is cured mullet roe, prized in Asia as an aphrodisiac.

But here is one of the first things I heard from elder relatives while fishing for croakers and whiting—not exactly trophy material themselves, but good eating—in north Florida. One of us accidentally hooked a mullet. It can happen, although mullet are far from hearty biters.* White folks don't eat that, I was told. Not in a mean-sounding way. But any other fish, except a toadfish or something else *patently* inedible, would have been called "him." A Southern friend of a friend of mine developed a taste for mullet recently and served some to his octogenarian mother. She loved it. "Why haven't we always eaten this?" she wondered. "Mom," he said, "that's one of the prices we paid for growing up white."

Mullet, I was told, was good only to be cut up for bait. Check out "Epic Mullet Migration in Florida" on YouTube. An enormous leaping melee of tarpon, sharks, snook, jacks, and—the featured attraction for all those big fish—mullet. Swimmers stand in the surf astonished, and you hear someone onshore yell at them, "Get out of the bait!"

Mullet is not a pretty fish, because its face is too small. You can almost imagine a redfish breaking into a smile (not in a boat, though), but a mullet's face amounts to big bug eyes and little squinched-up sucky lips. A mullet's body is sleek but also swarthy. Generally, its colors ("mullet" comes from the same Indo-European root as "melanin," dark pigment) resemble those of the old, piratical Oakland Raiders.

Conceivably, the quintessentially dumb-ass hairstyle—"business up front, party in the back"—is known as the mullet because of its resemblance to the fish's little-face, long-body look. But it's hard to imagine anybody in the hair business looking at the fish and thinking, "You know what? That would look right nice on an old boy's head." *The New*

---

*"Mullet are vegetarian," says Captain Rick Burns, a guide out of Citrus County, Florida, "so you won't catch them with any bait that has an eye." This makes mullet sound higher-minded than they are. In fact, they eat not only vegetable matter but zooplankton, which may have rudimentary eyes (the simplest eyes in nature), and animal detritus off the bottom—but try putting any of that on a hook. Captain Burns recommends tossing out carefully prepared dough balls of chicken mash and oatmeal as chum and dropping your hook, threaded through a bit of white plastic, into the cloud of dissolving dough. And be ready for a subtle, fleeting tug. If you want to take mullet seriously, get a net. (This may apply to the hairstyle too, I don't know.)

York Times recently reported that the mullet coif had become fashionable, but come on: the examples pictured were highly refined. The fish's image will never be improved by association with the do.

You may know that the fish (not the mammal) whose English name is dolphin is marketed by its Hawaiian name, mahimahi, so potential eaters won't think of Flipper. You may not know that in 1962 the Florida Board of Conservation tried to brand all mullet exported northward as lisa. *Lisa* is Spanish for mullet. This might have been a reasonable attempt to avoid confusion with a northern fish, the white sucker, which is sometimes called mullet and whose poochy, downturned lips are even less attractive than the true mullet's. But "lisa" didn't catch on. A mullet doesn't look like a lisa.

And it shouldn't have to. In the Mediterranean, mullet has been a staple since Roman times. Now it's a fish for the twenty-first century. Because it doesn't eat other fish, it's low in mercury content. Game fish eat it, so it's good for them. It's high in heart-healthy oils, so it's good for people. It reproduces like nobody's business, so it's sustainable. It dines on detritus, which is a service, and only in polluted water does it taste polluted, so it's a wake-up call.

Mullet is also of literary value. It inspired *Man and Mullet: An Elegy for a Lost Way of Life*, by Alan Frederiksen. Michael Swindle in his own good book *Mulletheads* calls Frederiksen "the Melville of mullet." A firsthand, vertiginous portrait of old-school gillnetters grappling with running mullet—each school of them a great "knot" collectively referred to as "he"—*Man and Mullet* does in fact evoke *Moby-Dick*. Here, behold the knot: "Fish on the move; surface appeared to come alive with escaping mullet . . . fused into a mass . . . like acrobats leapfrogging one another but with this difference: now hundreds in the air formed a solid wall of lunging bodies. The conglomerate melded . . ."

And here, within one mullet: "Deftly one removes the black membrane covering the fatty belly, then greases hands and fingers in the oozy substance reborn of the leafy detritus—black mangrove (gopherwood)— ancient tree planking Noah's Ark . . ."

But snippets don't do the book justice. Try to find a copy.

Another tip: Google "mullet gizzard."

FISHING HARD (AS OF 1976)

A man goes bass fishing in order to get away, breathe free, eat sardines, and suck on his teeth in peace, right? So why is that Cajun crop-duster pilot posing for pictures in front of a big tank full of lemon-lime-colored liquid, saying "Thank you very much, fish" to a bass in the tank, and holding up a check for fifteen thousand dollars?

Because he, Jack Hains of Rayne, Louisiana, has just won the fifth annual BASS Masters ("Mystery") Classic at Currituck Sound near Kitty Hawk, North Carolina. He has whipped eighteen of that fish's peers and twenty-nine of his own, including Jimmy Houston of Tahlequah, Oklahoma, who fishes in white pants with red and blue stars embroidered down the seams and . . .

He fishes in *what*? We'll get back to Hains. Let's take a closer look at Houston. Practice day, before the Classic proper. He stands vividly in the bow of his white-and-green-fiberglass-inlaid-with-glitter boat, casting toward one of Currituck's grassy banks.

He's throwing a Pico Pop. It looks like a chunky, scared-to-death baitfish or a legless, streamlined frog. Casts it and twitches it. "I just can't imagine something not coming up and getting ahold of that. I know they're up in under there. Up under them old stump roots. I don't know why a man couldn't catch a lot of fish in this water."

Casts, twitches. "This is pretty water."

He's operating his electric trolling motor with his knee and raising and lowering his electric anchor with his foot while consulting his sonar depth finder and his water-temperature gauge and the meter that measures the oxygen in the water. He works four different casting and spinning rigs. His tackle box contains 190 crankbaits, 80 spinnerbaits, 20 topwaters, and a couple hundred plastic worms. When one lure gets hung on the bottom, he switches to another rod until the boat moves to where the snag is.

"The same guys always win," he says. "They fish hard."

Fish hard! If a guy fishes hard, what is he going to do easy? People go into law or medicine to make enough money to be able to take off afternoons and fish. What will be the point of becoming a doctor or lawyer now? So you can go home and watch people fish on TV? Will people be watching television hard? Sleeping in hammocks hard? Whittling hard, humming hard?

Houston may not be as high gear a caster as Tommy Martin of Hemphill, Texas, who once was clocked at 12 casts per minute, or 5,760 over a full eight-hour day. But Houston does launch a lure about every eight seconds, underhand to save time.

After this practice day, Houston will be popping everything he catches as long as twelve inches into his live well. The fisherman who brings in the most pounds and ounces of keeper bass within the local daily limit during a three-day period wins fifteen thousand dollars and greatly improves the value of his face in ads selling lures, lines, boats, and motors.

Jimmy Houston is a professional bass fisherman. So is Jack Hains, which is why we saw him holding that check and thanking that fish.

"Pro bass fishing has its critics," concedes Bob Cobb, vice president of the Montgomery, Alabama–based Bass Anglers Sportsman Society, or BASS, which is the pioneering and still most prominent sponsor of big-time bass tournaments. "Some folks claim to fish for pay is as bad as bad women." Few pro bassers (as they are sometimes called) dress as colorfully as Houston, but some have been known to spray deodorant on their plastic worms and wash their hands with detergent every time they mess with their motors. Haven't they ever read that bestselling postcard that goes, "Old Fishermen Never Die . . . They Just Smell That Way"? Bass fishing has become nearly as tied up in money, tips from the top (pros hold "bass seminars" at men's clubs), official memberships, and shiny equipment as golf.

Ten years ago, Tom Mann of Eufaula, Alabama, worked for the state Game and Fish Commission, angled for pleasure, fooled around with a spinnerbait he called Little George (after his boss at the time, Governor

Wallace), and poured liquid plastic into worm molds in his wife's kitchen. His BASS exposure enabled him to build a bait company that makes and sells not only Little George (which *Popular Mechanics* named one of the Twenty All Time Great Bass Fishing Lures) but also extremely popular strawberry-, blackberry-, blueberry-, and watermelon-flavored plastic worms. You might think that worm-flavored strawberries would taste better to bass, but things don't seem to work that way.

When Bud Leavitt, the outdoor editor of the *Bangor Daily News*, first attended the BASS Mystery Classic, the annual grand championship tournament, he was skeptical: "Fishing you think of as a contemplative thing, with your son, with your brother, with your dad." But Leavitt saw a pro point to a Marlboro pack "and cast 80 feet and hit it. Then it drifted so he had to cast under a limb, and he hit it again. These guys know what they're doing."

BASS speaks often of its "Don't Kill Your Catch" program. An extra ounce is awarded for each live fish weighed in, special measures are taken to protect the fish from infection (that's why the water in that holding tank was lurid green), and the great bulk of a tournament's "harvest" is released alive every day. BASS has also attracted favorable notice by lobbying against water pollution.

As for commercialization, company reps are on hand saying, "Super sport, super people. Anything we can do for you?" Sew-on patches—"Rabble Rouser," "Sweet Okie Bug," "Mister Twister," "Bass Pro Shops"—are big. Non-pros send off for them; pros get considerations in return for wearing them.

Ricky Green, thirty-one, was a chemist till the fishing money got good. His father was an Arkansas revenuer who, when Ricky hooked his first bass at the age of six, made him land it himself. Green is not an outgoing self-promoter like Bill Dance of Memphis and Roland Martin of Broken Arrow, Oklahoma, the only two pros who rank ahead of him in all-time BASS earnings, but he has deals with a bait company, a boat company, an electronics company, a rod company, a trolling-motor company, and a company that makes "a liquid that you put in your trailer tires. There are eight or ten things it does for your tires."

Bass fishermen used to be loners. Tournaments are drawing experts out of the bushes to exchange techniques. One of those techniques is lying. Or, more precisely, being less than wholly straightforward about answering other competitors' questions when they try to expand their knowledge in time to beat you the next morning.

"Where'd you catch that big fish, Billy?"

"Like to had another'n too," says Billy. "Bigger. Had him right up to the boat."

"Where'd you catch him?"

"Throwed a purple-and-yellow worm out there."

"Where, though?"

"One 'em little pockets."

"Which pockets?"

"Yep, one 'em little pockets in there."

"Where? Which end of the lake?"

"You got any frog chunks?"

"I had a terrific problem today," said Roland Martin one evening during a tournament at Lake Texoma, on the Texas-Oklahoma border. "A guy followed me the entire day. Some local bass club guy. Then, when I started catching 'em, the guy started talking to me on the CB. 'Hey, that's a good one, Roland.' I hung a gigantic fish. 'What was that, Roland?' Then I see him writing things down. 'Roland,' he says, 'I got what I come for. To see you fish structure.'

"'I don't appreciate that,' I said. He got all huffy. I don't mind somebody watching me, but he's stealing my effort."

All of which carries bass fishing a long way from the days Jimmy Harris remembers. The other pros call Harris "Skinny D." One afternoon when he was wearing a pair of voluminous waterproof pants, somebody told him, "You look like a straw in a paper sack." He owns a lot of Mississippi cotton land now and competes in tournaments for the enjoyment. But back in the 1930s, when he and his friends would fish along the Mississippi River levees, "we'd take the string off packages for line, and we'd have one plug to cast so we had to go in after it when it was lost. We caught a lot of bass. And then we'd take an iron skillet, some lard, some meal, build a fire, and throw those fish on it. Some hush puppies, too. That was good."

John Powell, who looks like a well-seasoned Howdy Doody, has been fishing for bass for forty years and has been associated with BASS since its earliest days. At a cocktail party during the 1975 Classic, he told a couple of reporters, "I don't have the killer instinct anymore. I used to catch twelve thousand fish a year. Now, about two thousand. Maybe keep half a dozen a month. Work up and down that bank over there. Compete against Mr. Bass. He's the only one that's a pro. He don't read your cotton-picking Solunar Tables—he got his own computer. If I get a big strike and lose him, I'm not going to throw back in that same spot. We played that one, he won. But in a tournament . . . gotta get that meat in the boat."

Powell has his hand open, gesturing. Ray Scott, president and founder of BASS, comes by and closes Powell's fingers into a fist. He is kidding but also hinting that Powell is waxing heretical. Scott, big, energetic, engaging, moves on. "The people in this room," says Powell after grunting slightly, "are responsible for all the bass boats, all the monofilament line, the hooks, the techniques. You go into a store and buy a rod and reel today, there was some influence on it from this room. This guy Ray Scott, the guy that just come over here and made fun of me and folded my fingers down, he's the greatest thing ever happened to bass fishing."

Powell looks off into the distance, as if scanning the days ahead for structure. "I hope it's always fun and not commercial. I caught my first bass when I was six years old, took the day off from working in the fields, and caught an eight-pound bass with a cane pole and a spotted minnow. Fished thirty-five years without a depth finder. Now I've got in the habit. Soon as I get a strike, I'm looking right at that depth finder."

A couple of corporate monofilament types are edgily summoning Powell away. "Don't ever get obligated to anybody," he advises, and he joins them for dinner.

A good deal of the evening entertainment at the Classic is provided by the fishing stars, choreographed by Scott. After a big buffet dinner, Scott summoned the men with the biggest stomachs up front to dance the hula shirtless. After winning the most applause for his hula and the prize of a Johnson spoon, Bo Dowden of Natchitoches, Louisiana, asked for the microphone. "Let me talk over that thing."

"You can't talk over this thing!" cried Scott in mock dismay. "What you mean? You a fisherman."

The fishermen went out on the last day of the 1975 Classic in cold forty-mile-per-hour winds and flat-bottomed bass boats not designed to cope with ragged swells. The night before, one pro was asked whether he thought the boats would go out if the weather turned out as bad as expected. "Scott would send us out if it was raining pitchforks and Chinese babies," he said. One year at Lake Eufaula, Oklahoma, a norther blew up and started sinking boats. Wes Woosley of Tulsa had to be saved from drowning, twice.

On that final Classic round, waves knocked several boats out of commission, and a number of the competitors went all day—7:00 a.m. to 3:00 p.m.—without catching a fish. That evening when he checked in, Al Lindner of Brainerd, Minnesota, the only prominent northern bass pro, was asked, "What'd you get?"

"In," said Lindner.

"We've had those bluebird days," said Scott. "Bluebirds singing, wives sitting out making goo-goo eyes at the weather. And then we've had it turn bad. I've seen it so cold I saw a flag sticking out frozen." Scott was selling a lot of insurance in 1967 when he got the idea of bass tournaments that were on the up-and-up. Before BASS, tournaments were chaotic local affairs, invariably won by locals—that aspect wasn't chaotic. BASS tournaments are policed and aboveboard. When one competitor was caught bringing in fish he had previously stashed in a basket on the water, BASS suspended him for life and suspended another fisherman, who failed to report him, for a year.

Many of the best-known fishermen are big, beefy men with county-sheriff bellies. "When I get thin," says Roland Martin, "I get cold, sick, nervous." Many of the pros are marked by suntan from the cheekbones down; cap brims and dark glasses keep them pale on the forehead and around the eyes. Their hands are horny as farmers'. Scott speaks proudly of "two-fisted hairy-legged knotheads."

The only two men who have won the Angler of the Year award since it was first given in 1971 are Martin and Bill Dance. Dance seems to be the fair-haired boy. Scott introduces him as "bass fishing's first superstar" and is pleased that he represents the sport so personally. "He could've been one of these old harelip country boys with snuff running down both corners of his mouth," says Scott.

An intensely cordial fraternity-president type, Dance, thirty-five, says, "I've never been in a boat with a man in my life that I didn't learn something. I may have learned not to ever get in the boat with him again, but at least I've learned something. I love trying to figure fish out, seeking the unknown. But competitive fishing—the pressure really wears on me. I can't sleep. I remember when I was six years old and my granddaddy was going to take me fishing the next morning, I'd wake up every two hours. It's the same now. And there's a lot of traveling, with the TV show and appearances. But if I don't promote Bill Dance, no-body will. My fishing has improved 500 percent since I started fishing tournaments, and my income is ten times what it was."

Roland Martin, thirty-six, is shaggier than Dance. He's brawny, clever looking, prepossessing, intense. "I'm trying to be more amiable lately, in the boat," he says. "I've been accused of being a real ass. Won't talk to my partner. The guy you're paired with is supposed to control the boat 50 percent of the time. But I just tell him, 'Let's go catch a bunch of fish. If you have something to contribute, fine.' A guy is going to go for my deal.

"When I was nineteen, I caught a big fish, by accident, and entered it in a local contest and won a little trophy. My father was a professional man, never fished a lick, and my mother was a drama major. One time I missed dinner fishing, came in late, and Dad got so mad, when I walked in with my solid fiberglass rod, he yelled, 'I'm going to bend that thing!'

"He bends it. It springs back. He hits it into the wall. It lays grooves in the wall. He throws it down and jumps on it. It keeps its shape. Then he runs out of the room. I picked up the rod. It was bent a little bit, but it would still work. I loved my dad, but I never fished with him."

Martin couldn't vow to show his parents by becoming a bass-catching star, because there was no such thing then. After college, he went off to a reservoir in South Carolina where he stayed for five years, fishing, doing a little writing and guiding, building his bass-catching rep, and being "a bachelor bum." In 1970, he started fishing tournaments. At one of them, he met his wife. "She had on a big stocking cap and a snowmobile suit and was carrying a big stringer of fish," he says.

"He thought I was a little fat man walking up the hill," says Mary Ann.

"I said to Dance, 'Hey, that's a funny-looking guy.' Dance said, 'That's Mary Ann Colbert, twenty-five-year-old whiz-kid fisherman.'"

"Roland and I courted so much during that tournament, Bill Dance beat him by one ounce," says Mary Ann.

"Seven ounces," says Roland.

Mary Ann fishes in tournaments herself, but not BASS ones. No women are allowed. Competitors are paired by lot, and, well, what if a man and a woman, unmarried, were sharing a boat and one of them experienced a call of nature? "He can just turn his head," says Mary Ann, but BASS doesn't agree. She has done some figurative boat rocking on this count, but the gender bar remains unlifted.

Racially, too, BASS competition is homogeneous. The whole operation, and much of the bass boom, have a white Southern flavor. The University of North Carolina English professor Louis Rubin, a non-competitive bass fisherman and longtime student of Southern literature and ways, goes so far as to say, "The artificial impoundment has done more for race relations in the South than anything else. It has gotten the good old boys away from the general store stirring things up and out onto the water chasing the black bass."

And coming back in to shoot the shit. "When I was a boy," said Scott one evening as conversation at dinner turned to wart remedies, "people said the only way to lose warts was to take something like a button and hide it and then forget where you put it. As soon as you forget, the wart falls off. I still remember where I put that button. I can see it right now on that top shelf in my uncle's house. I can't forget it to save my life." The wart went away, though.

Okay, back to Jack Hains, winner of the Classic, fielding reporters' questions in front of the tank holding his final-day haul of eighteen bass, forty-five pounds four ounces. They look a little disoriented but otherwise unimpaired.

"Do you eat bass, Jack?"

"Nearly every night. Fillet 'em out and save some for breakfast."

"What color worm today, Jack?"

"Purple with a yellow tail."

"What length worm, Jack?"

"Six-inch. That's about as long a worm as I throw."

His regular job is flying for his father, who owns a crop-dusting service. "I work rice and soybeans, dusting." Yes, crop dusting is daredevil seat-of-the-pants precision work that a man can take pride in, and he likes it, "but not enough." Not now that he has a fishing career.

"Why don't you take off your waterproof suit for the pictures?"

"Ain't got no britches on. Had to get out and wade, and got 'em wet."

"That bass behind you in the tank—he's talking to you."

"I told you I wouldn't hurt you," Hains tells the bass.

The bass swims away. Scott comes forward to ask the other fish in the tank, "Anybody else in there want to be interviewed? Pooly," Scott says to the black man he brings from Montgomery to help out at such moments as this, "swirl a stick around in there, get us a fish who'll talk."

A lady with three different colors of semiprecious stones on her eyeglasses is watching. So is a man wearing a patch advertising a patch company and another wearing a jumpsuit advertising jumpsuits. Nearby, a fat man is challenging a skinny man to go quail hunting: "I'll show you how a fat man can walk. I've done walked two bird dogs to death."

Another fish looks out toward the camera. That is when Hains, holding up his first-prize check, says, "Thank you very much, fish." The fish swims away.

"Just look at Jack," says somebody. "Grinning like a cat eating yellow jackets."

"And talking to a fish. Only in America," says another man. He is wearing a hat that says "Field Tester, Yum Yum Worms."

SHARING OYSTERS

I'm at Felix's oyster bar. Across from each other on Iberville are two venerable oyster bars, the Acme and Felix. You are either an Acme person or a Felix person. I am a Felix person. New Orleans oysters are big, hearty fellows from the brackish waters where the river approaches the gulf. When the river has been low, they have more flavor, because their habitat has been saltier, but you can't tell a Felix one from an Acme one. And there is often a line outside the Acme, whereas you can almost always walk right into Felix's and lean against the place where the shuckers are shucking and call for a dozen and an Abita amber beer.

Okay, so there I am in Felix's, alone, eating 'em as they're shucked and working the *New York Times* crossword. The Saturday one, which is the hardest. And the shucker is condescending to talk to me. They won't, always. Generally, people in service occupations in New Orleans are happy to talk to you as if they've known you for years, but the shuckers in Felix's I have found to be a taciturn lot. Then too I have had long conversations with them in which the only word I understood was "shuck," but this one is telling me about a man who, he heard, ate forty-eight dozen oysters one night over at the Acme. "I don't know if he even leaves the shells," he says.

"Fat?" I inquire. Half my attention is into the crossword.

"Yes. But not *extree-ordinarily* fat. About my heighth, with your stomach."

And in comes Becca. With husband. I know her name is Becca and he is her husband, because he says, "Aw, Becca," and she jerks her thumb over at him and says, "My husband, Kyle."

It's late fall, crisp for New Orleans, and she's wearing a sweater. Striped, horizontally, which on a flat surface would be straight across, but on her the effect is topographical. "Shuck us a dozen," she tells the shucker, and with a look over at hubby, "Let's hope one of 'em works."

If I had not seen *Double Indemnity* enough times to be all too familiar with how these things turn out . . . Because here she is over close to me now saying, "I work that puzzle every damn day of this world."

Alice Pitts of Staffordshire, England, convicted of poisoning her husband's porridge because he accused her of poisoning his ferrets, appealed to the judge for mercy. Ferrets do not have a soul, she argued, and neither does anyone who cares more about ferrets than about her. So she could be guilty of attempted murder "only in a narrow legal sense, not in the eyes of God. Moreover you, Your Honor, meaning no disrespect, have the small, dark eyes of a ferret fancier yourself."

"Undoubtedly God's eyes," replied the judge, "are larger and brighter than mine, but if his eye is on the sparrow, it must be on the ferret and even the husband." He gave her five years.

In fact I had just been reading how it was in New Orleans that Walker Evans, the great photographer, fell in love with the woman who would eventually become his wife, though he disappointed her in New Orleans by leaving town after her husband brandished a gun at him. One look at Becca and I'm into a noir-narration frame of mind, thinking to myself, *You know a man has always got to be promoting getting some, and a woman has always got to be promoting getting something out of giving some up, but a woman who is giving you some to get back at her husband can just enjoy it and let you just enjoy it because her ulterior motive is covered.* Problem would be when she gets her message through to the husband, gets tired of that, and starts figuring out how you, too, are letting her down. I'd say Becca's daddy had money till she got halfway through high school and he lost it all; daddy's girl whose daddy folded.

And now, this husband, Kyle. A weedy sort. He nods distantly, looking like he hopes it's not coming across as miserably. "And two Ketels on the rocks," she says, and he says, "Aw, Becca," again. They're both fairly sloshed, but he's fading and she is on the rise.

"'A little hard to find'? How many letters?" she says. She's up against my shoulder looking at the puzzle. Husband's leaning against the counter, studying the first oyster shucked for them. Without moving away from me or looking away from the puzzle, she reaches over, takes the oyster from in front of husband, puts it to her lips, gives me a little half look, and slurps it down.

I say, "Eight."

She says, "A good man."

"But where's the 'little' in that?"

A woman who was just in it for the giggles would have made a coy face and said, "I'm not touching that one." Becca gives me another half look and grabs my pen and starts writing "A GOOD MAN" in.

That doesn't appeal to me, on one level. On another, it brings her up against me even closer.

She smells like her corsage—they're in town for the weekend for a football game from somewhere in Mississippi—and like her lipstick, maybe, which is certainly red enough to be aromatic, especially now that it is set off with a fleck of horseradish.

"No," I say, "'A GOOD MAN' can't be right—see, fourteen down, 'Greek love,' would be 'AGAPE,' and—"

She looks at me with both eyes and rolls them. "Ooh, I don't think so, hon," she says. "Let's just jam it in there. We'll make it fit." She writes "AGAPE" in so that the *E* is on top of the *N*.

She slurps another oyster. That fleck of horseradish is still there on her lip. I could reach over and flick it off for her. Or I could point to the same spot on my own lip so she could get it off herself. I don't do either.

Now she has one of my oysters. "Slurps" is too blatant. She takes it in juicily. Now she's filling things in willy-nilly, free association and spontaneity being the key more than strict interpretation or even in some cases the right number of

> You know how your cat will yowl and scratch to be let out, and then when you do go open the door, the cat will stop right on the threshold and sit down, half in and half out, so you can't close the door? Is this just a cat's way of keeping its options open? No, Puff is fully aware that in a moment you are going to nudge her or him unceremoniously on outside and shut the door. What Puff is doing, according to the Stanford zoologist Hsaing Wu, is laying the old feline freeze on you. It's a control thing. The primary feline stalking technique is to corner prey, then wait for it to move one way or another so the cat can pounce. Instinctively, Puff will seize any opportunity to hold another animal suspended. While you are standing there saying, "You wanted to go out! Why won't you go out?" for that delicious moment Puff is in charge, defying human logic, mouth watering.

Jocelyn Wofford of Milwaukee was turning forty. And she was laid off from her guidance counselor job and laid up with a broken leg. And her husband, Travis, insisted he had to leave town on business. To make up for it, he lined up surprise presents: a home-visit massage and membership in both the wine-of-the-month and the fruit-of-the-month clubs. When he returned from his trip, there were four strangers in his house, sobbing and hugging Jocelyn.

See, when the masseur arrived, the delivery guy was waiting with a box of pears. When Jocelyn hobbled to the door, smashed pears were everywhere, and the guys were wrestling on the ground. Turned out, small world, they were both seeing the same local woman. Jocelyn's counseling instincts came out. She brought the guys in to talk things through. Which they did. And the wine delivery guy arrived and took an interest. The four of them talked, and the massage guy admitted that the fruit guy was right for the girl, so they invited her over, and they all sang "Happy Birthday" and drank some wine and had massages and ate the rest of the pears and stayed the night, and there was more fruit in the truck, so they stayed another night, and Jocelyn and the massage guy decided they were right for each other, and they were all five crying they were so happy and that's when Travis came home. All this came out in divorce court this week. "If only I had given her just the massage, or just the wine, or just the fruit," said Travis, "there wouldn't have been this aftermath."

letters. I am far more tolerant of this than I would be in other circumstances.

"You know we could do this all evening," she says, and in spite of my reserve I'm beginning to have the same thought. At this time, I am unattached, and I am not thinking as sharply as back there in that noir-narration frame of mind. But there's Kyle. She turns to him and says, "Me and this man could do this all evening, keep on going till another puzzle comes out." She takes the last of their dozen. "Kyle doesn't do the puzzle," she says. "Kyle could eat ever' got-damn oyster in New Orleans, and he still couldn't do the puzzle. Let's go, Kyle, put some money down." He does, and my weight sags just a bit farther than I'd prefer in the direction of her abruptly removed shoulder.

Becca and Kyle turn to go, her arm in his, but she looks back long enough to lick the fleck of horseradish off, finally, and to say, by way of farewell, "They like it when you dog 'em out."

I look at my puzzle, which is a mess, and don't say anything.

"'They'?" says the shucker.

PART FIVE

PLANTS

SONG TO ONIONS

They improve
   everything, pork
   chops to soup,
And not only that
   but each onion's a
   group.

Peel back the skin,
   delve into tissue,
And see how an
   onion has been
   blessed with issue.

Every layer produces
   an ovum:
You think you've got
   three, then you
   find you've got fovum.

"Guys don't want to eat leaves, okay?" says Gunner Gundy, owner and chef of Gunner's Grille in Kenosha, Wisconsin. "A pile of crinkly leaves and a lot of purplish leaves mixed in with light green leaves and ruffled leaves, with whiffs of vinegar and herbs, and a few raw-carrot swirls, and sprouts, and something that looks like acorn bits? Whose ribs does that stick to?" But if you're a guy who lives with a woman, chances are the concept "salad" is very important to her, and she can't see why you can't share her enthusiasm. So Gunner suggests you get that lady a copy of his new cookbook, *Lad's Salads: The Masculine Mesclun.* Included are recipes for tossed sausages salad, a bacon-and-biscuit salad, a piña colada salada. But what about greenery? "Yeah, okay," says Gunner, "we cover that under Garnishes."

Onion on on-
Ion on onion they run,
Each but the smallest one some onion's mother:
An onion comprises a half-dozen other.

Some, then, might say an onion is less
Than the sum of its parts.

I'd say it's full of selves to express.
In food or the arts,
Give me pungent, not tony.
I'll take Damon Runyon
Over Antonioni—
Who if an *i* wanders becomes Anti-onion.
I'm anti-baloney.

Although a baloney sandwich would
Right now, with onions, be right good.

And so would sliced onions,
Chewed with cheese,
Or onions chopped and sprinkled
Over black-eyed peas.

Black-eyed,
Gray-gravied,
Absorbent of essences,
Eaten on New Year's Eve*
Peas.

*Actually, black-eyed peas with onions chopped up in them are traditionally eaten on New Year's Day. On New Year's Eve, onion dip is eaten. I put "Eve" here for the sound, and so that I could go on in the next stanza to wonder what would have happened to human nature if "old years' Eve" had bitten an onion instead of an apple in the Garden of Eden. However, I was advised by a succession of readers, editors, biblical scholars, and feminists that Eve had even less place in an onion poem than Antonioni. So out she went.

SONG TO OKRA

String beans are good, and ripe tomatoes,
And collard greens and sweet potatoes,
Sweet corn, field peas, and squash, and beets—
But when a man rears back and *eats*
He wants okra.

Good old okra.

Oh wow okra, yessiree,
Okra is okay with me.

Oh okra's favored far and wide,
Oh you can eat it boiled or fried,
Oh either slick or crisp inside,
Oh I once knew a man who died
Without okra.

Little pepper sauce on it,
Oh! I wan' it:
Okra.

Old Homer Ogletree's so high
On okra he keeps lots laid by.
He keeps it in a safe he locks up.
He eats so much, can't keep his socks up.
(Which goes to show it's no misnomer

When people call him Okra Homer.)
Okra!

Oh you can make some gumbo wit' it,
But most of all I like to git it
All by itself in its own juice,
Lying there all green and loose—
That's okra!
It may be poor for eating chips with,
It may be hard to come to grips with,
But okra's such a wholesome food
It straightens out your attitude.

You can have strip pokra.
Give me a nice girl and a dish of okra.

"Mm!" is how discerning folk re-
Spond when they are served some okra.

OKRAPHOBIA

When the rock-and-roll band of authors known as the Rock Bottom
Remainders got together recently, I learned that my friend and band-
mate Stephen King is horrified by okra. Someone—not me, maybe Greg
Iles, the only other Southern member of the band—happened to bring
up okra, just in passing, you know, as one will. And Steve reacted as
another person might to a vengeful psychokinetic wallflower, or a runaway rabid Saint Bernard, or an insanely jealous Plymouth Fury.
"Nooo," he said. "I don't want okra. No okra. No."

Not an unusual response, among people who didn't grow up with okra, also among quite a few who did. Even the definition in *The Oxford English Dictionary* sounds unsettling: "a five-sided 'pod' (actually a capsule), harvested when immature and mucilaginous . . . Also called . . . *lady's fingers.*"

To me, there is nothing much more savory than cross sections of okra dusted with cornmeal and crispy fried, but I like okra boiled, too. Jerry Clower said the longest dogfight he ever saw was over okra. At his mama's behest, Jerry dumped a potful of boiled-down left-over okra into the dog pen. "A big old hound run up there, *fsllppllp*, and it just went down so fast, he thought the other dog got it and jumped on him. Them dogs fought the whole rest of the evening and didn't but one dog know what they was fighting over."

Okay, okra is slick. But can't we appreciate slick? Ernie K-Doe, according to Ben Sandmel's biography of the singer of "Mother-in-Law," was proud to say, "I'm so slick, grease gotta come ask me how to be greasy." In GQ recently, an emcee named 2 Chainz was quoted as observing that "Atlanta people always say *slick* when we really mean it: 'It's slick hot outside.'"

"Okra gets a bad rap," says Poppy Tooker, author of the *Crescent City Farmers Market Cookbook*, on YouTube, where she demonstrates "how to keep okra from getting slimy." (Fry it in "hot-hot" oil.) Someone from the Philippines has posted a comment: "If you don't want your okra to be slimy then go pick another vegetable because it is made THAT way."

Also on YouTube, Sarah Sawadogo—slickly hot in a little black off-the-shoulder dress and three strands of pearls—shows us "how to cook okra the most delicious way." If the gumbo she stirs up, involving octopus, looks a little questionable, she sells it by tasting it so well, *mmmmm*, and then shouting, *"I see my grandmother!"* Comments range from "I am from louisiana i love okra its good 4 da body and yours look delicious" to "Most delicious wayyyy are you crazy!!! look whoever taught you to cook okra soup this way have wrong you big time miss ladie. NONSENCE!!!" And then of course another commenter has to blurt out, "DIRTY NASTY STANKIN'"—which bears out what another member of the Rock Bottom Remainders, Matt Groening, remarked when we were all in Los Angeles: "Never read online comments, because about the fifth one down will make you hate all humans."

But okra runs deeper than commentary. In Ghana, okra is not only a dietary staple but essential in other ways. There's a reggae-hop band called Okra and a singer called Okra Tom David, and the word for a mess of okra is *nkrumah*—the name of Ghana's founder, Kwame Nkrumah. Ghana's dominant ethnic group is the Akan people. They believe, according to the *Encyclopedia of African and African-American Religions*, that one of the three major spiritual components of a person is "the immaterial divine spark from God that is immortal and so vital that life cannot be sustained without it," and the word for that "soul from God" is *okra*. "If a person is faced with intense disgrace or attacks by evil, the *okra* is believed to react by temporarily leaving the person . . . In such a situation certain rituals are required in order to restore the *okra*." I like the notion of, say, John Edwards having to woo his okra back. I don't like thinking of the soul as slimy. But slick, yeah.

SONG TO LOVE APPLES

Slice 'em, juice 'em, broil, puree 'em:
'Maters, yessiree and mayum.

But:

The tomatoes you see in the stores
Are not tomatoes.
They are no more tomatoes
Than a Wiffle ball
Is the old apple.

They are no more tomatoes
Than the Rev. Norman Vincent Peale,

Who wrote *The Power of Positive Thinking,*
Is the Rev. Jonathan Edwards,
Who wrote *Sinners in the Hands of an Angry God.*
You don't have to think positively about a tomato.
You get caught up in it.

These other things,
Their fathers were neoprene lemons.
Far better share a lumpy
Scarred garden tomato with a worm
Than eat these celluloid things
With no life in them.

They are clean, symmetrical, and—because
Nothing bloodless bruises—all unbruised,
But still haven't got any virtue.
They've spent more time being transported
Than getting good. Like bland
Quasi-mystical young rich girls
Who've been
   humped all over
     Europe
And in and out of
   finishing schools
But never got well
   enough started.
They taste like the
   traveling
   salesman's
Spindly daughter he
   drags around.

Think of all the
   ripeness
Working its way
   through vines

> Houseplants get bored and need emotional sustenance. That's the conclusion reached by Amanda Fleece, a forensic botanist at the University of Rochester, after she lost patience with a droopy ficus in her apartment. "It had been a fairly happy plant before," she told the *Rochester Herald Leader,* "but it wilted. I gave it water, plant food, new soil. Nothing helped. So I yelled at it: 'You're a plant! What in the hell do you want from me? Blood?' I could actually see that ficus perk up, on the spot. So I mooned it. It perked up further." Over the next several days, Fleece sang bawdy songs to the ficus, decked it in Christmas-tree tinsel, and threatened to send it away to military school. It soon had doubled in size. "Wouldn't you get blue," says Fleece, "if you stood around all day in a pot? All my houseplants are flourishing, now that I'm feeding them some drama."

To where these arrested tomatoes were,
Before they were taken green
And carted off. The ripeness
Sighing into the air.
Get your tomatoes from a plot,
Roadside stand,
Farmers' market,
Or get something else,
Or use them for something besides food.
(But these other things
Would bounce off politicians.)

Real tomatoes I would compare
To a lover's mouth. Take them
Round and warm from the sun
As her round shoulder.

Slice 'em, juice 'em, broil, puree 'em.
'Maters, yessiree and mayum.

A PAEAN TO SOUTHERN PEAS

Though English peas or snow peas
Have their appeal,
Southern folk who know peas
Are going to tell you, "We'll
Have black-eyed peas, yellow-eyed peas,
Butter peas, white acre peas, crowder peas,
Zipper peas, mush peas, pink-eyed peas,
Purple hull peas, lady cream peas,

Or medium early or very young small sweet peas,
Please.
Or perhaps
Fancy tiny field peas with snaps."

BOILED PEANUTS: BE NOT AFRAID

And now, at last, the new health food: boiled peanuts.

I know, I was surprised myself. Boiled peanuts may be the murkiest Southern delicacy. People who didn't grow up with boiled peanuts see them simmering in that dark brine in that black pot tended by that sad-eyed man on the side of the road, and the voice of reason whispers, *"What kind of people boil nuts?"* The esteemed Serbian-American poet Charles Simic tosses exotic elements into his stew: "a beer-bottle full of blood," and "tongues with bones in them, / Bones of a wolf gnawed by lambs." In a dispatch from the South to *The New York Review of Books*, Simic said some nice things: "It's not a cliché that people are courteous in the South. Many of them tell memorable stories, love words, and can make something unexpected out of the simplest verbal ingredients." But one Southern ingredient defied his imagination: "The roadside fruit stands were overflowing with baskets of ripe peaches, tomatoes, and watermelons. There was also something called 'boiled peanuts,' which I was wary to try."

Simic had evidently not read "Changes in the Phytochemical Composition and Profile of Raw, Boiled, and Roasted Peanuts" in the American Chemical Society's *Journal of Agricultural and Food Chemistry*, which reported that boiled peanuts have fewer calories and less fat, a higher percentage of good fat, more fiber, and up to four times more antioxidants (which are good for your heart) than raw or oil- or dry-roasted ones. Boiling in salty water draws vitamins and flavonoids, not to mention

> A man once said to me, "I will show you, in the palm of my hand, three things you have never seen before. And will never see again. Are you ready?"
>
> "I believe so," I said.
>
> In his hand lay a three-chambered peanut shell. He cracked it open. He showed me the three nuts. And then he ate them.

fun-to-pronounce polyphenolic compounds, from the peanut's shell and skin.

Fortunately, boiled peanuts are luscious. Online you can find recipes for boiled-peanut hummus and boiled-peanut beurre blanc, but I don't know why in the world you would want to. Half the experience of boiled peanuts is in how you eat them.

Over the sink is not a bad idea; at any rate, you'll want to have a dishrag handy, because boiled peanuts are juicy. (Peanuts aren't nuts, by the way, they're legumes. Boiled ones have aptly been called redneck edamame.) One approach is laid out on, yes, YouTube (*how did we function as a people before it?*) by Sarah Pope, the Healthy Home Economist: "First of all, you take the peanut, put the whole thing in your mouth. Bite it, suck out the juice, *then* you take it out of your mouth, and open it up, and take out the peanuts. That's the correct way. If you eat it any other way, people will know you don't know how to eat boiled peanuts."

I am less prescriptive. For as we know, there are boiled peanuts, and then there are boiled peanuts. Some of them are still a little crunchy, and some of them are, okay, mush. Some of them have a soft lining of the shell, which I like to call the polyphenolic layer. Others partially adhere to the shell so you have to gnaw them out with either your upper teeth or your lowers, or you may want to use a fingernail. There are little single-unit ones that you'll eat hullistically (heh-heh, I mean hull and all), but otherwise I think you'll want to open up your boiled peanut and look at it, see whether you're getting a nutty one or a peasy one, before you slurp it. Do you lose some of the juice that way? Not really, you get it all over yourself. Another sign of a lasting relationship.

SONG TO BEANS

Boston baked, green; red, navy, lima;
Pinto, black, butter, kidney, string—I'm a
Person who leans
Toward all kinds of beans.
I hope that plenny
Of farmers sow beans.
You're not any-
Where till you know beans.

No accident "beans"
In common speech means . . .
Are you anything other than prim?
Have you keenness, spirit, vim?
Can you make all kinds of scenes?
Then we say you're full of beans.

"Eat no beans," Pythagoras said.
Where was his head?

Yankee, pole, mung; Kentucky Wonder;
Wax, soy, speckled: they all come under
The heading of beans. Flavor apart,
They are good for your heart.

SONG TO THE LENTIL

If we are good basic people, then one can assume in us
An affinity for the leguminous.
And there is no more fundamental
Legume than the lentil.

"Lens" derives from "lentil"—due
To the flat/round shape. It's true
The lentil is opaque, but who
Wants soup that he can look down through?

Lentil soup's as clear as fens,
But just as the ocular is eased by the lens,
So by the lentil
Is the gastric and dental.

That image may be inexact. In essence, what's meant'll
Glow through the lentil—
The hearty but gentle,
Almost placental,
Simmered-to-soft-focus lentil.

SONG TO LEGUMES IN GENERAL

A legume in its pod is
Like a pulse.
Absorbed into our bodies
They demulce.

CARROT WHIMSY

What started out as a bit of whimsy . . . has brought me in touch with lots of interesting people around the world . . . I regularly correspond with several people who have collections of carrot items in their thousands. One lady has 36 carrot tattoos! . . . The Museum [is] attempting to be a storehouse for all information about carrots around the world.

—JOHN STOLARCZYK, www.carrotmuseum.co.uk

(1)
"When one of my hippopotami
Gets a parsnip in its bottom, I
Call on the man
With the carrot in his hand—
Ohhhh . . ."
—a snatch of song, overheard, backstage at the zoo

(2)

In 1856, when Jean-Luc Thierry attempted to introduce the carrot stick, he was rebuffed. Etienne Bearnaise, Thierry's hoped-for patron, famously informed him, "It is neither a carrot nor a stick [*Il n'est ni une carotte ni un bâton*]." Having clearly (to us, today) missed the point, Bearnaise went on to explain: "It is too small to beat a horse with [*Il est trop petit pour battre un cheval avec*], and it cannot lure him forward [*Il ne peut pas attirer un cheval en avant*], because it does not look like a carrot [*parce qu'il ne ressemble pas à une carotte*]." Not until 1884, with La Belle Époque in full swing, seeing development of the blue-cheese dip (*dip de fromage bleu*), was the carrot stick's potential realized. And by then Thierry had been reduced to sweeping out bistros for all the butts (*tous les mégots de cigarette*) he could salvage.

(3)

If it's left up to carrots,
They keep growing down
Till they come up in China,
Wrong end around.
—from "If It's Left Up to Carrots," by MURIELLE BINKS

(4)

"Why is gold measured in carrots?"
"It isn't, you know."
"It isn't? Why not, then?"
"There's no point in it."

SONG TO A NICE BAKED POTATA

Say to yourself, or spouse, or waita,
"I'll have a nice baked potata."

It'll do you good, there is no question.
There's nothing it takes better to, than digestion.

It fits
You like pajamas do,
Your favorite pair.
It sits
On your stomach
  like you
On your favorite
  chair.

But on the other
  hand,
Just because it's
  bland,
Don't think that
  feeding yourself
  potata
Is just like feeding a
  processor data.

No, it's thoroughly
Existential.

Once I was served a baked potato with a small triangular cardboard notice stuck in it that said, "I Have Been Rubbed, Tubbed and Scrubbed. You May Eat My Jacket."

No doubt we have moved on beyond that today. No doubt the National Tuber Council is developing a baked potato that addresses the diner aloud:

"Hello. My—name—is—Tatum—and—I—am—your—choice—of—potato—for—the—evening. May—I—suggest—that—the—best—part—of—me—is—my—"

Jacket! But it won't work. Any more than the old print version. Butter won't melt in this quasi-sentient potato's mealy little mouth. What kind of person, even this potato might wonder, would go ahead and eat an entity that says, "You may eat my jacket"?

Say your stomach's as blithe as Shoroughly
Temple and brazen as Walter Wential.
It can handle hot dogs three
With onions and impunity.
And then, with both sangfroid and relish,
Chili that's so hot it's hellish.
Derma stuffed till it explodes,
And then four strudel à la modes—

The stomach of an alligata!

It will still appreciate a
Baked potata.
(With sour cream, butter, bacon bits, chives.)
We have felt *fuller*, and so have our lives,
Whenever we ate a
Baked potata.

And you know it's a sin
Not to eat the crumpled, crusty, butter-tin-
Ctured, vitamin-
Rich skin.
It looks like a shoe,
Or a bark canoe,
But there is no richer, more manifold chew.

Oh!
Idaho.

SONG TO BEETS

A freshly picked and hairy beet
Seems a daunting thing to eat,
Yet it adjusts, when
    groomed and
    worscht,
Most agreeably to
    borscht.

> When a preacher in Pascagoula, Mississippi, denounced the sustainable food movement as "satanic," the local organic grocer Bronwyn Vail saw green. "Business has been slow," Vail said, "and I figured this would click with Pascagoula's progressive, arts-centered community."
>
> By "this," she meant her promotional "Healthy as Hell Week," which featured everything from little red pitchforks in the pickles to shrieks of the damned issuing from the leeks. And all employees decked out in vegetable costumes from hell.
>
> "I was supposed to be a possessed beet," said a produce specialist who preferred not to be identified by name. "Not processed, of course, we wouldn't go near that, but *possessed*. People would look at me and say, 'What are you?' And I'd have to say, over and over, 'A possessed beet.' And they'd say, 'A what, what?' Or they'd just back away. What I want to know is, what possessed Bronwyn to come up with this?"
>
> After just two days, Healthy as Hell Week fizzled.

THE FALL OF CORN

I was born in October. Arose in the fall. "Welcome to the world," said the doctor as he held me up by the feet and gave me a whack. "Too bad you weren't here for the green leaves and sunny weather—and the corn! The sweet corn this year!" He got a dreamy look on his face and forgot about me.

Now I, too, in my autumnal years, can look back on corn fondly.

Alas. Corn, as an object of innocent delight, is over.* When summer floods in the Midwest devastated the corn crop a few years ago, it almost seemed like Judgment. Even the Mississippi had scorned corn.

From way back when I myself was a wee nubbin, until, it seems, like only recently, corn was a Great American Thing. No juice so uncloyingly sweet, no crunch so tender, no dish more convenient (not that you even need a dish, much less utensils) than recently picked sweet corn on the cob. And nothing was so altogether gritty and savory as real corn bread (as opposed to the fluffy sweet perversion). How about just cornmeal:

> Oh anything that lives
> Is sweeter gilded with grit
> That savorously gives
> When you bite down on it:
> > Cornmeal.
> Don't bury me
> When I have died.
> I'd rather be
> Cornmealed and fried.

Corn is the American grain. Native Americans invented it. Some pre-Revolutionary American—according to lore, a Baptist preacher—invented bourbon, whose mash is on average 70 percent corn, with no additives but water, and by law it must be aged in new American charred oak barrels. "Tell me where a man gets his cornpone," Mark Twain quoted a natural philosopher as saying, "and I'll tell you where he gets his opinions." It was from a TV cornfield that *quintessentially* corny Americans rose up, on *Hee Haw*, to deliver dialogue such as the following:

Junior Samples or somebody: "How's that new baby y'all got over at your house?"

Archie Campbell or somebody: "Oh, fine. But I can think of some things we could use a lot more."

---

*Unless you're a pig in the Polyface farm's Pigaerator—see "Steak, Environmentally."

By-products of corn include a musico-beautiful morning: "The corn is as high as an elephant's eye." A standard for being in love: "as corny as Kansas in August." A handy euphemism: "Shucks."

Without corn chips, what would we eat guacamole with? A spoon? Yuck.

Corn provides a symbol for roughness ("as a cob") and for blondness ("corn-silk hair"). Did you know that each strand of corn silk leads to a particular kernel? Corn silk is sort of like Rapunzel's hair, in that it receives the pollen shed by male tassels and channels it, one grain per strand of silk, to the female flower within. Oddly enough, the botanical word for this fine fetching strand is "stigma." Until recently, we might have wondered how on earth any stigma could be attached to . . . corn?

And yet an unignorable consensus has arisen around me up here in eco-conscious Massachusetts to the effect that corn is a threat to our way of life, or vice versa.

Corn stands accused of being the reason the love handles of the people next to us on airplanes overflow onto our armrests. The most fattening, least health-giving, and most carbon-consuming foods are sweetened with corn syrup, fattened with corn-fed beef, bulked up with cornstarch, or fried in corn oil.

Ethanol, a fuel whose mash is equal parts corn and tax dollars, offers only false hope as an alternative to gasoline, because growing corn ties up more real estate than any place but Kansas can spare, and anyway producing ethanol consumes about as much energy as it yields.

Then there's genetic modification. I don't know that I am purist enough myself to oppose breeding

According to a report commissioned by the Wisconsin Board of Education, the extraordinary upsurge in rowdiness on the state's school buses is attributable not to any psychological or sociological factor but to the fact that Wisconsin's schoolchildren have become too obese to fit two to a bus seat. Seats that were wide enough for previous generations no longer accommodate an average pair of kids. Hence the rising incidence of shoving and elbowing for seat room, resulting in noise and violence levels that in turn have created a critical shortfall of drivers willing to transport children squeezed into buses that are bursting at the seams. "If something is not done to make Wisconsin schoolchildren slimmer," says the report, "every school bus in the state will have to go double wide."

Since 1932, the Vienna, Tennessee, High School sports teams—the boys', that is—have been the Vienna Sausages. The boys have been right proud of that name, and so to all appearances have the cheerleaders, who still lead with unabated enthusiasm cheers such as this one:

> We are the sausages,
> We know what we're made of.
> To you our message is,
> We know what you're afraid of:
>> Us! Us! Us!

From time to time, however, players on the girls' teams have expressed displeasure over being called the Sausagettes or, alternatively, the Lady Sausages. At the end of the 2013–14 basketball season, when the girls finished number one in the state and the boys didn't even make the play-offs, that displeasure became public. After the championship game, Tenaysha Dee, Vienna's star center, was asked by the local paper, the *Bunch County Clarion-Bugle*, how she felt. "Not like anything to do with sausage," she said. The next day, as president of the student council, Tenaysha called for a school-wide referendum on a new name for the champs.

First came a school-wide assembly. Among the suggestions discussed, Vienna Austrias was criticized as too foreign and Vienna Aussies as not really connected, but Vienna Awesome Ladies was attracting a great deal of support until someone pointed out that that was an awful lot to read on a jersey. At that point, Tenaysha's counterpart on the boys' team, Bunky Sweatt, arose to suggest, "Hey, what do you get when you put Sausages and Awesome together? Kind of. What I mean is, how about y'all being the Vienna Saucies?"

"Oooooooh," cried the cheerleader co-captain Fiesta Highwater (who happens to be Bunky's girlfriend), and when all the votes were counted, Saucies it was.

bugs out of corn. But if, after eating a rat that ate corn that was gene-tically modified, your cat has six-legged, rapidly ripening kittens, don't blame environmental activists.

I'm not saying corn hath lost its savor. Butter and Sugar or Silver Queen from a farm stand still makes my mouth water. I have not lost my taste for the corn cakes at Jimmy Kelly's in Nashville; in fact, the reason I had fourteen of them just the other night, or maybe eighteen, was that I was thinking of all the near-starving people elsewhere in the world who can't afford to eat corn anymore because the price has gone so high.

As a commodity, however, corn has been pushed too far. Yet another golden oldie bites the dust. Remember when sunshine was good for us?

SONG TO GRITS

When my mind's unsettled,
When I don't feel spruce,
When my nerves get frazzled,
When my flesh gets loose—

What knits
Me back together's grits.

Grits with gravy,
Grits with cheese,
Grits with bacon,
Grits with peas,
Grits with a minimum
Of two over-easy eggs mixed in 'em: um!

Grits, grits, it's
Grits I sing—
Grits fits
In with anything.

Rich and poor, black and white,
Lutheran and Campbellite,
Southern Jews and Jesuits,
All acknowledge buttered grits.

Give me two hands, give me my wits,
Give me forty pounds of grits.

Grits at taps, grits at reveille.
I am into grits real heavily.

True grits,
More grits,
Fish, grits, and collards,
Life is good where grits are swallered.

Grits
Sits
Right.

HOLD THE CHEESE

Consider the delicate balance of power
In cauliflower:
Such a subtle collusion of really
Nice just-off-white musks comelily
Have filled it,
Why gild it?

PART SIX

DRINK

SONG ON DRINK

I know it is wrong, it gets out of hand,
I don't recommend it, isn't it grand?

WHISKEY

You should never drink whiskey alone, unless there's nobody else around and for research purposes. The research in this case being to get to the bottom of why I like whiskey so much. But not to the bottom of either of the three bottles I am researching in. If I were to reach bottle bottom and enlightenment simultaneously, or concurrently, I might not feel the same way about my conclusions, or even remember them, in the morning.

My research so far: a sip of Jack Daniel's, a sip of Wild Turkey, and a sip of Bulleit Bourbon, which is new to me. They were all good. Plenty good enough. I like those single-malt scotches and special reserve bourbons, but unless somebody else is serving them, they cost too much for me to enjoy.

One thing about whiskey is, it has so many great names. Old Overholt, the Famous Grouse, Black Bush, Heaven Hill, Tullamore Dew. And let's face it, it's what they drink in cowboy movies. You don't see white hats or black hats tossing back shots of vodka or rum or taking a bottle of sauvignon blanc to the table.

Usually, when I drink whiskey, it's Jack Daniel's, Tennessee sipping whiskey. I just had a sip from the bottle, and it was good. But you know what Jack Daniel's doesn't have that Wild Turkey and this Bulleit Bourbon do? A cork.

A cork is a great thing in a whiskey bottle, for the pleasure of pulling it out. Let's see if I can spell the sound: *f-toong*. That's if you pull it straight out. If you give it a little twist as you pull it, there's a squeak—no, a chirp, a tweet even—that drowns out the *f* and even some of the *t*. Interesting. That never really registered with me before. Sort of *squee-(t)oong*.

A good thing about whiskey is that you can drink more of it than you can martinis. "Razor-blade soup" is what somebody called a good dry martini, and I enjoy one (*not* flavored with chocolate or whatever, *bleh*), but two of them is about a half of one too much for me. I can't remember ever doing anything rousing or having any very interesting conversation after two martinis. On the other hand, I can have two or three whiskeys, occasionally (never more often than six or seven nights a week), and get relaxed rather than poleaxed. I can even write. See? Drive, no, but there's no way you can run over anybody while writing.

Maybe I should work up something to say when I take a sip or, okay, a slug of whiskey. In *Easy Rider*, Jack Nicholson says this: "NICK . . . NICK . . . NICK, *ff ff*, INDIANS!" That's a little too elaborate for me. Not to mention ethnically insensitive. Here's to everybody! Whoops! Or, no, this is more cowboy: whoopee!

I like Wild Turkey, and this Buillet, no, Bulliet—*Bulleit* (why put an *i* in it for God's sake, there is no *i* in whiskey; okay, there is literally, but)—isn't at all bad, and by the way the Bulleit comes in a flask-shaped bottle that is pretty cool. Jack Daniel's (okay, there's an *i* in that too, and, all right, an apostrophe—but *you know where to put them*), however, is just 80 proof, whereas the Buillieit is 90, and this Wild Turkey I have is—*whoa*—101. So you can drink more of the Jack Daniel's. How much more? Well, I never said I—*Here's twenty dollars says no man ever lived who*—could drink and do percentages.

Love those corks, though. Too much, for their own good. I've pulled

Swansea University, Wales, has sold at auction, for £798,000, a heretofore unknown manuscript in handwriting certified as that of the great Welsh poet Dylan Thomas. Those verses that are mostly legible go as follows:

A gentleman never boils his handkerchief for soup.
He knows that he is part of a sophisticated group,
And though they may be fun,
Some things are just not done,
So . . .
A gentleman never boils his handkerchief for soup.

A gentleman seldom farts in company aloud,
Especially when surrounded by a closely gathered crowd.
And when he does, he has the grace to own up to it proud—
Oh . . .
A gentleman seldom farts in company aloud.

A gentleman never carries cheese bits in his hat.
He knows what will develop as a consequence of that:
Soon there will be mice in there and after that a cat.
Oh . . .
A gentleman never carries cheese bits in his hat.

A gentleman never drinks to excess home alone.
Behavior such as that is something he cannot condone.
But surely others elsewhere can, so—off to parts unknown!
Oh . . .
A gentleman never drinks to excess home alone.

Proceeds of the sale will go toward renovation of the university chapel.

them so many times now tonight, trying to decide which one has the better tone, that they've lost their music. At most, one of them may go sort of *foop*. It's sad. I've worn them down; they're not tight anymore.

I am, though. To the point where I'm feeling sorry for corks and have forgotten what I was researching. But how many researchers can say this: I thoroughly enjoyed it. Do I live near here?

DRINKING WITH KATE SMITH

It lurked, for many years, in the back of my mind: that weird drink Kate Smith served me. Her special drink. I was determined, as God was my witness, to summon that drink from my own raw memory, eventually. No longer.

You want to be able to reach way back in your mind and . . . and . . . bingo. It's a rush. But that doesn't always happen. At the Nashville Public Library recently, Rick Bragg and I held forth jointly about the writing life. After many years of reporting, he said, he had lately been getting paid for *remembering*. I hear that, I said, but here's my problem: I might have already written everything I remember.

Of someone whose former life as, say, a majorette-slash-assassin has come to light, we say, "Her past has caught up with her." At least she has stories to tell. I am haunted by the notion that I have caught up with my past.

Oh, there was breakfast this morning, but that's already a little hazy, nowhere near unforgettable enough to turn into literary fodder. The next thing I recall from this morning, I was looking at the clock and it said 9:30. That memory is pretty dern vivid, I must say. I can feel the texture of the kitchen tablecloth against my elbows. But that could be because I'm still sitting here.

Just live in the moment? Nice if you can afford it, but it doesn't work for a Southern writer. The past is our bread and butter, or at least our indigestion. "The past is never dead," Faulkner wrote. "It's not even past." (I have always wanted to come up with a variation on that famous utterance. How about, if you get a gerbil for Christmas and the cat eats it. You could say, "My present is not alive. It's not even present.")

And yet the past may be this much like the future: you can run out of it.

Had I been prudent, I would have stashed away some nostalgia to trot out in this my anecdotage. But what if I hadn't lived this long? What if I had gone to my grave without getting mileage out of, for instance, all of my dogs? How could I know I was recalling them prematurely, so when *Garden & Gun* suggested I write a dog reminiscence, I had already squeezed every conceivable word out of every blessed dog I ever had, from Sailor to Pie. What I did was, I wrote about *not* having a dog, in these my fool's-golden years. Down that rabbit hole, not much left to sniff.

Time for a flashback to Kate Smith, the Songbird of the South. FDR once introduced her to King George VI of England: "This is Kate Smith. Miss Smith is America." Her head was a moon, the rest of her a mountain; and her theme song was "When the Moon Comes over the Mountain." She also had huge hits with "God Bless America" and, God help us, "That's Why Darkies Were Born." In the 1930s, 1940s, 1950s, she was Taylor Swift, Miley Cyrus, and Lady Gaga rolled into one—except Miss Smith was actually from the South, unlike Miss Swift, and Miss Smith would never have ridden a swinging wrecking ball naked, like Miss Cyrus, and Miss Smith didn't need to wear an outfit made of meat, like Miss Gaga, because she was packing plenty on her own big bones.

In the mid-1970s, I was working for *Sports Illustrated*, and Kate Smith had become an icon of ice hockey. Her "God Bless America" before games had inspired the Philadelphia Flyers to triumph after triumph. She was notoriously wholesome, a spokeswoman for Jell-O and for Swans Down flour. (There's something nice about the image of flour as swan featherlets. It makes you want to go *tp*, *tp*, but so does eating, say, popcorn.) The Flyers were not wholesome. They were known as the Broad Street Bullies. So I could have taken a snarky slant. But I liked her. I liked the way she belted "God Bless America." During my visit she was

> Milk,
> Unless you are lactose intolerant,
> Is a universal swallerant.

cheery and sociable and said not one quotable word.

So I didn't write anything. Then one day I was drinking with other reporters, and one of them claimed to have had scotch and milk with Adam Clayton Powell. Another one claimed black coffee, two sugars, and Dutch gin with Ray Charles. I thought I could top them. "Kate Smith and I had her special . . . ," I said. And I had forgotten what it was. Over the years, I racked my brain. I would lie on my back pretending not to care, hoping that drink would drift accessibly by. It was like trying to get your late great-great-grandfather to remember where they buried the silver.

Finally, just moments ago, I gave up. Typed in "Kate Smith drink," and there it was, in an old AP story. A London Fog, she called it. Half milk, half Coke. "It looked awful," said the reporter. I had remembered it as weirder than that.

The past is not dead; it's Googlable.

PART SEVEN

FOOD IN THE ARTS

FOOD NAMES FOR BANDS, I

Gravy Flavored Kisses, the name of a blues-rock-reggae-etcetera New Orleans band, has everything a normal person really needs: food, sex, music, and interior rhyme. The band's bassist, Damon Motto (a good name right there), says the name's origin is "a closely guarded secret. But what I can tell you is that it's Popeyes related." Maybe the name is borderline off-putting, if you dwell on it. How about Pie-Flavored Kisses. Kiss-Flavored Pie.

No, Gravy Flavored Kisses is sweet and savory enough as it is. Which is not to say that all the good food-related band names have been taken.

For old guys doing oldies, how about Gin-Soaked Raisins—you've got your wrinkles and your alcoholism, plus, altogether, a remedy for arthritis.

How about a group specializing in *bad* old favorites: Popular Cheese, or Yesterday's Specials.

Ambiguous boys: Bubble and Squeak
Country goth: Death on a Cracker
Psychedelic polka: Shroom-pa-pa
Swamp pop: Flamingo Puree (if that's not the next Carl
    Hiaasen novel)
Cajun two-step: *Boudincin'*
Ballroom: Creamy Dip
Emo: Pity Patty
Bounce music: Hampop
Soft rock: Roll
Punk: Baby Ruthless
Crustpunk: Dumpster Divas
Enigmatic Southern: Q

LOUIS, LOUIS, LOUIS, FATS, AND SLIM

If music be the food of love . . . Or is it the love of food? Salsa is hot sauce, zydeco comes from *les haricots*, and jazz was invented (at least according to the man himself, Jelly Roll Morton) by a man named Jelly Roll. Rock groups have had food-associated names from Cream to Korn. (Not to mention Neutral Milk Hotel, Pomegranates, Jimmy Eat World, Slobberbone, and Half Man Half Biscuit.) Many people call an ocarina a sweet potato. The African juba beat, one of the most essential riffs of rock and roll, has been more popularly known as the hambone. How would we talk about jazz without the use of "chops," "cooking," "tasty," and "jam"? And if you don't think "jam" as in "jam session" has anything to do with food, you're forgetting Fats Waller's "Black Raspberry Jam" and his verbal asides thereto, like "Spread that jam around, yehhhhh."

Waller is the fourth most prolific recorder of food-related music. If you want to challenge that statement, show me your database. Mine is 2,961 taped recordings of food-related songs. Fats appears, singing and playing the organ or piano, on 25 of them, including three different versions of what I venture to call the most recorded food song ever, "Honeysuckle Rose." I have thirty-five versions of that song, three of them featuring Fats himself. He wrote

The "Sweetie CD," which has proved so popular among Tokyo teenyboppers, is on its way to our shores. It was only last summer that the Japanese firm Oishi Ongaku (in English, "Delicious Music") developed a process for burning songs onto hard caramelized sugar discs, but already the label's first release, "Tired of Listening Eat This," has sold over a million copies. And now American music lovers will be able to hear, and munch on, the same Nip-pop number in English translation. "Doesn't taste as bad as it sounds" is *Rolling Stone*'s capsule preview.

the music; Andy Razaf wrote the lyrics: "When I take a sip / From your tasty lips / The honey fairly drips," and so on.

Fats smacks his lips over that song like nobody else. And yes, to get this out of the way, food songs *do* tend to be about sex. But they're also about food. Waller's propensity for swaying women's thinking along the lines of one of his songs, "You're My Dish," got him into plenty of trouble, but his appetite for food was what killed him at thirty-nine. (Well, for food and drink. The eight fingers of whiskey he took in the morning, four before shaving and four after, he called "my liquid ham and eggs.") Once, while dining with the orchestra leader Fletcher Henderson, the story goes, Fats ate nine hamburgers and found he had no money. Pay for the burgers, he told Henderson, and I'll write you nine songs. Henderson agreed. Waller called for paper and dashed off the melodies right there at the table.

Among the food songs Fats recorded are "You're Not the Only Oyster in the Stew" (nor "the only wrinkle on the prune"), "Rump Steak Serenade," "Hold Tight (Want Some Seafood, Mama)," and "Eep, Ipe, Wanna Piece of Pie." If his music—the rolling-thunder left hand, the right hand like a band of pixies, and the comparable wicked-ingenuous, meaty-sweetie range of manner and voice—were food, it would be a roast rack of lamb with plenty of au jus and mint.

Perhaps Bulee "Slim" Gaillard—who ranks fifth in food-music production, with twenty-four recordings—was jiving when he said, "I invented the word *groovy*." But he did make up a language, called Vout, which consisted largely of the word "vout," other words that resembled "vout," and the widely applied suffix "o'roony." And the following are cold facts: that a copy of his first hit song, "Cement Mixer, Putti, Putti," was buried along with "The Stars and Stripes Together" and "Rhapsody in Blue" in a time capsule at the 1939 New York World's Fair; that he appears in the Jack Kerouac novel *On the Road* as someone whom the arch-hipster character Dean Moriarty regards as God; and that—more to the point here—he was composer and co-performer of "Avocado Seed Soup Symphony" (in two parts) and many other songs that one critic characterized as "musical mixtures of avocado, chicken, rice, lamb and grapeleaves garnished with Greek and Arabic speech patterns" and other elements.

What do folks ingest these days when they're raving all night to technopop? Benzodioxyl-methyl-propanimine, popularly known as Molly. Or so I'm told. But if an extra oxygen molecule slips in there, you've got benzo*tri*oxyl: the accidental offshoot known as O'Molly. Whereas Molly makes you feel all ecstatic and rubbery, O'Molly induces an intense craving for weepy old Irish ballads. Understandably, O'Molly has caused havoc on club dance floors. When you're gyrating to electroclash, with the laser lights and all, the last thing you want is people standing there glaring at you and crooning "Danny Boy," or worse. According to a study issued this week by the Drug Enforcement Administration, no fatal overdoses of O'Molly have been reported, but a Boston DJ was beaten and thrown through a plate-glass window for refusing to sample "My Cheek on Mother's Tattered Shawl," a song virtually impossible to twerk to.

We don't know how much of what we know about Gaillard's life is true. He claimed Cuba as his birthplace, but apparently Detroit (in 1916) is more likely. His father, a steward on a steamship, took twelve-year-old Slim along on a round-the-world cruise. And accidentally left him on the isle of Crete. There the boy is said to have remained for a year or so, broadening his horizons culinarily and otherwise, before finding his way to (or back to) Detroit, where he was adopted by an Algerian family. Somewhere along the way, he picked up smatterings of Yiddish, which stood him in good stead when he came to compose "Matzoh Balls," "Drei Six Cents," and "Dunkin' Bagel." That last number, as recorded by the Slim Gaillard Quartet, moves from an initial tango feel, with a backdrop of sort-of-African-sounding drums, through lots of noodly piano arpeggios, a dash of snake-charmer/hootchy-kootchy, and lyrics that repeat the title very often and sprightly, and also bring in gefilte fish, pickled herring, and "Lox o'*roony!*"

Gaillard played guitar and most other instruments with eminent groovers such as Charlie Parker, Dizzy Gillespie, and, eventually, his son-in-law Marvin Gaye. His voice was a hummus-smooth baritone, and on piano he could play the blues or "Clair de Lune" with the backs of his hands. But the man who served up "Eatin' with Boogie," "When Banana Skins Are Falling," and "Mama's in the Kitchen, but We've Got Pop on Ice" was more than just a jazz virtuoso. He stocked our fridge with soups as strange and yet assimilable as a marooned American twelve-year-old must have found food in Crete. In 1946, his song "Yep Roc

Heresay" was denounced as subversive of moral values. Its lyrics are his rendering of an Algerian restaurant's menu.

Of Louis Jordan's twenty-six food-song records, at least four topped the rhythm-and-blues charts in the 1940s and early 1950s: "Ain't Nobody Here but Us Chickens," "Boogie Woogie Blue Plate," "Beans and Cornbread," and "Saturday Night Fish Fry." He sang and danced, played strong alto sax, and led his own bands with an iron hand, but most notably he was a caper-cutting showman. From his small-town Arkansas background and early experience in both minstrel shows and serious jazz, he developed hospitable jump-shuffle rhythms that helped pave the popular way for several genres of African-American music: Nat King Cole, Ray Charles, Chuck Berry, and James Brown have all cited him as a primary influence. Perhaps, it must be said, his identification with food music overshadowed his greater contributions. Describing one of Jordan's late albums, his biographer John Chilton (who is English) reveals a certain exasperation:

> On "Chicken Back," Louis again struts around the barnyard, but this time ends up in the kitchen to present another "food" song, sharing vocal duties with Dottie Smith. Dottie also joins Louis on "Texas Stew," which at least has tastier lyrics than many of Louis's other culinary offerings. The gormandizing ends with "Bananas," which has a charming, light calypso feel. Several of the songs are spiced with rock-and-roll seasoning, but are mercifully not connected with food.

Elena Llewellen, newly named poet laureate of Delaware, says she often orders from a menu for the sound of the words. "Last night I asked for 'raw wahoo,' just because I liked saying 'raw wahoo.' Like Walt Whitman's 'barbaric yawp' but so much smoother. 'Raw wahoo'—what happens when you rub two *w*'s together. And you know there's a soupçon of *w* at the end of 'hoo,' too. Too wit too woo. Once, when I decided to limit myself to items that had a *k* sound, I was able to order a quatrain:

"Cucumber pickles,
Chicken kabob,
Chocolate ice cream
And corn on the cob."

"We're counting on Elena to be a hoot," says the Delaware Arts Council's president, Cesare Rose.

But you just track down Jordan's jumping version of "I Get the Neck of the Chicken" and see if that doesn't make you hop up and go looking for breasts and legs and wings.

The only one of the top five food musicians who was not African-American was suspected of being partly so, both by white club owners in New York who at first refused to hire him, in the segregated 1930s, and by black audiences, at the Apollo for instance, who took to his singing and horn playing right away. Hey, he had olive skin and kinky hair and came from New Orleans. What Louis Prima was, was French Quarter Sicilian-American. By 1923, when he was twelve, he was an established local jazz trumpeter. By 1969, when a stroke forced him to retire, he was a longtime Vegas headliner whom some called the primogenitor of the lounge act (not to mention lounge-in-cheek).

When Prima appeared at the Strand Theatre in New York, fans streamed down the center aisle to lay pizzas and pans of lasagna at his feet. I have him on twenty-nine food songs, from "Banana Split for My Baby" to "Please Don't Squeeza da Banana." Maybe his biggest food-oriented hit was "Angelina," addressed to the waitress who caused him not only to "eat antipasto twice / Just because she is so nice" but also to rhyme "matrimony" with "spumoni." If you want something more to chew on, try Prima's "Closer to the Bone" (where you find the sweetest meat).

And now we come to the greatest food musician of them all, who happens, fittingly, to be the twentieth century's greatest musician. It's a cliché to discuss the culture of New Orleans in terms of gumbo, but Louis Armstrong, who came from that city, does call that improvisational dish to mind. There are many kinds of gumbo and within each kind many levels: gumbo can be down and muddy and also too finely ambrosial to be deserved, and both things going on in the same bowl.

Certainly no one who fails to appreciate New Orleans food can be regarded as having any taste in American music. When James Lincoln Collier's absurdly condescending biography of Armstrong came out, the jazz scholar Dan Morgenstern busted it on that basis. Satchmo generally signed his letters "red beans and ricely yours." This, wrote Morgenstern, "is proof to Collier that he was 'obsessive' about food. Armstrong's favorite dish is dismissed by Collier, who has already demolished gumbo and fishhead stew, with 'and red beans and rice are—well, beans and rice.' Quite so. And wine is fermented grape juice."

Even for a New Orleanian, though, Armstrong was more than averagely focused on in- and digestion. Here's how he recalled falling in love with Lucille, who would become his fourth and ultimate wife:

> "After all [she said], I'm just a little small chorus girl, lucky to come in contact with a bunch of lovely, well-hipped people." That's when I stopped her from talking by slowly reaching for her cute little beautifully manicured hand, and said to her, "Can you cook red beans and rice?" which amused her very much. Then it dawned on her that I was very serious.

Early in his career, after watching a fellow musician nearly starve himself trying to save money, Armstrong resolved, "I'll probably never be rich, but I will be a fat man." As he grew older, and portlier, he developed firm ideas about dieting as well. He swore by orange juice, which "softens fat," and an herbal laxative called Swiss Kriss, which became a larger part of his life than we have space to go into here.

He recorded at least thirty-seven songs significantly involving food—in their titles (three of his greatest instrumentals, "Potato Head Blues," "Struttin' with Some Barbecue," and "Cornet Chop Suey"), their lyrics, or both ("Big Butter and Egg Man," "All That Meat and No Potatoes"). With Ella Fitzgerald (who is the sixth most prolific food-song recorder and with whom Louis Jordan cut a tasty version of "Patootie Pie"), he recorded five great food duets: "The Frim Fram Sauce," "I'm Putting All My Eggs in One Basket," "Strawberry Woman" from *Porgy and Bess*, "Let's Call the Whole Thing Off," and "A Fine Romance." If the importance of food references in the last two do not occur to you immediately, you have a perfect excuse to take a break, make yourself a tomato sandwich, and give those lovely vexed-relationship numbers a listen.

What do these food-music immortals have in common? All their careers, aside from Gaillard's low-profile comeback in the 1980s, were encompassed by the period between 1914, when Armstrong got a steady red-light-district gig at the age of thirteen, and 1971, when Armstrong died. They were all fine musicians, great comedians, and enormous

If you've seen the movie *Saving Mr. Banks*, about the making of the movie *Mary Poppins*, you know that the Sherman brothers, Richard and Robert, who wrote the songs for *Mary Poppins*, got frustrated trying to win over the super-severe P. L. Travers, who wrote the book in which Mary was created and who retained right of approval over everything in the movie. So—did the brothers work off their frustration in a hitherto undiscovered song for Dick Van Dyke, as Bert, the chimney sweep who is sweet on Mary? Was Bert to be dancing and shopping at the Covent Garden food market? Had he somehow learned that Mary had a soft spot for a certain crunchy snack food? All we know for sure is that *Entertainment Tonight* has posted online an image of a wrinkled piece of circa-1960 Disney stationery with the scrawled heading "Bert's Pistachio Song," followed by these lines:

> You can bite me sweet strawberry,
> And me teacakes? Take your cuts.
> But I'll be saving *these* for Mary—
> Hands off me nuts.

hams. They all liked to roll words and sub-verbal enunciations around in their mouths—Prima laid claim to "gleeby rhythm," Jordan had a big hit with "Choo Choo Ch'Boogie," Armstrong was the first great scat singer. Each of them recorded "Honeysuckle Rose." Slim was the only thin one; the others were all good, funny dancers; Slim was perhaps too laid-back. Except for Jordan, who was brought up by his father, and perhaps Gaillard, who for all we know was not of woman born, each of them was extremely, fondly attached to his mother and her down-home cooking. And yet every one of them was out in the world, performing and exploring, before he was old enough to shave.

All five helped shape jazz in the 1920s, 1930s, 1940s, and 1950s, when it was about making cultural history, yes, and tasting sips from lots of tasty lips, yes, but also about getting fed. Up in Harlem, great players jammed on Monday nights at Minton's Playhouse and after hours at Monroe's Uptown House because Minton and Monroe were good to musicians—didn't pay them, but did lay on plenty of ribs and chicken. On the road, the same musicians, playing for cheering white people, were often hearing their own stomachs growl for lack of a restaurant that would serve black people, even takeout. (Gaillard gave up touring around 1960 because "I was eating one, missing ten. I'd start a hamburger today and finish it the day after tomorrow.")

They all had appeal that notably crossed racial lines. There was something universal about each of those guys. See if you can supply the *f* word I've left out of what the *New York Post* once quoted Gaillard as telling an audience: "F—— is such a pleasure to enjoy. I think f—— is a good invention."

Nope, it was "fun." But "food" would have fit just as well.

FOOD NAMES FOR BANDS, II

The Dead flashback: Second Joint
Remains of the British invasion: Crust
Italo-Mexican opera: Salsa Verdi
Calypso/Gaelic: McCoco
New Orleans klezmer: Oyoyoyster!
Radically crunchy folk: Cob Salad
Sweet oracular metal: Icing the Body Electric
Cordial Christian: Haybaby
Not folk*ie*, but folk: Dewey (Do It Up) Brown

MISSISSIPPI MUSIC NOTES

• What's up with the alternative story of how Conway Twitty got his name? All agree that he was born Harold Lloyd Jenkins, in Friars Point, Mississippi, and that he felt the need to come up with something catchier (although he'd been named after the silent movie star) to sing under. According to the official Conway Twitty Web site, he picked town

> In 1927, E. O. Armistead of Roanoke, Virginia, suffered what is known as a "running-in-the-road death." Having over-imbibed on a cold night, he ran out onto the warm asphalt and was run over by a minivan. This was not like him. A prominent attorney, he had served in the legislature and published reflections on the book of Ruth. To preserve his memory in the proper light, his granddaughter Alva turned his home into the E. O. Armistead Bed, Breakfast, and Museum. Today, for sixty-eight dollars, guests may spend the night surrounded by portraits of Armistead, framed tributes to him from other prominent attorneys, and his extensive collection of stuffed squirrels. For a hundred dollars more, they may dress up in his clothes and imagine being him. "At 8:00 p.m. in his smoking jacket," reports one who took that option, "I felt transported to a more gracious age. At midnight in his pajamas, I longed for the highway." (Alva's niece, Iris, stands guard at the door to make sure you're around for Armistead's favorite breakfast of squirrel and eggs.)

names from maps: Conway, Arkansas, and Twitty, Texas. You'd think he might have come up with a more resonant combination: Eureka S. (for Springs) Galveston maybe. If he'd been diminutive, he could have been Little Rock Laredo.

But that is all beside the point. I'm wondering about the other story, which abounds on the Internet: that he *might* have borrowed the name of a man he met named W. Conway Twitty Jr. of Richmond, Virginia, who later, himself, recorded a song called "What's in a Name but Trouble?"

The first story is surely the right one. But the countermyth is intriguing, with regard to the original Conway. How would you like to go through life explaining to people—in Arkansas or Texas bars, for instance—that you are in fact *the* Conway Twitty, or anyway your daddy, W. Conway Senior, was, and that the famous Conway Twitty *isn't* Conway Twitty, he is Harold, oh never mind.

I'll tell you one thing: Conway was a funny-looking old boy with that frizzy hairdo, but I love some of those duets he and Loretta Lynn recorded, like "Louisiana Woman, Mississippi Man" and "You're the Reason Our Kids Are Ugly." ("Oh, but looks ain't everything.") Despite the spicy implications of such lyrics as "We've been busy makin' merries, and pickin' wild mountain berries," Conway and Loretta, according to them both, were not romantic in real life. But they were the best of friends. "I never knew how to use a credit card," Loretta discloses in her memoir *Still Woman Enough*, "until the late 1970s when Conway Twitty taught me." That might have inspired a song:

> I'm leaving these old cotton fields
> To start out living large.
> I got me one of them plastic deals,
> Now show me how to charge.

• An excellent CD from Old Hat Records, *Barbecue Any Old Time: Blues from the Pit, 1927–1942*, includes the 1936 instrumental "Barbecue Bust," by the Mississippi Jook Band, which consisted of Blind Roosevelt Graves, on guitar; Cooney Vaughn, on piano; and on tambourine, Roosevelt's brother, whose given name is perhaps the oddest in the history of the blues: Uaroy.

Was Uaroy forever being asked, by people who didn't quite catch his name, "You're Roy?" to which he would have to respond, "No, Uaroy," to which his questioner would say something like "Me? Naw, I'm Lucille Elizabeth."

• According to the liner notes of *Barbecue Any Old Time*, the great Mississippi-born singer Lucille Bogan's husband was named Nazareth Lee Bogan. But here's the best-named Mississippian on the album: Bogus Ben Covington. He not only sang ("I Heard the Voice of a Pork Chop") and played harmonica but also performed as a contortionist, the Human Pretzel. Why was he called Bogus Ben? Because he insisted on pretending to be blind. Sometimes he is referred to in fact as Blind Bogus Ben Covington. So . . . Was he *billed* as Bogus Ben? Did people call him that to his face?

> "Hey, Bogus Ben. Is that short for Bogalusa?"
> "Naw. It's from me pretending to be blind. Okay?"
> "Okay, okay. Don't get bent out of shape."

• The creator of the Muppets, Jim Henson, was born in Greenville, Mississippi. Does he belong to Southern music? Well, Kermit the

Frog, Muppeteered and voiced by Henson, sang "It's Not Easy Bein' Green" with Ray Charles. Then there's the TV special *Emmet Otter's Jug-Band Christmas*, in which the band, which includes a possum, plays "Barbecue" ("The sauce Mama makes just sits there forever / If it ever gets under your nails") and "Ain't No Hole in the Washtub." Paul Williams, from Nebraska, wrote the songs, but Henson produced and directed the show.

And how about the greatest music video ever made: "Put Down the Duckie." The celebrity participants include Wynton Marsalis, of New Orleans, and Joe Williams, of Cordele, Georgia. And Kevin Clash, an African-American man from Baltimore, whose people surely did not come there from the North, is the voice and the manipulator of Hoots the Owl, who convinces Ernie (Henson) that he'll never play blues saxophone without a squeak until he puts down his rubber bathtub duck. And did I mention that "Put Down the Duckie" is the greatest music video ever made?

• The Jackson that Johnny and June sing about talking about going to, is it Jackson, Tennessee, or Jackson, Mississippi? I guess we can take our pick. The songwriter Billy Edd Wheeler picked Jackson, he told *Country Music People* magazine in 2005, "because it's snappy and they are hard consonants. I tried more mellifluous titles like Nashville at first but I didn't need a pleasant sound, I needed something snappy." It's such a great song, you might think any city would do.

> We got married in a fever, hotter than a pepper sprout,
> We've been talkin' 'bout Twitty, ever since the fire went out.

No. See. Doesn't work.

FOR CHAMPION CRICKETS, NO WHEATIES

Ancient Chinese fighting crickets were fed rice mixed with fresh cucumbers, boiled chestnuts, lotus seeds, and mosquitoes. Sometimes a cricket fancier would allow himself to be bitten by mosquitoes, which he would then feed to his cricket. When time for a fight drew near, the cricket might be deprived of food for a while, until its movements became slow, whereupon it would be fed, according to a 1927 pamphlet on the subject, "small red insects in water." Which would make the cricket feel like kicking cricket butt.

I did not know any of this until I took in the show of cricket cages and other cricket paraphernalia at the Asian Gallery in New York. I had not even known that there was an ancient Chinese sport of cricket fighting. The only form of cricket fighting I had known about was in connection with crickets' understandable reluctance to be bait. Nearly every time I go fishing with crickets, someone turns over the tricky wire bait box they are kept in, and in a flash everyone in the boat is covered with crickets. Fishing is relaxing, in theory, but not when the crickets are out. My friend Vereen Bell once came home from a fishing trip, sat down at the table, and a cricket hopped out of his shirt pocket into his chicken gumbo. His Siamese cat at the time, Beep, saw the cricket jump and went after it. A cricket can add shouting and grappling to your life.

The ancient Chinese fought crickets, however, in the sense that the Vanderbilts race horses. According to *Insect-Musicians and Cricket Champions of China*, a 1927 pamphlet by Berthold Laufer, which Richard Ravenal of the Asian Gallery showed me, it was a peculiarity of the ancient Chinese that they "were more interested in the class of insects than in all other groups of animals combined." Hence, silk; and hence also the great enthusiasm, as early as the tenth century, for watching prized crickets fight each other in a pottery jar. As late as 1927, the sport was so big that wagering on a single cricket match in Canton might go as high as $100,000, and a national *shou lip* (winning or victorious cricket) would bring his home village as much honor as LeBron James brings to Akron.

I am not making this up. Crickets with black heads and gray body hair, Laufer says, were held to be the best fighters. Next were those with yellow heads and gray hair. The trainer of a first-class cricket would keep the temperature in its cage just right. If the cricket's mustache started to droop, it was too warm. A cricket enthusiast might carry a caged favorite around in his breast pocket so that the fighter could keep warm and all the world could hear it sing. A strong chirping voice was an attribute of the best cricket gladiators.

How it was possible for more than a few fans to watch a big cricket bout Laufer does not explain, but the event would take place in a demijohn-sized jar placed in the middle of a public square. Opponents were matched according to size, weight, and color. Before each set-to they were carefully weighed on a pair of tiny scales. Crickets are natural fighters in defense of their own turf, but in the ring, or rather the jar, they had to be provoked. The referee, using a device made of hare or rat whiskers inserted into a reed or bone handle, would twiddle first the contestants' heads, then the ends of their tails, and finally their large hind legs. Then the crickets would stretch out their antennae and jump at each other's heads. An antenna would break off, then a leg. Usually the struggle would end in the death of one fighter; often the winner would manage to land with its full weight on the other's body and sever its head. Do we have too much compassion for every living thing to enjoy such a spectacle today?

At any rate, the sport has died out, at least on the mainland, since the revolution banned gambling; who wants to watch crickets fight if you can't bet on them? But in the old days, emperors and other high officials put a lot of money and artistry into cricket cages and accoutrements, and these were the objects at the Asian Gallery. In winter the crickets were kept in cages made of gourds that were about the size of a swallow. The beauty of these cages resides in their perforated tops and the designs on the gourds themselves. The caps were carved into flowers or dragons or intricate vine-like tangles, from sandalwood, elephant or walrus ivory, coconut shell, green jade, white jade, ebony, bamboo, or tortoise shell. Some of the designs on the bodies of the cages were etched, but most were raised. Molds with inner indentations were fastened around gourds still on the stalk so that the gourds would grow into patterns.

Some of these gourd cages were exquisite antiques and more interesting to explain to guests than, say, a Tiffany lamp. Their prices ranged from $250 to $550. Ravenal implied that he might well throw in one of the cricket ticklers, cricket water bowls, cricket beds (singles), porcelain cricket-bout scorecards, or hard-to-describe small decorative items (apparently trophies or memorials to cricket champions) that are also part of the collection. Another nice piece is a sash worn by a cricket-fight referee. Evidently, judging from the size of this sash, the referee was a man. I had hoped he was a field mouse.

FOOD NAMES FOR BANDS, III

Chamber with a twang: Stringbean
Vintage country disco rap: BUႪBAPHAT
Tongue-in-cheek lounge: Smoothie
Philosophical rock: Reason Bran
Fusion: Apples and Oranges
Art rock: Two Plums and a Peach
The new sincerity: Playin' Potatoes
Punk enviro-protest: Poached Elephant
Feminist mocprovocroc: Extra-Virgin (a.k.a. EVOO)

SOME SPICY LIMERICKS

A good cook otherwise, Ella
Pooh-poohed "so-called salmonella,"
    Till during her Jethro's
    Consequent death throes
It struck her she'd need a new fella.

A lady I know named Elaine
Finds all endeavors inane
    But fucking and cooking.
    If you think I'm looking
For anyone else, you're insane.

A toothsome lady named Faye,
When told by a spindly gourmet,
    "You, dear, to me
    Are a delicacy,"
Said, "Stuff it. I'm a buffet."

An unfussy lady named Cecily
Likes to horse around messily,
    As long as her lovers
    Will help with the covers
And dine with her afterward, dressily.

Though she put herself down as "a chub,"
I liked when she called me "Hey, Bub,"

Just a little
deep-throated,
And the way
that she floated
When she leaned way
back in the tub.

A full-bodied lady
named Linnea
Discovered that she
could get many a
Man in a lather
By staying
plump rather
Than forcing herself
to get skinnea.

An abundant lady
named Lala
Murmurs, "Come into my pahlah,"
And through her peignoir
Shows flashes of Renoir,
And shrugs her shoulders, and voilà.

A bait-shop proprietor, Kate,
Tells randy fishermen, "Wait
Just a damn minute.
Your boat: go get in it,
And fish. Cause I ain't the bait."

A lady named Donna Sue Bird,
When her beau spoke of "fondness," demurred:
"If you're wanting some
Of my yum-yum,
Come up with some yummier word."

A stay at the Valleyhill Spa in Van Nuys, California, can be a bliss of herbal baths, massage, and guilt-free micro-nibbling. Or it can be something much darker. If you need drastic help with weight loss, you can sign up for Fat-Cam. You know how television cameras add five pounds? Fat-Cam adds fifty. And that's not all. At breakfast on the first day, you eat as you please. Then you watch yourself doing so as video'd by Fat-Cam. Fifty high-def pounds adds quite a lot of flesh bunched loosely around your face, neck, shoulders, upper arms, and so on. But that's not all. You know how they make the babies talk in the TV commercials? Fat-Cam makes you slurp, and belch, and moan, and breathe deep, and get a second wind complete with guttural yum-yum noises. Then, at the end of your meal, you squint, and your eyes disappear into your fat, and after a lengthy strained pause, *VAROOM*, what a fart. You can take the DVD home, to watch just before mealtime.

There once was a lady named Dot,
Who said as we found a nice spot,
    "I never undress
    At a picnic, unless
It's warm, and it is, so why not?"

There once was a lady named Eleanorsomething—
Men were always teleanorsomething
    She already knew:
    "It's . . . like honeydew
Or maybe Catawba meleanorsomething!"

Our next-door neighbor, Nancy,
Dabbles in necromancy:
    Fresh-baked bread
    To raise the dead,
For instance—nothing fancy.

There once was a lady, Clothilde,
Whose swimsuit barely concealed
    Her impatience to get
    More *deshabille* yet.
From her core she appealed to be peeled.

"In bed," boasts a lady named Shelly,
"I'm noisy and tasty and smelly—
    Yes, touchy, too.
    No hoochy-koo
Till the jelly roll bowl's full of jelly."

At Communion, a lady named Bev
Said to the minister, "Rev,
    It's grape juice, not wine—
    Would you like to have mine?
And the cracker could use something. Chèvre?"

"I do not need," says Valerie,
"To *avoid* a single calorie.
    I *burn* 'em, man—
    All that I can
Afford on a Walmart salary."

"Tonight," says my vegan friend Blanche,
"I'll be serving myself, root and branch.
    And you can be guessing
    Which mode of undressing:
French, Thousand Island, or Ranch."

PIMENTO EASTER EGG

"Take a moment," writes Sven Beckert, the Laird Bell Professor of History at Harvard, "and imagine, if you can, a world without pimento cheese."

No, actually, what Beckert writes, in his magisterial book *Empire of Cotton*, is "a world without cotton." But until recently, most of the world—that portion of it lying outside the American South—*was* without pimento cheese. This was something Southerners came to realize, to our consternation, if we ever remarked, outside the South, "You know what would be good right now? A pimento cheese sandwich." And the local person we were addressing responded, "A what?"

And that non-Southerner was *typical*. "Pimento cheese," I would tell such a person, "is the last thing y'all haven't caught up with up here." I enjoyed that.

But now pimento cheese has moved on. Quick chronology:

1955. Stanley Donen directs *It's Always Fair Weather*. Gene Kelly and friends dance in the street with garbage-can lids on their feet. Dan Dailey gets drunk and dances with a lampshade on his head. Cyd Charisse's moves give the boxing fellas in Stillman's gym such a charge that they break into a big production number, "Baby, You Knock Me Out." And for the first time in movie history (by my reckoning), pimento cheese appears.

A character who tends to overeat under stress starts calling for lots of food. "Here," says a man who doesn't want her to get fat, "take this."

"What is this?"

"A pimento cheese sandwich," he says.

"I don't want a pimento cheese sandwich," she says, but she takes it. How did pimento cheese get into a movie set in New York City? The director is from Columbia, South Carolina. Will pimento cheese become an established movie trope, like rooftop chases or the line "We gotta get outta here"? Will *everybody* know about it?

Not yet. This is before the Internet.

2000. In *Dr. T and the Women* (screenwriter Anne Rapp from Texas), Richard Gere asks for a pimento cheese sandwich. On Food.com, someone writes, "Mmmmm. I had never heard of Pimento Cheese until I was watching a movie and they mentioned pimento cheese sandwiches. I searched and found a recipe . . . The spread is addicting."

2003. Southern Foodways Alliance sponsors a "Pimento Cheese Invitational," producing a two-hundred-page book of recipes. (The best pimento cheese recipe I have read, by the way, is from SFA founder John T. Edge: "In Oxford, Mississippi, my friend Mary Hartwell Howorth concocts a devilish tub of pimento cheese about twice a week, adding yard onions and sage to a mix of shredded cheese, chopped pimentos, and mayonnaise. She likes it spread on rye or rough wheat." Yard onions! The best store-bought pimento cheese I have had is at Cochon Butcher in New Orleans: ten dollars a pint, and worth it.)

2008. Having embarrassed himself at another SFA gathering by revealing his ignorance of pimento cheese, Ari Weinzweig, co-founder of

Zingerman's Roadhouse in Ann Arbor, Michigan, sells excellent pimento cheese by mail order, nine dollars for a six-ounce tub.

2010. *Time Out New York*: "A century after its birth, pimento cheese is finally finding a foothold in New York." One eatery is already taking "a revisionist approach, deconstructing the snack into deep-fried crispy."

2011. *Breaking Bad*, about a mousy chemistry teacher in Albuquerque who becomes a drug lord, is a red-hot TV series. Mike, the lovable hired killer, and Jesse, the apprentice drug lord, are staking out a house so they can retrieve some hijacked blue meth. Jesse is bored. Mike offers a sandwich: "How does pimento cheese sound?" Jesse is so irritated he bolts from the car. What is pimento cheese doing in New Mexico? Vince Gilligan, creator of the series, is from Richmond, Virginia.

2012. Gothamist.com: "Where to Get the Best Pimento Cheese Sandwich in NYC."

2015. An episode of *Better Call Saul*, the series that is a prequel to *Breaking Bad*, is titled "Pimento." Our friend Mike gets a gig as one of three bodyguards for a guy doing a drug deal. Mike is old and bald and small. The other two are big badasses. One of them makes fun of Mike, wants to know what he's packing. Mike indicates a small paper bag, which contains, he says, a pimento cheese sandwich. Badass guy is incredulous. "Pimento," says Mike. "It's a cheese." Then of course he knocks the badass down and takes all three of his guns and throws them away. The other badass cuts and runs. Mike handles the gig by himself unarmed.

So pimento cheese has become what TV obsessives call an Easter egg: a hard-to-notice touch harking back to something earlier in the series. Only this Easter egg harks to *another* series. And because this latter series is a prequel, this Easter egg harks *forward*. An in-joke within an in-joke. Wiseguys all over the world will be cracking, "Pimento. It's a cheese."

I thought I was an authority on pimento cheese. And I didn't even know it was funny.

FOOD NAMES FOR BANDS, IV

Retro turntablism: Natural Scratch
Trad jazz: Chestnuts Cooking
Fat man and backups: Meat and Three
Creole Vietnamese: Pho Ya-Ya
Nostalgia: Our Own Sweet Corn
Synthpop: Inorganic Avocado
Cutting-edge power ballads: Alt-Schmaltz
Shoegaze: Spilt Milk
Archly allusive fish-camp ditties: Catchin' Anything?
Rootsy: Beet

PART EIGHT

INCIDENTALS

RO*TEL IT ON THE MOUNTAIN

Say you look in your pantry and find a can of RO*TEL diced tomatoes and green chilies that says, "BEST BY JAN 2011." What does that actually mean?

    A. DO NOT OPEN; ENCASE IN LEAD; CALL HAZMAT.
    B. THE ODDS ARE GOOD THAT THESE GOODS ARE ODD.
    C. PROBABLY STILL NOT ALL THAT BAD.
    D. WE HERE AT RO*TEL URGE YOU TO THROW THIS CAN AWAY AND GO BUY A NEW ONE, EVEN THOUGH A CAN OF RO*TEL, UNOPENED AND KEPT OUT OF THE MIDDAY SUN, WILL BE THERE FOR YOU PRETTY MUCH FOREVER, THAT'S WHAT THE CAN'S FOR.

Left to my own devices, I would assume (*c*) and (*d*). However, I am married. Recently, my wife went through the pantry and took out everything that had been in there for quite some time. These items, in various containers, included the following:

dried "One-Step Garlic Basil Entree"
Karo syrup
only legible words: "Meat Rub"
cream of coconut
pine nuts, by volume about 30 percent pantry-fly larvae
olive spread
"Stuff's Chicken Marinade"
hard to tell: "Yamaki Soba" and a word like *Tsuyn*

sesame seeds

"Inner Beauty West Indies from Hell Spice Rub 'Go Ahead, Rub
   It In'"

some kind of gray-green oil

Of these, I voted to keep all except the pine nuts, which I was willing to concede had gone off, and, grudgingly, the gray-green oil, though
there might be a way to make your car run on that. But there was something to be said for pouring all that into one bucket to see how nasty
the result looked and then heaving it, larvae and all, into the compost
heap—where, freed from jars and bottles and boxes, these heretofore
unappreciated comestibles could find new life, by contributing right
merrily to future homegrown collards and beets. Our cat, Jimmy, func-
tioned mostly as an observer.

But I did hate throwing out that 2011-vintage RO*TEL. The marking was evidence, no doubt, that RO*TEL doesn't always jump off our
shelf, but let me say this: if I ran a hotel, the sign outside would say
HO*TEL. And you combine RO*TEL with Velveeta cheese product—
what a couple they make: he full of swash and buckle, she a lissome,
even slippery blonde. I got a craving for some of that dip.

The first fancy food market I tried had no RO*TEL, and when I asked
the man in the cornucopious cheese department (fifteen kinds of gouda—
you'd think three or four would be goudanough) for Velveeta, he looked at me the way the father of twelve beautiful daughters might look at you if—well, one night long ago a fellow college boy and I found our-selves for some reason in Tullahoma, Tennessee. We asked a local man where we could "meet some girls."

> At last week's American Cheese Council convention in Kauai, Hawaii, a resolution was passed deploring "the media's increasing tendency to use the term 'cheesy' to mean of inferior quality. There is no intrinsic connec-tion between cheese and inferiority. On the contrary, 'cheesy' should connote 'flavor-some, rich, nutritious.'" In a spirited discus-sion leading up to the resolution, a panel of cheese experts proposed various public-information efforts to counteract the current meaning of "cheesy," including an ad cam-paign featuring "beautiful, healthy young people snacking on cheese products and us-ing the catchphrase 'Mmmm. It's cheesy!'"

He reflected. "You mean loose hangers?" he asked.

Our reply was to the effect of, Well, uh, not necessa—sure.

He said, "We don't have any loose hangers in Tullahoma."

The cheese man looked at me the way the father of twelve beautiful daughters might if I had checked out all his daughters and then asked if he had any loose hangers.

Before I did pour out that old RO*TEL, I found online that RO*-TEL had a promotional connection with Crazy Sam Higgins, proprietor of the highly rated Chuckwagon Inn Bed and Breakfast in Fredericksburg, Texas, and author of a cookbook, *Snake, Rattle & RO*TEL*, in which he says of himself, "If old Crazy Sam tells you a chicken can dip snuff, just go ahead and look under his wing, and . . . there'll be a can hidden there." I met Sam many years ago, through my Waxahachie, Texas, in-laws Johnny Pearson and Rusty Marchman. I called him up and put it to him: Can't you eat RO*TEL that's two years past its theoretical prime?

Turns out Sam and RO*TEL have parted ways. The current corporate owners "didn't understand what I did" for them, he said. In fact he maintains that RO*TEL isn't as strong as it used to be. He now favors a local brand, Hill Country Fare. And he wouldn't recommend that anybody eat post-best-by cans of either one. He did, however, say, "Context is all. If you're on a deer lease, you might eat 'em and be okay. But around the house, you might be sick for two weeks."

I found fresh RO*TEL and Velveeta, and the dip was good. But with a bittersweet overlay: if RO*TEL gets too old, even Velveeta might dump him.

SONG TO CATSUP

(For Young, Particular Eaters)

My father was a very religious man who believed in the hereafter, that you're marking time here, that this earth is not the real thing, the real thing was where you'd go after you died. But I didn't believe that at all because I liked catsup too much.

—George Burns

If every food your parents hatsup
Tastes like something to matsup
With something not even a buzzard would snatsup,
Add catsup.

Catsup will fix up all kinds of yuck.
You'll find a way to pour it on your turnips, with luck.
And if you can't—
Since children can't
Turn turnips down—
Find a way to pour
Your turnips on the floor.
And if your mother sees you, move to another town.

Catsup makes you well.
It's tangy, gooey, red.
Pour it on your shirt and tell
Your parents you are dead.

SONG TO BARBECUE SAUCE

Hot and sweet and red and greasy,
I could eat a gallon easy:
Barbecue sauce!
Lay it on, hoss.

Nothing is dross
Under barbecue sauce.

Hear this from Evelyn Billiken Husky,
Formerly Evelyn B. of Sandusky:
"Ever since locating down in the South,
I have had barbecue sauce on my mouth."

Nothing can gloss
Over barbecue sauce.

BRUNSWICK STEW: SCALABLE?

I am the first to admit that Brunswick stew, which I think the world
of, lacks the mystique of chili. I don't admit for one minute that the
Southwest produces real barbecue (don't they have any pigs in Texas?),
but I will admit freely that those folks out there have generated more

mystique around their chili than southeasterners have around Brunswick stew.

You never read about Brunswick stew-offs, where people compete to put the finest, hottest, hairiest (figuratively speaking), and most natural ingredients together into the most definitive bowl of mushy, tangy, reddish-brown-with-yaller-specks goodness.

This is partly because, what kind of hat would you wear to a Brunswick stew-off? And partly because Brunswick Stewoff sounds like the son of an Anglophile movie agent.

"Chili" is a sexier term than "Brunswick stew." If you doubt this, try saying "chili-chili-chili-chili-*hoo*-pah!" in a bouncy, finger-popping way, and then try the same thing with "Brunswick-stew-Brunswick-stew-ick . . ." I don't think you will get as far as the "*hoo*-pah." No one enjoys setting out toward a "*hoo*-pah" and bogging down.

On the other hand, a long slow rolling "Bruuuuuuuuhn-z-wick stoooo" has resonance. So if the Brunswick stew industry (should there be one) were to hire the right marketing people, and change the name slightly so that someone could throw in a lot of extra hot sauce and put out Third-Degree *Burns*wick Stew, it would likely become commonplace within the next few years to find out your daughter is rooming with a former stew princess at some fancy college.

But I would hate to see Brunswick stew blown out of proportion. I think that's what has happened to chili, frankly. Chili to me is like peaches: even out of a can it's not bad. In fact that's the only way I ever had it until I was twenty-three years old. That's why you have to make a mystique of chili, to justify not eating it out of a can.

Whereas Brunswick stew isn't put out by Hormel; it just crops up, at barbecues and in barbecue places. No one knows what is in it, other than corn and tomatoes and pulled pork and chicken and garlic and *maybe*, if squirrel is available, squirrel. It may be a by-product of the hickory-smoking process—resulting when a small animal running with an ear of corn in its mouth tumbles into the open pit.

And sometimes it's not good. Sometimes. I will urge some people who have never had Brunswick stew (no one but a North Korean has never had chili) to try it, and I'll tell them it's named for General Lionel Brunswick, who discovered that anything is good that goes with a side of corn bread, and I'll assure them that boy, howdy, do they have a treat in store for them. And then it will arrive and it won't be good, sometimes.

Which means I can be authoritative about it. When people complain that this Brunswick stew I have touted them onto is not good, I can roll a bite of it around against my upper palate, gaze off into the middle distance with my eyes closed except for tiny contemplative slits, and observe, with no tinge of defensiveness, "Yeah, this is a little off. Prob'ly used a rabid squirrel."

I DON'T EAT DIRT PERSONALLY

Not long ago, *The New York Times* reported a scientific discovery: that significantly more people who were told not to think about a white bear had more thoughts about a white bear than people who were not told not to think about a white bear. I forget the figures involved, but someday I expect the *Times* to disclose research establishing that some strikingly low percentage of people know you when you're down-and-out.

So when the *Times* runs something that reflects on me as a Southerner, I can't just dismiss it as off the wall. I have to explain it to the people I live among, which is to say Northerners. One morning, I picked up the *Times* and saw my work cut out for me. Here was the headline: "Southern Practice of Eating Dirt Shows Signs of Waning."

"While it is not uncommon these days to find people here who eat dirt," the story said, many Southerners "are giving up dirt because of the social stigma attached to it."

Now, I would be willing to argue, in a quasi-agrarian way, that the giving up of dirt is part of the downside of modern life. The giving up of eating dirt, however, is a subject that I frankly resent having to discuss. And not because it hits too close to home. The truth is, I never started eating dirt. The stigma attached to dirt eating is one of a handful of stigmas that I have never even considered feeling. But try telling that to people whose source of information about dirt eating is *The New York Times*.

The very evening after the dirt-eating story came out, I was in a chic salon, gamely eating arugula. A woman with a crew cut heard my accent.

"Ah, yes," she said, "Southerners are all natural storytellers. Sitting on the old screen porch, dog under the rocker, flies on the baby, everybody spitting and spinning yarns compounded of biblical cadences and allusions to animals named Br'er.

"One thing I never realized, though," she went on, "was that you eat dirt."

At that point, there were two tacks I could take. I could say, "Well, I know there are some folks down south who like to chew on clay, for digestive reasons, but I never ate any myself, and neither did any of my relatives or friends. In point of fact, I never even saw anybody eat dirt."

The response to that tack would have been a knowing look. "Here is a man who comes from people who eat dirt, and he thinks he is better than they are." She would be thinking I couldn't handle stigma. Or that I was inauthentic. Southern and inauthentic: worst of both worlds.

So I took the second tack, which, if you recall the Carter administration, might be called the Billy tack: "Hell yes, we eat dirt. And if you never had any blackened red dirt, you don't know what's good. I understand you people up here eat raw fish."

You know how sushi got started, don't you? Some Tokyo marketing people were sitting around, thinking how they could create a whole new American market, and one of them said, "Restaurants."

Another said, "What would these restaurants serve?"

"Oh, fish."

"How would we cook it? The most cost-efficient way."

And the eyes of another one lit up, and he said, "You know what we could do . . . ?"

And they got away with it. But of course sushi was over now, I told this Northerner, and people were Cajuned out, and even New Zealand cuisine was about to go the way of Finnish, and now this hot New Guinea place, Yam Yam, was so overpraised, I figured the time was ripe for investing in dirt restaurants.

None of the Northerners I tried this tack on had realized that it was time to be Cajuned out, even. The best way to get a Northerner to believe something is to talk to him as if you assume that he knows it already and that most people don't. Without half trying, I raised more than three thousand dollars. I figured that when these investors came to me wondering what had happened to their money, I could admit that dirt eating wasn't quite happening yet, after all—that when they had invested in it, it had been ahead of its time. Which would have consoled them more than you might think.

Then the *Times* came out with another headline: "Quiet Clay Revealed as Vibrant and Primal." According to some scientists, the first forms of life might have begun in clay. This was too close to what I had learned as a boy back in Sunday school for comfort. And I didn't want to be explaining why Southerners eat life at its very source. But then I thought, what the heck. "Yep," I told Northerners. "In fact, if there had been a Southerner around at the time when the first forms of life were getting under way, we'd have been nipped in the bud." People who weren't put off by raw fish were certainly not dismayed to learn that dirt was, in a sense, their mother.

The *third* dirt-related *Times* headline was the one that made my position difficult.

"Clay Eating Proves Widespread but Reason Is Uncertain," it said.

"Uh-oh," I thought, and I was right.

"The practice of eating dirt, usually fine clays, is so common in so many societies," the story began, "that it must be regarded as a

Regular customers of the Memphis-based Home Folks chain of cafeterias noted with some bemusement this week that one of the most popular items on the menu, the Redneck Blue Plate Special (a different entrée every day with choice of sides), is now known as the Meat du Jour and Three. Explained Home Folks International's CEO, Jackson Wheat, "My daughter Shana came back from college and Europe and wanted me to know that 'redneck' was an ethnic slur I shouldn't perpetuate. And I wouldn't hear anything about it, and she said, 'See? People would say you're being typical, when all you're being is hardheaded like you always are.' Or something. And her mother agreed with her, so I gave up."

normal human behavior rather than an oddity, according to scientists who are studying it."

Dirt eating, the *Times* had now decided, was known by experts as geophagy and was no more peculiarly Southern—or, for that matter, peculiar—than rabbits. "Historical records of earth-eating in Europe go back to 300 B.C., when Aristotle described it," said the newspaper of record.

Now, Northerners had no reason to believe that I knew any more about how to get rich off dirt than they did. They wanted to know what I had done with their money.

I had sunk it all into development. That is to say, I had sent it to my uncle Mullet, who did eat dirt. When I said I never had any relative who ate dirt, I wasn't counting my uncle Mullet, who is not my blood uncle, and I never felt responsible for him, because he did everything, up to and including teaching his dogs to dance. He wasn't typical of anybody's family. He kept armadillos and lived with a woman named Valvoline. He always did just exactly what nobody wanted him to. So no wonder I feel entitled to say I have never had any relatives who ate dirt.

Why did I send that money to Uncle Mullet? It just seemed right. I didn't want to be taking advantage of Northerners for *mercenary* reasons. It was more of a cultural thing with me. Sure enough, Uncle Mullet spent all that Northern money on snakes.

But one afternoon he went over to his favorite clay hole to dig some up, and a man dressed all in just-ordered-looking L.L.Bean clothing came out from behind a tree to wave a "Posted" sign at him.

"Stranger," the man said in a Northern accent, "you are eating my land."

"What do you mean, *stranger*?" my uncle Mullet said. "I been coming here for generations."

The Northerner looked at him in a certain way.

"What do you mean, *your land*?" my uncle Mullet said. "This spot has been free for folks to come to for clay ever since I don't know when."

The Northerner looked at him in a certain way.

"And what do you mean, *eating*?" Uncle Mullet said. "I wouldn't . . ."

And that's what broke his spirit. After a lifetime of doing every awful thing he felt like, proudly, Uncle Mullet had denied to a Northerner that he did something that he always had done, because the Northerner had looked at him in a certain way enough times to make him feel looked at in a certain way.

And Uncle Mullet was shamed to the point that he stopped trying to shift for himself, and everybody in the family had to start sending my aunt Rayanne money to keep him up. (Valvoline dropped him.)

And of course the reason the man in the unbroken-in L.L.Bean outfit was protecting the old clay hole was that he had just bought up all that area in through there so he could get in on the ground floor of the chain of fine dirt restaurants that I had led him to believe, late one night in that chic salon, was about to happen.

We reap what we sow.

(Update, Amy Fleming in The Guardian, *July 29, 2014: "Japanese chef Yoshihiro Narisawa . . . was surprised to find he liked the soup he had made with distilled soil which, cooked properly, tastes great. As well as the earthiness, it is rich in umami. The Girona [Spain] restaurant Celler de Can Roca . . . has also successfully dabbled with soil. It is only a matter of time before the trend reaches critical mass and Heinz baked beans bring out a limited-edition soil flavour.")*

THE W WORD

To every magazine writer, if he or she is lucky, comes one beautiful idea, both topical and evergreen, that will forever establish writer and subject, together, in the firmament of great stories. Gay Talese on DiMaggio, A. J. Liebling on Earl Long, me on worms.

It was 1977, when I—who shouldn't be the one to say so, but who else remembers?—was hot. Magazines were hot, and I was freelancing for the best ones. Even my home state was hot, because Jimmy Carter, a Georgian, had just become president. And worms were hot.

Worms as in red wigglers, night crawlers, and so on. The trendiness of worms owed something to the fact that President Carter's first cousin Hugh operated a big-time worm farm back home in Plains, Georgia. Hugh's son, Hugh junior, told *The New York Times* that his father "started out with a wooden coffin . . . full of gray crickets and a washtub full of worms. He probably sells 30 million worms a year now." At that point, Hugh junior, whose master's thesis at the University of Pennsylvania had been on the worm-raising business, was in charge of organizing the White House. As I recall, the can-of-worms angle was fully exploited by media.

But worms—which Aristotle called "the intestines of the earth"—transcended the presidency. "You would not be here and I would not be here today if it weren't for the worms," said an architect and worm fancier in Atlanta. "The only reason we're alive is because of that eight inches of topsoil the worms created." It was said that worms would eat anything even remotely organic—cardboard, baby diapers—and excrete it as four-hundred-proof loam. It was said that the sportfishing market required some eighty million dollars' worth of worms annually, and that there was an inexhaustible demand for worms as garbage disposers, as companions to large potted plants in industrial offices, and as food. The 1976 earthworm recipe contest staged by North American Bait Farms in Ontario had been won by an Applesauce Surprise Cake that edged out earthworm patties and earthworm curry. Worms were said to be 70 percent protein, high in vitamin D, and—this had the ring of truth—free of bones and gristle.

"It's a billion-dollar-a-year business," according to a man who claimed worms had made him a millionaire. "And probably growing faster than any other business today." On the other hand, said a headline in *The Atlanta Constitution*, "Worms a Slippery Business." The story quoted the Georgia Office of Consumer Affairs: "Questionable sellers may misrepresent potential profits, the skill and time required to care for the worms and the commercial demand."

I suspected the worm boom was, in effect, a Ponzi scheme. People were selling worm-farm starter kits on the promise of an ever-expanding market for worms, when the truth might just be that there was a so-far-expanding market for worm-farm starter kits.

One way or another, there was a lot of worm stuff going on. According to a story out of Casper, Wyoming, "A deputy investigating the theft of eleven million worms hopes a reward offered in the case won't produce any more tips like the one suggesting he question the nearest 500-pound sparrow."

I had already been interviewing people in bait shops. "I was using a *gob* of worms in my speckled perch hole, when I got a *big* bite, and I yanked, and nothing. Yanked again, and nothing. Yanked again, felt *something*, and there was an eyeball on the hook the size of your thumb. Just what it was, I do not know."

There was a place in Albany, Georgia, whose sign said, "Wormy's Bait and Tackle. Wormy Sez: Wiggle On In." The best way to get the worms Wormy specialized in—sold as Louisiana Pinks—was to "grunt them up." Drive a stake in the ground and rub it with something that caused "viberation," and the worms would rise to the surface. "First time in seventeen years, I found one with two tails. Both of 'em was alive and well."

So you had politics, economics, natural science, and Americana. I figured it for a three-parter in *The New Yorker*. When I sent a proposal to my editor there, Roger Angell, he liked it. He sent it on to William Shawn, the magazine's legendary editor.

Mr. Shawn's reaction, more or less, was *"Eww."* He couldn't stand the thought of worms.

A DARK SWEETNESS

Grandma, she had only scorn
For syrup took from trees or corn.
For ninety years, what got *her* up,
Up and at 'em every morn,
Was biscuit soaked in good *cane* syrup.

When I was a boy, in the family car, on a Southern highway, we would fairly often drive past a mule going in circles. That mule, my father would point out, was *working*—turning a mill that ground stalks of sugarcane. The people in the yard were working too—cooking the juice in that open kettle.

Even while my father was in that expansive frame of mind, I never asked him to explain Eelbeck.

At home, we sweetened our waffles with Log Cabin, which was translucent and tasted more or less maple. At my grandparents' house in Jacksonville, Florida, we had Eelbeck cane syrup, which looked like motor oil overdue to be changed. Eelbeck tasted sweet but also *murky*. On biscuits with butter, Eelbeck was the strongest thing I had ever put in my mouth. It evoked that *unh . . . unh* noise King Kong made when he was running around with Fay Wray. I liked it.

But why "Eelbeck"? The image on the bottle wasn't bland and reassuring like the log cabin on Log Cabin. As I recall, it was a hillbilly-looking man sitting on a creek bank fishing with a cane pole and at that moment getting an eel on his hook. The eel was labeled "eel," and the creek was labeled "beck." The man might have had exclamation points leaping from his head; at any rate, he looked as if he'd been struck by a lot more than he'd angled for. Maybe the eel was not meant to evoke the power and darkness of the syrup and vice versa, but it worked that way for me. I had not yet heard any song about a blacksnake moan, but I had been in a skiff with a fresh-boated eel lashing and thrashing and twining upon itself, and I had been glad that Daddy, not I, had to deal with it. And what was a beck? I had heard my mother complain of being at someone's "beck and call." The call of the eel?

I was never one to pipe up with possibly embarrassing questions. If there was something sufficiently work related for my father to explain, he would bring it up. That's the way things still stood between us when he suddenly died. Eelbeck remains one of a number of things I can't imagine being cleared up in a fatherly voice.

Today, there is the Internet. Online I have learned that *beck* is an old English word for brook or stream. Eelbeck is a settlement in south Georgia (now part of the Fort Benning reservation) named for Henry J. Eelbeck, who was associated with a mill, built mostly by slave labor, that produced grits and cornmeal as well as syrup. Google provides a faint image for Eelbeck grits; a man is fishing, but that is all you can tell. It can't be the same drawing that preyed on my imagination. The mill no longer produces; the Eelbeck brand is dead.

Cane syrup lives, though. On the Internet, it even shines, at least in comparison to the high-fructose

> Honeybees, alas, are a threatened species. So maybe it's a good thing they no longer have a monopoly on making honey. This week the Food and Drug Administration announced approval of a new form of honey induced from rabbits. Put Peter Cottontail in a cubicle with room only for him and a conveyer belt carrying a mixture of carrots and nasturtiums, and the rabbit will continue to chew long after he is sated and ceases to swallow. The resultant overflow is conveyed to special vats where it steeps along with organic enzymes and natural sweeteners, and voilà: bunny honey.
>
> The ick factor too much for you? How do you think bees make honey?

corn syrup that gets a lot of blame for American obesity. Too much of any sweetener is bad for you, I gather, but cane syrup is too pricey, in bulk, and too bold, in any amount, to be slipped into the processed foods that seduce the contemporary palate. Pure cane syrup—nothing but sugarcane juice boiled down until it's deep and dark—lacks the bitter taste of molasses, because molasses is what's left after sugar is crystallized away. Pure cane syrup retains the sugar plus some of the iron and other nutrients for which people have traditionally taken molasses.

And the big name in pure cane syrup is Steen's—a staple of Louisiana culture, like crawfish or Fats Domino. The C. S. Steen mill, founded in 1910, still thrives, in Abbeville, Louisiana. Charley Steen III, who runs the mill, is the founder's great-grandson.

This was the man, surely, who would talk to me of cane syrup in familial terms. I telephoned the mill and chirped, "Hey, I want to write about your syrup." Whoever answered said, "No. No. He doesn't do any of that. And I *know* he's not going to talk to you now, because his father died last night."

A couple of days later, an obituary of Albert Steen, father of Charley III, was online. "He loved to work," his widow was quoted as saying. "I figured he would die because he worked so hard." My dad, the same.

PART NINE

PROCESS

Bishops eats elders, elders eats common peopil; they eats sich cattil es me, I eats possums, possums eats chickins, chickins swallers wums, an' wums am content tu eat dus', an' the dus am the aind ove hit all. Hit am all es regilur es the souns from the tribil down tu the bull base ove a fiddil in good tchune, an' I speck hit am right, ur hit wudn't be 'lowed.
—SUT LOVINGOOD (George Washington Harris),
"Rare Ripe Garden-Seed"

Even with a perfect computer emulation of the stomach, you cannot then stuff a pizza into the computer and expect the computer to digest it.
—JOHN R. SEARLE, "What Your Computer Can't Know,"
The New York Review of Books

DREAM SONG

I dreamed in the night I had gone on to Glory,
And found it was full of loose women not whory—

Whose faces were sweet, whose bodies incredible,
Whose sweat was white wine and whose few clothes were
    edible,

And all of them naturally knew special arts,
And along with the wholes there were sumptuous parts:

Great legs, cherry lips, and deltas aglow,
And breasts you could nibble and cause them to grow,

And buttercream voices expressing their gratitude
To me on account of my marvelous attitude.

"Oh boy," I was saying, but then I said, "Look,
It's all very nice, but can someone here cook?"

"I *thought* this," said one of the women, "was *too good*
To be true." Came a chill. "We were told *you* could."

YELLOW SQUASH CRISPS

The only cooking I have *had* to do over the years is for myself, or for children. The children were harder to please. But I can turn out spaghetti sauce or soup that discerning adults find palatable. And I can make these reliable crowd-pleasers.

We didn't call them "crisps" when my mother made them, when I was growing up. We called them fried squash. But "crisps" has a nice ring to it, and they are crispy. Except for the ones that turn out floppy—but still good. Either way, they are not like batter-heavy sports-bar fried-zucchini strips. Much finer, as to texture and taste. In fact they're even better than good fried zucchini in a good Italian place.

Take, say, three or four small to medium yellow squashes and slice them width-wise into disks maybe three-eighths of an inch thick. (Some thinner than that, for diversity.)

Let the disks sit and sweat as you pour olive oil maybe five-sixteenths of an inch deep in a heavy, seasoned-over-the-years iron skillet.

While your oil is heating to medium heat, put a double handful of cornmeal and a smidgen of salt into a paper bag. Then put the squash disks into the paper bag and shake it.

Then flick a little cornmeal into the oil to see if it's hot. If it sizzles fairly fiercely, as if resenting the intrusion, start removing the cornmealed slices (they'll be mostly covered with the meal but not thickly) from the bag. And place, one by one, the first batch of disks side by side into the oil. Flip them after a couple of minutes.

As they brown, take them out and put them on a paper towel and put others in the skillet. Add more oil as needed (the oil doesn't have to be a constant depth or temperature, as long as it's sizzling and lubricating). You'll lose some cornmeal into the oil, but plenty will stay on.

They'll get a little browner after they come out. Even if they're bordering on burnt, they'll be fine. In fact I would slightly overcook some of them, and let some others be floppier, for diversity.

Eat no more than 10 percent of them right off the paper towel yourself, because otherwise you'll eat so many of them that there won't be any point in putting what's left out on the table, so you'll eat them all. Use elbows to keep anyone else in the kitchen from eating more than 5 percent.

Hot or warm or cooling or cooled, they'll be gritty-crunchy from the cornmeal, delicately moist on the inside, and in taste uniquely salty-squashy-olivy-corny-sweet. They could be an hors d'oeuvre, or—in fact they will be an hors d'oeuvre, if your guests catch sight of them on their way through the kitchen.

EATING OUT OF HOUSE AND HOME

"Why is it that things taste so much better outside?" is a question people are always asking, and unlike most questions people are always asking ("Do you really love me?" "What is truth?"), this question springs from *satisfaction*.

Outdoors your senses perk up. And the smells of pine, honeysuckle, grass, and wood smoke are like extra spices: sauce of the outdoors, which isn't fattening. And you have so much room in which to eat. A mouthful becomes a heartier proposition.

I don't say there is no downside to eating outdoors. My daughter, Ennis, when she lived in San Francisco, reported that it took some of the zest out of a picnic when you saw, and were seen by, people who were living in the park.

Another thing that will mar outdoor eating sometimes is rowdiness. Once I was attending an outdoor event called the Steeplechase in

Nashville, Tennessee, with my friends Slick and Susan Lawson, when a man with no shirt on fell into our lunch, where we had it spread out there on plates on our blanket, and he got up with the bulk of our cold cuts sticking to his upper body. That was awful. It wasn't anybody the Lawsons knew well. I didn't know him at all. That wouldn't happen indoors.

Eating outdoors is somewhat like going naked outdoors. Animals do it. You know why Manet's *Le déjeuner sur l'herbe* is so sexy, don't you? Not just because one of the people in it is outdoors naked; I wouldn't be surprised to learn that half the people in the entire history of French painting are outdoors naked. It's because she is outdoors naked *eating lunch*.

Sexy, and perfectly natural. Most foodstuffs come from outdoors, and cook fires had to be outside originally. In the scheme of things, more eating goes on outdoors than indoors even today. "The whole of nature . . . is a conjugation of the verb *to eat*, in the active and passive," said William Ralph Inge. Here is an outdoor eating poem I wrote after reading in the *Hartford Courant* that "the smallest meat-eating animal is the least-weasel." I call it "End of the Line":

> So on what creature does the least
> Weasel feast?
> Say a herbivore—
> One which, furthermore,
> The least weasel at least
> Does not eat easily.
> Still, that meal must feel,
> When finished,
> Greatly diminished.

FAME

You may be hot, but that
Don't mean you're in control.
The jelly said to the butter pat,
"Hey, we're on a roll!"

The least weasel, on the other hand, can just let its belt out a notch.

Take a hike up a hill and get out your ordinarily ordinary sandwich and look around at the bird with its worm, the frog with its fly (and here come the ants for your crumbs), and what do you think?

My. (What a good spot on the food chain *I* lucked into.) This is a *fine* sandwich.

One thing you want to look out for, eating outdoors, is that you don't eat bits of the outdoors itself. Bark, pine straw, dirt. I ate a fly once, in some baked beans. Until you have bit down on a live, beans-sated fly, don't talk to me about what it's like to have a trashy-greasy taste in your mouth. It lingers. I realized what was happening before my molars quite meshed, but that was too late. Actually, it might have been better if I had briskly chewed and swallowed and then realized. But, as I say, I realized just before I quite finished biting down. A buzz, some movement.

I'll tell you what's *good*, though. Baked beans without a fly in them, outdoors. Even the memory of having eaten a fly in them is not enough to put me off outdoor baked beans. Or deviled eggs. Or potato salad. My friend Lee Smith, who is from Virginia, says, "Northern people on a picnic take whole things. A whole chicken. A whole loaf of bread. Southern people have to have things that have had things done to them."

But simple is good too, outdoors. On the island of Lamu, off the coast of Kenya, a lady named Christabel and I ate just-caught fish roasted whole on the beach on a grid of green twigs.

Ooh.

Say you do find a little something in your outdoor food that you wouldn't have found if you and your food had stayed indoors. I am reminded of a time in a Paris

Prejudice, says the Stanford biologist Dr. Terrell Fleming, prevents our learning much from the housefly. True, *Musca domestica* carries disease in the digestive sputum it deposits indiscriminately on garbage, manure, and the food we eat, and its eggs do become maggots, which to our eyes are nasty, but in other ways, Fleming recently told the Association for the Advancement of Science, the fly is worthy of human emulation. If we could harness the fly's multifaceted vision, we might still not be able to see maggots as cute, but we could vastly improve our own optic systems, and the fly's uncanny ability to avoid being swatted may hold the key to preventing airplane collisions. And the fly is a model of metabolic efficiency. Says Fleming, "A housefly after consuming nothing for days still has the energy of a three-year-old child on a sugar rush. But even scientists hate flies. And science is the poorer for that."

restaurant when I cast a warm eye on a raw oyster on the half shell and saw a tiny wormish life-form swimming in the liquid.

I called the waiter over, but by the time he arrived I was unable to point out any swimming thing (*chose nageuse*). It had evidently succumbed to the lemon juice I had squeezed on the oyster.

I addressed a second oyster, and there was another one of those things. I summoned the waiter again, and this time he had to admit that he saw the thing swimming.

He shrugged and said, "C'est la mer."

You want to be mindful of what you're eating outdoors. I know a man who was eating potato chips out of a bowl at night in a semi-enclosed picnic area, and somebody said to him, "You're bleeding all out of your mouth, there."

It turned out he had been eating handfuls not only of potato chips but of lightbulb fragments, from a bulb that had broken in an overhead fixture.

That wouldn't have happened if he had been *entirely* outdoors. Then too he had been drinking a great deal. He doesn't drink at all now, and that's one of the reasons.

Anyway, say you are serving something outdoors and someone complains that there is something unexpected in it. A bee wing or a wind-blown seed. Here is what you could say: "C'est le grand air."

I don't know why there have been so many French references in these remarks so far. Perhaps because "picnic" comes from the French *pique-nique* (as opposed to the English "pyknic," which means "fat"). I had better bring in some counterbalancing Americana.

So here are some alfresco cooking hints from the late Slick Lawson, who was deeply involved in outdoor food affairs up to and including annual goat roasts featuring goat gumbo, nude swimming, and helicopter accidents:

"Things cooked inside are eaten with elbows up; things cooked outside, the elbows are on a table.

"Inside, you stand up and stir; outside, you bend over and peek.

"Inside, guests tell you how famous chefs do things. Outside, they tell you how they do things. They have secret recipes that they share with everyone.

"Inside, they help with the dishes; outside, they help with the ice.

"Inside or not, women always help with the bread. Instead of nice hot French bread that you break off, they are compelled to slice it and put garlic and butter on it, wrap it in foil, and turn it into a mush of dough that won't sop.

"Outside, men want to pick up things. Chairs, beer coolers, and your best client's wife.

"Inside, people try to make interesting conversation and are dull. Outside, they remember the most deplorable things you did in the good old days.

"Outside, if you discard a chicken lip or the left front paw of a hamster (hamsters have more dark meat than gerbils), someone will tell you that you threw away the best part.

"Outside, someone you don't much like will leave a dish and follow up with three messages on your answering machine while you are in London.

"Outside, it's hard to clean up after dark.

"Boy Scouts and Girl Scouts are *forced* to eat outside.

"Outside, anything that falls to the ground belongs legally to the dog.

"Outside, medium rare has a wider latitude.

"After you finish serving from the grill, someone always points out that the fire is just now getting right."

In San Francisco, my daughter, Ennis, taught three-year-old kids who had various handicaps: Down syndrome, deafness, parental sexual abuse, drug addiction in the womb. When the 1989 earthquake hit, her workday was over and she was at home, but many of the kids were still at the school. After the earth stopped moving, the teachers on duty took the kids outside while someone checked to make sure the building wasn't about to collapse. It was suppertime. The next day Ennis wanted to give the kids a chance to talk out any traumatized feelings they might have.

"Okay," she said to her class, "now what happened yesterday?"

"We had a picnic!" the children exclaimed.

SONG TO COOKING OUT OVER AN OPEN FIRE IN THE OPEN AIR WITH CRICKETS GOING GEECHY GEECHY

Food gets brown, wood gets rose,
Eyes join hands with ear and nose
To handle all of this that goes

     Fume rise
        juice drop
    Fpss pif
      ssfpop

To thee, O Lord, we lift the praise
For all this air in which to braise.

COMPOST HAPPENS

However progressive, in other respects, the many Southerners of my acquaintance are, and however down-to-earth, many of them treat *salade fatiguée* and moldy oranges like trash. I have seen dear friends toss precious organic materials right in with popped bubble wrap and outworn socks. Blithely they throw away eggshells, banana peels—even *coffee grounds* . . .

After I moved up north to rural Massachusetts, my mother came to visit and took note of my compost heap. She rolled her eyes. As an underloved child on a Mississippi farm, she said, she *had* to do such things. She gave me a look that said only a perverse smarty-pants eco-freak who had left the church would devote his time to getting the good out of corncobs in this day and age. "Everything your father and I worked so hard to *preserve* you from," she said, "you *like*."

When I was a child, I loved to play in dirt. Little did I dream that someday I would *produce* dirt, good, black, and crumbly. I will never be wealthy, but I have made my share of rich soil. My father told me that his grandfather, in cracker Florida, was "poor as owl dung." If you've ever seen one of those owl droppings, hard little pellets of mouse hair and bones, you know they're not going to contribute much to your prospects for waxing fruitful, but I have added some of them to my compost, in acknowledgment of my roots. They have mingled with collapsed jack-o'-lanterns, buggy cornmeal, maple leaves, and lobster shells to create loam.

Even some of my current neighbors, who tend to be, if anything, whole-earthier-than-thou, have accused me of caring more about compost than about the eventual phlox and tomatoes. That is true only in the sense that I may devote more time to fussing with the compost than to fussing with the phlox and tomatoes. I offered my wife a similar explanation recently when she asked—lightly, but you never know—whether I cared more about my sinuses than about her. That was insensitive of me, I realize now. I should not have drawn an analogy between my sinuses and my compost, because I love my compost. My sinuses follow me around, nagging. My compost stays out in the yard and works. My cereal dregs and dead daffodils decompose together, that my phlox and tomatoes might thrive.

And those tomatoes I do appreciate. They are red and robust and—try to find this in the stores—they taste extraordinarily like tomatoes. (Not to mention the beans, lettuce, collards, onions, squashes, garlic, cauliflower, eggplant, carrots, peppers. *Dirt*, in your own backyard, producing stuff that sticks to your bones. Makes you wonder.) But I admit, compost appeals to me in and of itself, for I have always been tickled by *e pluribus unum*. Spaghetti sauce or soup can incorporate considerable diversity, but there are limits. Compost is almost a wide-open town. Broccoli stalks lie down with shreds of *The New York Times*, stale Ritz crackers with herbal tea bags, gone-musky garlic cloves with blown rhododendrons. Give me your tired, your poor, your stringy, and your mildewed, the wretched refuse of your teeming fridge.

Sometimes our heap seems to resist breaking down. "I like compost," I will yell at it, "but not very mulch!" Or, "Dust thou art, to dust returneth, was not spoken of this soil!" Our compost never—at least while I'm watching it—steams. You hear about piles that emit visible rays of heat, but that is a gratification I have been denied. Still, I take pride in our down-to-earth clump of decadence:

Flat beer, bones, fireplace ashes, burned popcorn, struck matches, spoiled hay, black zucchini, lobster shells, fish eyes, incompletely devoured cat kills, finger blood, hair from our combs and brushes, dish-rinse water, peels, hulls, parings, stems, twigs, leaves, bark, sawdust, eggshells, pencil sharpenings, moldy applesauce, weeds (if seedless), sand, month-old bread, live worms, corncobs, apple cores, pine straw, wine dregs, string, crusts, crumbs, sardine oil, melon rinds, artichoke chokes, shrimp legs. A heterogeneity of tissues, coming together to create a richness, like unsavory influences forming a style.

And of course I keep an eye out for dung. Years ago, I had an old horse, and more manure than, honestly, I needed. Now I have to make do with road apples of opportunity. Do you know how Aunt Betsey Trotwood, in *David Copperfield*, runs out and waves a broom to chase off donkeys whenever they pass her house? When people ride horses past mine, I am glad. If I thought I could run out and startle them, the horses, into making a deposit as they go by, I would. That stuff makes your compost *strong*.

I fuss with my heap, yes, but I have a gimme cap that says "Compost Happens," and so do I believe. Someone sent me a video put out by Alameda County, California, titled *Do the Rot Thing*. Exemplary Alamedans are shown systematically turning out compost that, by the looks of it, might be packaged as a breakfast cereal or knitted into a nice nubbly sport jacket. My compost is stranger than that. Over the years, I have buried in it three snakes and untold fingernail clippings. I used to add a lot of cigar butts and Red Man leavings. My system won't tolerate tobacco anymore, which is a good thing, but no quid ever fazed my compost. My compost is eating, at its leisure, a pine log eight inches thick that I put in there as a friendly challenge. Maybe I could have consoled my mother if I had expressed my feeling for compost in hymnal terms: What once was waste, now is ground.

Ah, Church of England clergywear: dog collar, surplice, cassock. As that Austin Powers fellow might say, not exactly what's happening, baby. Members of the Southwell diocese of Nottinghamshire (pronounced Suth'l-disNoshersher) feel that it's high time vicars serve Communion as their parishioners take it, in casual dress. Draw in young worshippers in increasingly secular times, sort of thing. Otherwise, studies suggest, for every one hundred children who went to church in 1930, by 2030 only four. Who'll fill the pews, you see. The bishop of Maidstone was game, said he'd consider wearing jeans. Traditionalists were aghast. "If you are standing behind the altar as the Eucharist," argued one (happened to be a designer of ceremonial robes), "you are standing there as Christ. Difficult to imagine Christ in jeans and T-shirt." Point there. This week, General Synod convened. Church's governing body. Whole matter brought up for debate. Bang: jeans and T-shirt thrown right out. Anglicans taking their transubstantiated wine and bikky will continue to imagine Christ in dog collar and so on. Do them good, too.

WEED DATING MAY WORK FOR SOME

I heard on the radio about weed dating. Single persons making one another's tentative acquaintance while weeding down a row of collards or something. A potential twosome will bend over and pluck along together for a ways, and then everybody will switch. Although she had met no one she wanted to see again, said one woman who had tried weed dating, she did feel that weeding people out, so to speak, between bean rows was more natural than in a bar.

It is a good thing I am not single myself, because I would be a terrible weed dater. I am a solitary weeder. Weeding helps me think. The last thing you need, when you make a living doing semi-creative work, is something else semi-creative to do while you are trying to focus. Weeding is in no way creative. Weeding is clearing away irrelevancies, so the vegetables, too, can focus. When you pull up all the weeds crowding a tomato plant, you can almost hear the tomatoes going, "Whew!" Which is not to say tomatoes want to chat—my impression is, they want to get on with turning red. When I'm weeding, my mind is safely a thousand miles away. Weeding as an icebreaker? I can't see it.

At any rate, I can no longer separate weeds from the context of my particular marriage. When our garden is producing, I weed every day—but sporadically, disjointedly. This is in part because I don't think straight but also because of the way my wife plants: lavishly, multifariously, nonlinearly. Basil, pole beans, and hollyhocks mingle with innumerable weeds. And many of Joan's favorite plants, at various stages of their development, resemble weeds to me. So I tend to hop from one incontestable weed to another.

But what if I were the kind of weeder who can stick to a row and would welcome a soul mate to do that with. As we weeded, what would be our conversation?

Incidentally, according to the *Dictionary of Smoky Mountain English*, an Appalachian version of "weeded" is "wed," as in "Did you-uns get them weeds wed out yet?" So if you find yourself weed-dating with a winsome mountain gal, and she says, "I wed with my brother just this morning," you don't necessarily have to write her off.

One thing you and a possible life sharer might discuss is what a weed is, anyway. Other languages don't mince words. French is *mauvaise herbe*, Italian *malerba*, Spanish *mala hierba*: a bad herb. German is *Unkraut*: a non-cabbage. But *The Oxford English Dictionary* says no one knows where the Old English *wéod* came from. Just growed, evidently.

Okay, etymology is too dry for romance. Let us, if we must, be creative. Let us picture a fellow, Vern. Scrawny and indistinct-looking. And a lady, Inez. Stringy-haired and uncurvaceous. Two nice people, with feelings, who have tended to be dismissed, over the years, as weedy. All afternoon Inez and Vern have been weed-dating fruitlessly. Every person she or he has come up against has given her or him a glance and then looked down, at the crabgrass, and then away, toward who the next prospect might be. Dusk is approaching.

Then at last the pairing-off brings Vern and Inez together. As it happens, they are English majors. There between rows of brussels sprouts, among picked-over burdocks and dandelions, they try to get the ball rolling, as is their wont, by quoting from literature.

Vern: "It was Emerson who said, 'What is a weed? A plant whose virtues have not yet been discovered.'"

Inez: "'A weed is but an unloved flower'—Ella Wheeler Wilcox."

And their eyes meet, and they know, and they pitch forward into each other's arms and tumble into the topsoil. All the cool weeders, hearing Vern and Inez thrash and whoop, suddenly feel less cool, or rather too. It was Shakespeare who wrote, "Sweet flowers are slow and weeds make haste."

BETWEEN MEALS SONG

I want to gnaw your ankles,
Root behind your knees,
Nip your bended elbows,
Browse your forehead, please.

Oh, let's make love and supper with-
Out washing off our hands.
Eat prairie oysters, turkey breasts, and
Other savory glands.
Let's make love and supper with-
Out washing off our hands.

I want to wrinkle your neck's nape
And stretch out your back's small,
Go "This little piggy" on your toes
And, honey, that ain't all.

I want to heft your two prize calves
And play like you're a farm
And I'm the farmer and my house is
Underneath your arm.

I'll cultivate your collarbone,
Achilles' tendon, palm
And ears inside and out and lobes
And hair on end or calm.

I like your eyelids and your hip
And relatives and friends.
Your navel is a constant source
As are your finger ends.

The bottoms of your feet rate high
Before and after bath;
I want to reckon on your ribs
Whenever I do math.

I'm taken by your vertebrae
And back behind your ears,
Your Adam's apple, temples, and
Most of your ideas.

Oh, let's make love and supper with-
Out washing off our hands.
Eat prairie oysters, turkey breasts, and
Other savory glands.
Let's make love and supper with-
Out washing off our hands.

GREEN PEA LOVER'S LAMENT

I tried to eat my English peas.
The peas they had their own ideas.

BEES OF THE ANTHROPOCENE

"Was you ever bit by a dead bee?" Walter Brennan keeps asking people (but Lauren Bacall beats him to the punch) in *To Have and Have Not.* In his book about writers in Hollywood, Tom Dardis assumes that William Faulkner—"because it *sounds* like Faulkner"—came up with that line. Faulkner did contribute to the shooting script, but the bee line has now been traced to an earlier draft by Jules Furthman. What Faulkner did write, in *Flags in the Dust,* was "the garden lay in sunlight bright with bloom, myriad with scent and with a drowsy humming of bees—a steady golden sound, as of sunlight become audible."

Bees themselves may not know they're buzzing; like human teen-agers before cell phones, they communicate by means of dancing and pheromones. In an astonishingly intimate documentary, *Tales from the Hive,* you can watch a forager bee doing the waggle dance, by which she gives the worker bees directions to a new source of nectar. Bees buzz because bees be busy. Their intense wing vibration makes sound waves to human ears.

And I don't know about your garden, but in mine I do not hear bees waxing Faulknerian. Every year for the past ten or so, the U.S. bee population has declined by a quarter to a third. And if you don't think you can get bit by a dead bee, consider this: according to the actor and conservationist Ed Begley Jr., "One of every three bites of food you and I eat is pollinated by honeybees." One bite thank you Lord, one bite thank you Mama (excuse me, Ed, that's mine), one bite thank you bees.

Without bees we'd not only be out of honey, we'd lose most of our apples, blueberries, blackberries, watermelons, cucumbers, squashes, almonds, cantaloupes, and so on, because—it's a sweet system. While gathering nectar and pollen for their hives, honeybees serve as little cupids for the fruits and vegetables. In graphic terms, the bees offhandedly (I don't want to say inadvertently—I think they kind of know) carry pollen from the male parts to the female parts of fruit and vegetable blossoms. And why can't the apples and cantaloupes do this for themselves? Because it would be weedy and unsocial; it's not how these fruits and vegetables roll. Do it for each other? That would make appaloupes. Well, couldn't we get undocumented workers to do it? Or the Internet? Nope. Other insects and the wind can do some of it, but mostly it's got to be bees.

Do you regard bees in a negative light? You may be thinking of "killer bees," which have made their way over from Africa and up from Brazil into terrible disaster movies and a real-life invasive presence across the South and the Southwest. Indeed you do not want to stir up these bees, because they will come out in full swarm and chase you for half a mile stinging you hundreds of times while you run, and if you dive underwater, they will wait for you to come up. Their venom isn't any stronger than other bees', they just have a hair-trigger all-in defense system. But far more Americans are killed by pet dogs every year than by killer bees. Some hope has been advanced that these bees might be bred with regular honeybees to produce a hybrid more resistant to what is causing colony collapse disorder.

If only we knew what the cause is. Beekeepers go out to their hives and find that their bees have disappeared. Wandered off to die scattered, where their bodies are hard to find. When little autopsies are possible, they do not lead to definite conclusions. Maybe it's the mites that get on bees; maybe it's the chemicals employed to kill the mites.*

Maybe it's the stress on bees from being loaded into trucks and dragged all over the land to service blueberries in Maine and almonds in California. Maybe a forager bee comes in and does the hell-I-don't-know-where-anything-is-anymore dance.

Of all the theories put forward, here's the one most appealing to my sense of non-fitness. Bees' immune systems depend on their foraging from diverse blossoms. Bees that have fallen into agribusiness are more and more being fed high-fructose corn syrup and, get this, "pollen substitute." Feeding corn syrup to honeybees is like feeding LeBron James a beach ball. And *pollen substitute*? No wonder our bees are leaving us; we're making them feel like they aren't really bees.

We know we are what we eat: venison puts hair on our chests, and we are very, very silly if we eat foam. We know, further, that we are what we eat eats: for our health, we should demand pork from pigs fattened on good organic swill uncontaminated by antibiotics. But we are also what brings what we eat into fruition. We are all part bee.

---

*"It's hard to kill a bug on a bug," says a beekeeper in Louisiana. But two beekeepers I talked to in Eureka Springs, Arkansas, said they'd had success dusting their bees with powdered sugar; the bees pick the sugar off each other and the mites along with it. That must be some mouthful, though, given that another Louisiana beekeeper told an interviewer that one of those mites "on you would be like a tick the size of a rat sucking your blood." The things that bees go through.

PART TEN

TRIPS

WHAT WE ATE IN JAPAN

No, we did not eat the fugu, the blowfish which if prepared incorrectly is fatal. We did not eat that. If you must eat a blowfish, I always say, find one that comes without a waiver. Nor did we eat eel on a stick, ice cream made from whale fat, or a bowl of tiny squirming live fish. We did eat raw chicken.

I know, I know. Tell people you have eaten fried armadillo, for example, and they may turn up their noses, but they do so with some grudging respect for your exposure to folk food. Then they ask, and not just out of politeness, what it tasted like. (A little like fried chicken.) Tell people you ate raw chicken—people who scour and bleach their cutting board for fear that some faint vestige of raw chicken may lurk in the grain—and they look at you as if you have sunk to the level of an egg-sucking dog, or a geek (actually that would require a live chicken—in Japan we saw a sign for "Living Ham Pizza," but that just meant "very fresh"), or a gerbil that devours its young.

Every day, a lawyer in Marin County, California, named Peter Buchanan does exactly the same thing for lunch: drives to the same restaurant and picks up the same take-out order: salmon grilled on one side, light olive oil no salt no pepper, well-steamed green beans, carrots, and four potatoes. And drives back to his office and eats. One day recently, a slight complication arose: as Buchanan left the restaurant, a road worker tried to wave him around a construction barrier. The next thing the worker knew, cones were flying and he was clinging—with what a witness called "a pretty shocked look on his face"—to the hood of Buchanan's car, which proceeded up Highway 101, as usual, at forty miles an hour. When, after several miles, traffic halted momentarily, the worker got off. Buchanan went on, as usual. Police found him in his office, as usual, having his lunch. "A crazy guy was on my hood," he said. "I told him to get off." Buchanan, seventy-three, faces charges that could get him four years of a whole new routine.

So, were we disoriented, so to speak? Japan is a long way from where we live. You cross the international date line, which means that you journey earlierward for the better part of a whole day, and yet when you reach the Land of the Rising Sun, back home it is currently yesterday. Although for some time in the night, it will be today.

Were we bemused by what happens in Japan to our native tongue? There are shops in Japan called simply "Let's." Or "Get!" On the other hand, there is a bar and restaurant in Kyoto called (with all the dots and quotation marks) "Pooh's? . . ." When you see a sign that says, "Relaxation Forest . . . For Rest," outside a place where you go to unwind by sitting among potted plants and looking at videos of woodsy settings, you know that this is a culture that has its own way of playing around with English words. And mixing them with other languages, as in "Le Monde des ONLY YOU," a private club in the Gion district of Kyoto. The Japanese word pronounced "taco" means "octopus," and the magazine named *B.L.T.* stands for "Beautiful Lady and Television."

But my wife, Joan, went to high school in Japan and remembered enough Japanese to keep us grounded and to order us several beers before we ate the raw chicken. True, she was not sure she was ordering them correctly because, since they were draft beers, in chunky glasses, she couldn't decide whether they were tall skinny things or not. In bottles, they would clearly have been tall skinny things. The Japanese for "two," when the two things in question are tall and skinny, is *nippon*. For two things that are not tall and skinny, it is *futatsu*. (For two animals of any shape, it is *ni-hiki*, for two people, *futari*.) Anyway, we had got several pairs of beers ordered.

And the fugu aside, how can you get poisoned, accidentally, in a country that produces such toothpicks? We brought home a package of five toothpicks (Japanese things never come in fours because *shi* means both "four" and "death"), dressed up, each one differently, in the wigs and kimonos of geishas. We also brought home Nice Day brand toothpicks. They come in a translucent plastic cylinder packed tight, not a micron of wasted space, so when you take off the top, you see a solid flat mass of blunt tips, ranging in color from burnt brown to tan. Together these tips suggest a cross section of a single many-stranded organism or cable. Or a beehive, but better organized. Eight hundred and fifty toothpicks, needle sharp and sturdy: I have been using one of them, off and on and respectfully but not gingerly, for two days now to see how long it will hold up, and so far it is only just a bit soggy at the tip. The blunt end resembles a chessman: a head, and where the neck would be, there's a groove or circumnotch that fits your fingernail, and then there's an elegantly beveled torso, and then a swelling like hips, and then another notch, this one less pronounced than the one above, and finally there's the long shaft leading to the business end. Each pick would appear to have been hand turned on a tiny lathe and then cured and tempered. I have encountered such toothpicks before, in Japanese restaurants, but to have a jam-packed quiver of them, which should last for two or three years of strenuous use, is to love them. And in tiny English beneath the Japanese for "Nice Day," we read the following message: "We wish to enjoy meals as we have them every day."

From Japan we also brought back containers of ground pepper. A four-inch bamboo section with a wooden stopper in the top, where the pepper went in, and a tiny stopper on the side, where the pepper comes out. A label on the side says, in Japanese, "Seven different peppers." Blended as to color and taste in seven-part harmony.

We brought from Japan stainless steel grapefruit spoons, very subtly serrated, engraved with Japanese characters that may be rendered phonetically, according to Joan, as "Gurepufurutsusupun."

We brought from Japan a drawstring bag, on the inside red silk, on the outside green silk with little white rabbits and, in Japanese, "Little silk rabbit bag." Nothing tricky there.

We brought from Japan a sumptuous spiral watercolor book. Opening its dusty-rose-colored boards to the white paper, just *faintly* creamy, inside, is like biting into a plum and finding gelato, or sliding a silk gown up over an even lovelier leg. "Human art materials," it says on the first page.

We brought from Japan smaller notebooks, three inches by four and an eighth, in various pastel colors, all of which say on the cover, in small type, "Let simple and

> A chill: They've turned on
> "Air-conditioning." I'll eat
> The philodendron.
>
> —Cat haiku

old-fashioned myself stay with you, while ordinary things have been disappearing in the world," and below that, in minuscule cursive, "Gratitude for you." We brought a larger notebook whose red-and-white-gingham-pattern cover says, "Be chic about a notebook. Facile/Tasty character is our basic criterion," and another notebook with a clear plastic cover that says on the second page, "The proof of a pudding is in the eating, and so start up right now without worry about."

We did have one worrisome food experience in Japan, in a small, inelegant inn on the Ise Peninsula, where we paid three hundred dollars for a room with meals and karaoke. Before we had a chance to order dinner, the proprietor showed up at our door with a spread consisting of an overbroiled lobster apiece; six baked clams of a certain type said to be named for the noise they make when alive (*bapubapu*); a cooked fish called, I think, *asagi*; heaping platters of octopus sashimi, tuna sashimi, salmon sashimi, and sea-bream sashimi; several enormous peeled grapes; some pale, unspecified sashimi in a boat of ice with a fake cherry-blossom bonsai garnish; and—sizzling sluggishly on a tinfoil platter over burning Sterno—half an onion, half a green pepper, and eight cubes of salami.

It doesn't take long for a small morsel of fatty pork to pass through a duck. Alton Emory, of Canardia, New Hampshire, who has ducks, noticed this, and it gave him an idea for a surefire viral video. He tied a piece of fatty pork to a greased length of twine and placed it in his duck yard, and soon he had a string of ducks—going on with their lives unruffled, because Emory allowed for adequate slack. But the video footage—four ducks, then five ducks, then six—didn't look like much. And the local humane society got wind of his project. Last week, as Emory stood in the yard arguing with the humane society guy, an eagle swooped down, grabbed the sixth duck, and flew off with the whole string—wouldn't you know it: as the other five ducks, one at a time, slid down the string, fell through the air, and landed on his pond, Emory's camera was in the house.

We couldn't eat more than half of this repast, and we didn't want to hurt the proprietor's feelings, so we hid much of the sashimi in a plastic bag. Next morning we walked down to the water, off behind some craggy rocks out of sight of the inn, and tossed sashimi in the direction of hovering seafowl. Which hated our manners and flew away.

After a long awkward pause, a single bird reappeared. Birders tell us it was undoubtedly a black kite. It had in its mouth what looked like a *tissue*. As it made a pass over the sashimi scattered on the riprap, the kite transferred this tissue thing to its talons, as if to wipe them off. Then the kite dropped the tissue-like thing into the sea, where it seemed to melt. Then the kite soared, spiraled down, grabbed a bit of our fish, and flew away.

In a country where seabirds are that fastidious, how risky can the restaurants be? Generally, we found the restaurant food to be less eerie than it looked. In a Kyoto restaurant called Agatha, for Agatha Christie, we were served skewered eggplant topped by what looked like lots of tiny wee wings, *moving* on it. Were they supposed to be on there? Were they some manner of near-evanescent beings which, having been undercooked, had revived? At the time we didn't have a cat back home, so we had to ask. They were flakes shaved from a chunk of bonito fish that had been dried in the sun, and they were moving because they were so thin they fluttered with every faint current of air in the place. The favorite treat of the cat we do have now, Jimmy, is a coarser version of those flakes.

It was also in Kyoto, in a mom-and-pop joint called Toridori, that we ate raw chicken. *Tori* means chicken and *dori* means street, but *toridori* could also mean chicken-chicken, because when the Japanese double a word to make a compound they always change the first letter the second time, as we do in "fuzzy-wuzzy."

All our favorite eating places in Japan—ones specializing in soba noodles, or ramen with soup and luscious *gyoza* dumplings with soy sauce and vinegar—were small, packed, and inexpensive enough that you could eat well for under fifteen bucks apiece. Toridori, after we entered through the traditional hanging curtain bearing the establishment's name, was just big enough to hold ten chairs along an L-shaped polished-wood counter, behind the counter a range and a cutting surface, and on a shelf the traditional welcoming cat: a plump poker-faced china figure holding up one paw in benediction. After we sat down, only one of the chairs was empty. Mom and pop sliced and diced and cooked and served and chatted with a cheery clientele.

We did not try to conceal the restaurant guide in which we had read about Toridori. We sensed an air of "Here come the *hen-na-gaijin*" (strange foreigners, a redundancy). Hosts and diners alike were undoubtedly bracing themselves for the sight of something barbaric, like a human being putting soy sauce on his or her rice, or pouring his or her own sake, or at least neglecting to lift the sake cup up from the counter while accepting more sake from his or her dinner companion. But thanks to Joan, we knew better than to do these things. And when she offered some pleasantries in Japanese, all present relaxed.

Our first course was excellent fried dried *yuba* (tofu whey). In a Tokyo restaurant specializing in all forms of tofu, we had made our own *yuba*. Big squares of tofu came floating in the whey, which was simmering over a charcoal burner. After you ate the tofu, with onions and various sauces, you took a bamboo-and-rice-paper fan and waved it over the whey until what formed was, to be frank, a layer of scum. And you picked it up with your chopsticks, and it was not at all bad, for scum, but nowhere near as good as Toridori's three-by-five rectangles of extra-thin *yuba* deep-fried to a crispness that melted as you chewed.

Then we ordered some yakitori—fried dark chicken meat on one skewer, white meat on another, livers on a third. *Oishii.* Means "delicious." Then we ordered steamed chicken dumplings. Very *oishii.* Then we ordered fried chicken dumplings. Even more *oishii.* And then . . .

The specialty of the house.

Chicken sashimi.

We watched pop slice raw chicken breast extremely thin and serve up the slices in precisely staggered stacks. We watched two stylish Japanese women, svelte in basic black and pearls—women who gave every appearance of being much further removed from a low animal state than I—dip these slices into plum sauce and enjoy them. We saw that these women did not die.

Pop took a break from slicing to tell us there was another pun involved in Toridori: he came from the town of Tottori. Multilevel wordplay with the locals! And mom presented us with gifts: a felt chicken on a chain, commemorating Toridori's fifth anniversary, and a series of chopstick rests, which she had made herself, some of them wine-cork halves wrapped in decorative paper, some of them origami cranes, and some of them paper-wrapped and lacquered *oshibori* ties—the strips of plastic that go around the wet towels served before meals.

You would have taken chicken sashimi from those nice folks too, or I would have been disappointed in you. It was pink, almost translucent, and each slice came with a slender ridge of raw chicken skin.

What did it taste like? Plum sauce, more plum sauce, and beer.

INCIDENT IN THE TIMES SQUARE NATHAN'S

Something that happened to me in the Times Square Nathan's still sticks in my craw, years and years after that Nathan's has ceased to exist.

Back then, I was living in New York working for *Sports Illustrated*. Often I would lunch on Nathan's hot dogs or Nathan's fried shrimp, which happened to be fried the way my mother used to fry them in Georgia, with Nathan's tartar sauce. (When asked what my favorite food is, I sometimes say, "Tartar sauce." Not strictly true, but there's something to it.) And Nathan's corn on the cob.

Ideal corn on the cob is from farm stands: sweet, white, exquisite little-crisp-kernel Silver Queen or alternating yellow and white Butter and Sugar. But Nathan's plump basic-yellow central-casting kernels were succulent too, in their way.

So one day I purchased fried shrimp, a vanilla shake, and a nice, juicy ear of that corn. And carried it all to one of the many Formica tables in the place.

In the Times Square of those days, you might well encounter fellow diners who were unsavory. But I have always had a strong stomach. I can count the times I have thrown up on the fingers of one hand. (I mean, I can count on the fingers of one hand the number of times I have thrown up.)

Once in college, from overintense pipe smoking.

Once in 1969, from having eaten chili after sustaining what was

> Vereen Elam, CEO of Inglow Inc., a Youngstown, Ohio, window-treatment firm, has urged his more than two hundred employees to have their auras cleansed at home. "It has come to my attention that many of you may have auras that restrict your full effectiveness," says a memo received by the Inglow workforce. "This can be corrected after work hours. Sit in a chair while a family member does a firm but gentle chopping action around the entire body, coming within one to two inches from physical contact. The family member should then be sure to shake their hands out thoroughly." Though the memo states that the cleansing isn't mandatory, rumbles of in-house dissent have reached the local media. "We are Presbyterians and do not recognize the aura," an unnamed employee tells the *Youngstown Eagle*. "Especially my husband. He doesn't even acknowledge herbs."

later diagnosed as a bruised spleen from a company-softball collision. To my surprise, the chili had not settled my stomach. I was trying to make it to the Time Incorporated infirmary, didn't want to throw up on Radio City Music Hall, scurried across Sixth Avenue while holding my toddler daughter's hand—"I don't want to hold Daddy's hand! I want to hold Daddy's hand when he's well!" Got as far as the base of the Time-Life Building, up against which I lost it. "It's all right," my then wife, Ellen, told a disgusted-looking man who showed up with a broom, "he works here."

Once in an Italian villa in 2003, from what must have been some extraordinarily bad mussels marinara *di amore*.

And once in Nashville, on a book tour, from the last ham-salad sandwich I will ever buy from a TV-station vending machine.

What's that, four? I might well be better off today, weigh less, have a lighter karma (if I understand Eastern religion at all; maybe I don't), if I threw up more often. But I don't.

So I could handle the Nathan's ambience. People milled around, the tables stayed full despite a rapid turnover, and they were shared by strangers. And I stress, *strangers*. Everyone was fully clothed and no one was lying down, or relaxing, but otherwise the Times Square Nathan's was much like the beach at Coney Island, without sand. As I settled in, a frazzled mother impelled her three children, aged about four, six, and eight, and hard looking every one of them, into the three chairs opposite me.

So. Okay. We all got to eat. But.

"Now, what do you want?" the mother queried over my shoulder—her intention evidently being to leave the young ones there while she went for food.

"That!" said the largest of the three, a girl, and she physically poked, with her finger, my ear of corn.

I sat there. Staring incredulously at my corn. As it rocked back and forth slightly in its butter. And then I stared at the trespassing girl, who sat—with an air about her of not having exceeded her rights, or even having begun to exercise them good—some fifteen inches away from my nose.

> Tim Philip Ditmars of Buford, Arizona, never heard of National Public Radio until two years ago. "At that time," he says, "I had been a Buddhist for eighteen months. Had achieved prolonged tantric ecstasy for periods up to four and a half hours, and was looking around for something else. Then I turned on this portable radio I had stolen from my macrobiotic nutritionist's office, just for the thrill, which gives you an idea where my head was, at that time. The radio was set at a station where people were just talking, in a normal tone of voice, for a long time. I was fascinated. A man in Kansas was saying something called secular humanism was a religion trying to take over America. Then a woman in Michigan said no it wasn't. Either way, I was hooked." Ditmars has started a group of recovering ultimate-truth addicts called Eureka Seekers, whose membership numbers over five thousand nationally. Among them is Ditmars's nutritionist, who has stopped pushing millet.

"Cynthia . . . ," snapped the mother then. And I figured the girl was going to get a lesson in the inviolability, in a civilized society, of another person's ear of corn. "That is *not* enough."

So, against her will, Cynthia ordered a hot dog and a large Coke as well as some corn, and the whole family continued to take no notice of me as . . .

As I ate mine. I couldn't even eat around the spot where Cynthia had touched it, because, as I say, she had caused my corn to rock a little bit in its butter, and I had taken my eyes off it to stare at her and then at her mother.

I guess you could say that by not speaking out, at least, by not standing up and saying, "Now, listen here. Now, listen here. People don't *do* that to other people's corn"—I guess by not doing that, at least, I was as guilty of ignoring their personhoods as they were of mine.

But I was *astonished*. And who wants to say anything to anybody in Times Square?

BUTTERED KITTENS

New York City, 1969. My daughter wasn't three years old yet, her brother was a baby, and they, their mother, Ellen, and I had two cats, Abyssinians, named Kobar and Bale. One day Bale, in a comfortable cardboard box, with Kobar pacing back and forth and occasionally peering in and muttering, delivered four kittens. The fourth born was weak. It kept getting pushed back away from Bale, where it cried in an odd voice and twitched feebly. Then Kobar and Bale began to shiver. Shivering in the mother might mean eclampsia; Kobar was being hysterical.

We were living in Manhattan and had no car. Nor did we have a cat carrier that could accommodate six cats (two of them shivering, four of them tiny, and one of those impaired) comfortably enough that they could be carried alive on foot by one person for long. Nor did we have whatever it might take to load two adults, two small children, and six cats into and out of a taxi.

So we put Kobar in the cat carrier, and him and the two children in the baby buggy, which Ellen pushed, carefully, and I carried Bale and the kittens, carefully, in the big cardboard box of the nativity, with a top on it and holes cut out for air and light. Eventually, we all ten made it the twelve blocks to the vet's.

The vet prescribed a lot of pills and powders that would make the whole cat family right, except for the feeble kitten. He would need to have butter smeared all over him. That would induce Bale to lick him, which would be stimulating.

And it worked. It felt pretty questionable, I can tell you, to smear butter, with a little calcium lactate mixed in, on a minuscule, faintly wriggling fur ball, but in the long run it lent him vigor. Soon the runt was tearing into the scrimmage like a tiger. Sometimes we would have to pull a larger kitten out of his way, but then he would latch on with a will and hold his own. In the process, he got butter all over his siblings.

Buttered kittens. Both parents enjoyed licking them. Let's have a chorus of "Wo-oh-oh-oh-oh . . . *fee*-lines."

LAST NIGHT

I dreamed that I
Was up to my knees
In my mother's mac-
Aroni and cheese.

MAN HERE TRIED TO BE A GOOD CITIZEN
OF THE D TRAIN

Years ago I did a bad thing on a New York City subway, and I still feel responsible, although it was owing to the difficulty of modern life.

I was living in Brooklyn at the time and working in Rockefeller Center. I was on my way from the former to the latter. I had had the foresight to leave tardily enough that morning to get a seat. Still the car was fairly crowded, several unfortunates standing.

We pulled in to the Grand Street station. I was absorbed in the *Park Slope News*, our weekly neighborhood paper, which reported the seizure of $200,000 worth of heroin in a house near ours (we didn't know them). Suddenly one end of the subway car was aflutter. It was the first time I had been in an even partially aflutter subway car. I was accustomed to subway cars' having the interior atmosphere of quarter-ton trucks carrying enlisted men back at night from long, pointless exercises in the rain.

My end of this car, though, was filled suddenly with people gesturing, pointing to a spot just over my head, and saying, *"The window."* Two men across from me had even risen from their seats and advanced in the direction the others were pointing.

I looked over my shoulder and saw what seemed to be the window in question—an adjustable horizontal vent over the big stationary pane. The doors had closed, the train was just beginning to move out of the station, and a young couple was running alongside, pointing at the window. It was open.

I can't *explain* my reaction. All I know is that I felt I had to react quickly, and I suppose the only previous situations to which my mind could relate this one at the moment were situations in which my car door was open and other drivers were shouting at me to close it. I knew, in my mind, that you couldn't be sucked out of a subway window the way you can, as I understand it, out of an airplane window, but I might have assumed subrationally that there could be something nebulously hazardous about a subway window left open. And I loved New York, even including its subways, and I wanted to be a good citizen.

With one reflex motion of my arm, at any rate, I shut the window.

The faces of the couple running along outside fell, as the train pulled away from them and a paper bag hit the inside of the window and dropped back, onto the woman beside me.

"He closed the window," from another woman across the car, was the only comment on my action that I heard; its tone seemed moderately surprised but too tired to be censorious. The man who had thrown the bag picked it up off the lady's lap and went back to his seat.

He and the man next to him opened the bag, revealing its contents to themselves only. The other people in the car murmured a bit and then lapsed back into their previous silences.

I couldn't put the thing out of my mind so easily. I went over to the two men, losing my seat to a blind woman as I did. "What was that all about?" I asked.

Both men shrugged, but then they showed me what was in the bag. A blond wig and a sandwich.

It came clear to me then. The young running couple had left his or her wig and lunch on the seat by mistake and had been calling for someone to throw the bag out through the window to them before the train departed.

The two men put the bag back down on the seat. They didn't want to wear the wig, and they didn't trust human nature enough to eat the sandwich.

By getting involved, not wisely but too well, I had prevented what might have been the only spontaneous and niftily coordinated friendly effort among strangers going on at that moment throughout the metropolis. I felt bad. I wanted to account for my actions. But nobody would look at me. I glared at the blind woman and stood there impersonally rattling and groaning on the underground the rest of the way to work. Urban life is too complex.

JUNE, SPOON . . .

Ever wonder what a baboon
Couple do on their honeymoon?
Nitpick. No, not being malicious.
Love's when your nits are most delicious.

TICKS DU PAYS

A few years ago, after eight years of unmarried bliss, the artist known as Joan Griswold and I were wed. People (that is to say, men) asked me why. She put her foot down, I said: unless I made an honest woman of her, she would no longer check me for ticks.

In that there was a germ of truth. To be sure, we were wafted to the altar (or rather, Sunset Beach, in Tarpon Springs, Florida) by forces so gossamer, mutual, and luminous as to render laughable any notion of mundane quid pro quo. If, however, my beloved *had* laid down the tick ultimatum, it would have been dispositive. On the green rolling swards of western Massachusetts, where we live in tick season, ticks dine on us.

With sophisticated people of the Northeast—sophisticated, that is, in their way—I have long had an unspoken compact. They get their props for growing up comfortable with things like fresh mozzarella (when asked what possessed me to move north, I often reply simply, "Real, fresh mozza-

At last someone has harnessed the digestive powers of that minute reddish larva of the harvest mite known as the red bug or chigger. At one-sixtieth of an inch in length, a chigger is almost invisible to the human eye, but when it crawls up onto you (it has six legs), it begins to devour you. It digs down past your outer layer of skin, breaks down your inner-skin cells with its saliva, and chews. This, as you well know, makes you itch like original sin. (In hell, I have been told, chiggers are the size of squirrels.) So have scientists at Clemson University discovered how to stamp out chiggers? No. But they have shown that the key element of chigger saliva can be isolated and reengineered to focus on hair follicles. Is Madame's down getting dirty? A little bit of repurposed chigger spit whisks away those unwanted whiskers for good. Because chigger saliva is almost laughably hard to gather in bulk, the commercial potential here may seem limited, but the researchers hope to synthesize that key element before long.

rella"), and I get mine for having grown up comfortable with things like ticks.

For many years, after moving up here, I was content in the notion that nothing in the New England countryside, except bears, was virulent or voracious enough to have much impact on a person who grew up in Georgia and Texas. I have been pretty brazen about Massachusetts poison ivy, for instance, because it doesn't seem to be anywhere near as strong as the Georgia variety, exposure to which may have blessed me, in retrospect, with the immune system of a boar hog.

In Georgia, we had copperheads, water moccasins, rattlesnakes, and chiggers, and our bees were strong. If a barefoot boy—even a barefoot Georgia boy—stepped on a Georgia bee, the arch of his foot would turn convex. I look at a Massachusetts bee today, and I think, *Buck up, little buddy.*

As for Texas, we lived there for just one year, when I was thirteen. But that was long enough to be faced with scorpions and . . . the asp.

The asp. Not the venomous snake from Egypt but a friendly-looking caterpillar, which, I was told by my eighth-grade peers . . .

Eighth-grade peers. Remember—shudder—them? Perhaps I seemed as unfathomable and potentially menacing to them as they did to me. But that's what people say about alligators. And alligators have never shown me any signs that they perceive me as either a threat or a meal. Neither did my eighth-grade peers, in particular the ones who told me that if you touched an asp, it would rot your flesh away down to the bone.

In later years, I have come to realize that it's eighth-grade peers who do that.

But the deer ticks of Massachusetts are bad. They can give you Lyme disease or worse. Georgia ticks latch onto you and suck blood until they get tight as a tick. And you find them and you go, yuck, and you pull them off. No. These Yankee ticks sneak in, little bitty things, and the next thing you know, they are gone and have left behind . . .

This is a bit much. They have left a bull's-eye mark.

They. Have left a bull's-eye. On me. After having their way with me and going off to wherever smug had-my-fill-of-that-*Homo-sapiens* parasites go.

It wasn't a sign my marriage was slipping. I had gardened and walked in the woods all summer, virtually tick-free, and I had got careless. At the side of a road that runs along a stream, I had discerned a fallen tree as a great source of free firewood. I had parked downstream, waded upstream, and, wearing shorts, had bow-sawed great chunks of wood off that trunk and floated them to my car.

But then one morning I felt rotten. At my age I expect to hurt vaguely all over, but this was worse. And under my arm: the bull's-eye. No joking matter. These ticks don't just take blood, they leave serious sepsis. My extremely hardy son had to be hospitalized with a fever of 105 after getting a tick bite and being dismissive of it. After being pumped full of antibiotics, he was okay, but since then he can't eat or drink lots of good things without severe indigestion.

A little bitty tick did that. Got between him and his *appetite*. So I embarked upon a three-week course of antibiotics—and yogurt, to restore the beneficial digestive bugs that the antibiotics kill along with the malevolent bugs. I had to pay for killing bugs by eating bugs! And you know what really gets me? Not so much that the tick is so little bitty it is able to eat and run. (Where does it go? Having got into my kitchen metaphorically, does it go there literally and make a sandwich?) What really gets me is that its great-great-grandparents are probably from Connecticut.

HYENAS FEEL GOOD ABOUT THEMSELVES

My assumption had always been that hyenas skulk because, something to do with a carrion diet, they feel lowly. They are said to have, literally, the worst breath in creation. But after observing hyenas in the East African bush, I am inclined to believe that mother hyenas say to their young, "How many times have I told you? Stop holding your head up!"

A hyena's laugh sounds like the whoop of an old boy who's just heard a good one. It isn't hard to imagine one hyena nudging another when a real jaw-dragger goes by and saying, "Look at that sumbitch skulk!" I'll bet hyenas fed fresher fare in captivity lose their sexual appeal to each other until they're given supplements of ripe offal. Hyenas are monogamous, by the way, and the male and female raise the cubs together. Oh, they'll rob a human grave, all right, and in Kenya I met a plastic surgeon, Dr. Peter Davis, who once made a new nose for a man who'd had his bitten off by a hyena as he slept (or, more precisely, as he abruptly woke) in a tent in the wilds of Zaire.

"Was he in shock?" I asked Dr. Davis.

"Oh, no, no. He was a real colonial. He didn't mind. Said, after it was over, he thought I'd given him a better nose. That's all."

At any rate, the hyena population of East Africa is thinning along with that of other, loftier animals. Crops and people crowding them out. The cheetah, in my experience, is typically surrounded by nine or ten Land Rovers and vans. From these vehicles people are taking photographs and inquiring loudly, "WHAT DO THEY MAINLY EAT?" At the moment the cheetah and her cubs are eating some type of antelope. Which type is a matter of audible disagreement among the vehicles' various guides.

"Do we need a constant comment'ry on the disemboweling of poor little whatsit?" asks one of the tourists. One of the guides is commenting so loudly that an earnest camera user in another vehicle shouts, "Shut up, man!" The guide takes umbrage and begins to yell, "Who are you? Who are you?" The guide in the vehicle with the shouting photographer begins reasoning in Swahili with the offended guide, but the latter yells, "I will talk! It is a free country!" The cheetahs give no sign that they notice all this, but you think they must.

Our guide, Richard, of Little Governors' Camp on the Maasai Mara in Kenya, quietly observes things that the other guides don't. "It is a Thomson's gazelle baby," he says of the cheetah's meal. "There is its father." Up on a rise fifty yards away, the father is staring at the devouring of the son. Once, the father stamps his foot, which is too small to help. Over the rise are another male and two females, one of which is the prey's mother. She is staring into space.

We drive on and see a young impala off to itself. A baboon is sitting patiently between it and the herd. "The baboon will eat the baby," Richard says. "There is the baby's parents. They know where the baby is. It was asleep. But they do not know the baboon is there. He is clever. He waits till the baby is used to him. It will take about one hour."

My image of a mongoose is of him killing a snake. But according to my observations from a Land Rover, mongoose parents are so preoccupied with keeping their offspring safe from predatory birds that you wonder where they find time for snaking. The mongoose family is living in a termite mound (having eaten the termites), which has ten or twelve tunnels and exits. Mongoose babies are popping out of first one hole, then another—squeezing out past their parents even—and the parents are rushing out, grabbing the babies in their mouths, and bringing them back, and the babies are popping out again. "I've seen it in a nature film," says a Land Rover passenger. "But I never dreamed it was actually *there*."

For a while we manage to be the only car parked next to a pair of sleeping lions, waiting for them to mate. A pair of lions will keep company for a week and have sex every twenty minutes or so, day and night, for that period. The male of this pair wakes up, licks the female for a few moments, and then mounts her. She growls. He lies back down acting as though it doesn't matter to him, he just thought she wanted to. It doesn't seem to occur to him that our presence may have anything to do with her attitude.

We watch another lion eating a fresh warthog's head. The roar of a lion is like a stone rolling away from a tomb. You've heard of a whiskey baritone. A lion's roar is warthog-head bass.

That night at dinner a woman cries in exasperation, "We did not see one copulating lion!"

You know how New York City has pigeons? That's how Kampala, the capital of Uganda, has marabou storks. Stiff-backed, five-foot-long birds resembling public officials, bald-headed except for straggly fuzz, they stalk or glide

> A lion, no longer in youth,
> Grumbles, "To tell you the truth,
> Hold the antelope,
> I'll just have cantaloupe.
> I've lost my carnivorous tooth."

through the midtown area, eating garbage and perching on used and disused buildings. Urban marabous may be the African fauna of the future. Scavenger birds. And there will be goats no doubt, and here and there a rogue hippo such as the one that "emerged from a sewage pond and attacked a bicyclist on the outskirts of Nairobi," according to *The New York Times*, just before I traveled to East Africa to see wild game before it's gone.

Here, far from the zoo, the hippo is a purple animal with big soulful eyes. Around the eyes and on the underside, pink. The tail looks like a nose with a stringy mustache under it. Hippos in the wild usually have scarred backs from fighting among themselves, biting each other. One hippo can come up under a small boat and flip it.

"I see no hope for it, really," says an old white Kenyan hunter, "it" being Kenya as a place to behold fabulous beasts. (I have heard a New Orleans oil-company lawyer say something equally dismissive about lower Louisiana.) Of course there is always a chance that he meant a place, *run by white Kenyans*, to behold fabulous beasts. White Kenyans have a deep emotional investment in their sense of Kenya as paradise lost.

Tourism is Kenya's number one industry. Tourism means coming to see the animals. And the minister in charge of protecting the game is no longer the one who escorted nine Arab sheikhs on a shooting spree—two hundred animals they bagged, including lion and water buffalo and cheetah—in a game preserve. So there may be room for optimism. Still, there is "less and less room," as the white Kenyan put it to me, "for the game."

"Game" is of course a speciesist term. Being a water buffalo is not a game to the water buffalo. Not a business either, more a way of life. Bit of cheek, really, calling oneself a big-game hunter or even referring to the taste of a fellow animal as gamy. But consciousness-raising along those lines won't help much. In most parts of Africa today, hunting is illegal, and the poachers who kill rhinos and elephants for their horns and tusks, or the odd giraffe or hippo for its meat (the former is said to taste like beef or horse, the latter like pork), are not patronizingly sporty.

The main reason the youth of today may be the last generation to see free-ranging lions is the African youth of today. The infant mortality rate in Kenya is no longer 50 percent, thanks to modern medicine.

Even with the AIDS epidemic, adults live longer too. And birth control is unpopular. Kenya's population needs more and more arable land—the already limited supply of which has been shrunk by drought—to grow crops and raise cows on, which leaves less and less land for the king of the jungle and so on.

On the other hand, a modern young Ugandan, a journalist of Kampala (one of whose slim newspapers, *The Evening Times*, was coming out quarterly when we were there), told me he had managed to get through his coming-of-age lion hunt without reducing the lion population. He and his friends had one surrounded, late at night, and were closing the circle, *hoomba, hoomba*, with their spears raised. He was feeling, I gather, like an American Little Leaguer who prays the batter won't hit the ball to him, when he felt more than heard an enormous uncoiling whoosh go right past him in the pitch dark.

"I didn't say anything," he confided. "I continued to move in, spear up, *hoomba, hoomba*, as did the others. I believe that in this period many lions may vanish mysteriously from hunters in that way."

As to zebras, they look so zebraic! You'd think they might feel too boldly patterned—wouldn't feel up to it all the time. Everything black and white! You'd think an occasional one would be gray. But no, zebra-striped as you please. They bray, or honk—a quick harsh hee-haw-heehaw that sounds almost like a bark—when they're deciding to move to a different grazing spot and spreading the word. "They only *seem* to have such big rumps," said a woman in our Land Rover, "because of the horizontal stripes." She had brought along her teddy bear so he could see the wild animals too.

A giraffe running—that neck pumping loftily along over cantering legs—is like several animals at once, but highly coordinated. A giraffe has tremendous eyelashes—talk about looking down on tourists superciliously. An old elephant looks like two men in an elephant suit that is far too big. It knows only too well that it's an elephant, you sense.

> Grandeur, yes . . . my magnificent ears . . .
> But looming large isn't all it appears.
> It's fine when you want to trumpet and amble,
> But something in me would love to gambol,

Make mellifluous cooing sounds,
Proceed, for once, by leaps and bounds.
Would love—don't laugh—to peep. To be
Able to perch in the boughs of a tree,
To burst, in short, this frame of mine.
An elephant's more than just elephantine.

A baby elephant looks cutest from a distance. Up close, it is already wrinkled, and you realize that what makes an elephant's visage is the ears and tusks. The rest is saurian and chinless. But when all is said and done, a baby elephant at any range is damn cute. And close to its mama.

I'm what? An elephant? No.
I'm a little teapot. Mama said so.

We saw one that had no tail. "A hyena eat it off," our guide said. "When it was little. There will be problems. With the flies."

WILD FISH RIPPED MY FLESH

Let me qualify that. A wild fish ripped my flesh. If there is one point that Ney Olortegui, Amazon guide, would like to clear up, it is that people go overboard when they talk about man-eating fish. *One* small man-eating fish ripped my flesh.

Traditionally, tales told by explorers back from the Amazon are hard to swallow. Those fierce women warriors for whom the Amazon is named? Fabricated by an eighteenth-century Spaniard. Those three-hundred-pound catfish that will drag children to the bottom of the river and gulp them whole? Well, those do exist. We ate part of one that we bought in a village.

But I won't sensationalize the man-eating fish. There I was, dog-paddling in the Huallaga, an Amazonian tributary in northern Peru. Our raft, the *Yacu-Mama* (named by Ney for a legendary Amazonian monster that is said to abduct people down into the depths), was at anchor. Several of us explorers were in swimming. Ney had assured us we needn't worry about what he referred to as "my piranha."

As long as we kept moving, he said, the kind of piranha that frequents this stretch of the river would rather eat something dead. "People come here, they make a documentary out of the piranha. They take a cow, they shoot pictures until they drown the cow. They use special pipes from the United States to blow bubbles. They buy one of the stuffed piranha, put it in the water, and make its jaws move. Then they strip the cow, so it look beautiful, to the bone. That's false. That's why my piranha have gained so much fame."

Special pipes? This did not dispel footage of cow devouring that held me rapt in my boyhood. But another explorer was asking about something even worse: the candiru, a toothpick-sized fish that introduces itself (strange phrase) into one or another of a swimmer's orifices, spreads open its set of spines, and sets up housekeeping. Was it true, in fact, that the candiru had such a yen for any old human entrance that it was capable of swimming up the stream of a person urinating into the river?

"Oh, yeahhhhhh," said Ney. "They do that. Can . . . *dee* . . . ruh. But thass just if you not wearing a bathing suit."

So there we were, treading water, energetically, in the brown-green, pleasantly warm, unhurriedly inexorable current. And I felt a nibbling on my upper thigh.

The last time you visited a zoo, were you surprised to see someone jogging there? Well, that jogger was testing a safety device—located in his or her shoes. In 1999 in this country alone, over fifteen thousand runners were bitten by dogs badly enough to require medical attention. Hence the development of Roveroff, a tiny device that, when stepped on, emits a squeak that is too high for humans to hear but just the right pitch to repel dogs. Trouble is, that pitch also attracts owls—by giving them the irresistible impression that someone is running along stepping on mice. This year alone, five Roveroff road testers have been mauled, in broad daylight, by hungry awakened owls. So test joggers are now running past every kind of caged bird and beast to find a pitch setting that turns dogs away without stimulating the taste buds of any other animal.

I should tell you who we were: the Emerald Forest expedition, booked through Sobek, a California outfit that specialized—this was back in 1986—in adventure vacations. Seven hundred miles in ten days along the Peruvian headwaters of the Amazon, through the heart of the rain forest, from Chazuta to Iquitos, on a raft handmade out of balsa logs, cane poles, wood poles, chainsawed planks, and palm fronds. Eight Peruvi-

"I'll tell you where I got the idea," says Wade Beacham, the Dallas oilman who founded Rain Forest Fellowships Inc. "I took a fishing trip on the Amazon, and I saw how our native guides lived. And I got back to Dallas, and a friend of mine said he was worried about his son, who was off in college and wanted to be an environmentalist—save the rain forest. I said, 'I tell you what. Let's set up a program.' So now any Texas college student who's developing environmental leanings, and whose daddy has thirty-six thousand dollars to spare, can go spend a semester seeing, as Beacham puts it, "what the environment is really like. With these Indians down there, who kill and eat everything they can and chop down everything they feel like. In other words, the rain forest is just as much a jungle as the bidness world. These kids go down there wanting to hug a tree and come back mean as snakes."

ans and nine gringos, including the distinguished sports photographer Heinz Kluetmeier, my son, Kirven, then seventeen, and I, then forty-four. The three of us were doing a story for *Sports Illustrated*.

We made our way down the river from village to village. Very appealing people. Clear handsome faces with smiles for us everywhere. At one time in history, the agency charged with protecting the Indians fed poisoned candy to inconveniently situated Indian children, and the kids in one village ran from us, saying (according to Ney) that we were Germans who would kidnap them for their fat. They were giggling, though.

On the roof of the raft, we had chickens clucking and scratching. We acquired these chickens for the equivalent of nine dollars each in the market at Yurimaguas (where chicken feet and chicken heads were being cooked as snacks on braziers). One by one, we ate our chickens. We didn't eat the rooster—who crowed early in the morning, when Heinz didn't grab him and throw him in a sack first—until the last day. Ney identified with the rooster and pouted when Heinz sacked him.

We also ate fillets from horrible-looking catfish of various kinds, some fresh and some dried (the one portion I had trouble warming to

Reed Duryea ate a cocker spaniel puppy once, okay? He was told he had to do it—find, clean, cook, and eat a puppy—to get into Sigma Alpha Epsilon fraternity. "They sprang it on us in the last stage of initiation," he told reporters. "Doesn't everybody do something in college they wouldn't do today?" Yes, but what Duryea did caused his chapter of SAE to create an award in his name, which is presented each year to the coldest-blooded initiate. It seems that the great majority of pledges when presented with the puppy requirement say they would rather forgo brotherhood than do that to a puppy, and they are congratulated. Those few who are gung ho enough to undertake the puppy quest are led by helpful hints on a wild-goose chase, so to speak, until a light begins to dawn. Reed Duryea is said to be the only pledge in history who, before he could be stopped, actually went off into the night for a couple of hours and returned with the bones. Now he is running for Congress, in northern Virginia, and the puppy thing has come out. "Here's what is key," says Duryea. "It was a secret, sacred ceremony. Whoever disclosed this violated an oath."

was from a batch of insufficiently dried that I'd seen Ney's assistant, Julia, scraping maggots off of), potatoes and potatoish yucca, mangoes with lime juice, beans, rice, a vivid beets-peas-and-potato salad, various hearty soups (one of which was augmented by swarms of melting gnats one unusually buggy evening), and some red meat that one of the crew, when asked, said was "bi'ef."

"It monkey meat," said Ney. "They change the name to protect the innocent."

On the *Sports Illustrated* expense account (those were the days in magazine journalism), I bought a monkey, which we named Blanca. And a turtle who never got named, a little green parrot named Rosita, a puppy named Tipico (to replace the puppy named Inca, who got so sick we left him with some coca dealers we uneasily encountered), and a marmoset.

The marmoset needed no name. He was a pistol. In the face he looked exactly like a movie gremlin. He was smaller than an explorer's hand but had more attitude than any four whole explorers put together. He would jump down onto the dinner table, wade right through somebody's beans, and go headfirst into the lemonade. So during meals we kept him in a bag, where he expostulated like an arrested diplomat. One night he sat on the rafter above one of the gringos' hammocks and screamed, as if hailing a cab, until the gringo stuck up his hand and the marmoset ran down his arm to his armpit, where he spent the rest of the night. The marmoset and the little green parrot were about the same size. Finding themselves on the same rafter, they fought toe-to-toe like King Kong and the dinosaur.

Some of us are hiking through a stretch of rain forest with a man from the nearest village. Ney hands one of us a guava fruit, he bites into it, passes it back to me without looking at it, I see it is crawling with worms. Local guy chops down a forty-foot palm tree with his machete at Ney's behest to get one heart of palm for salad. (I hit the tree a couple of licks and it's as hard as a railroad tie and clangs like metal.) We pass by a thorn tree with an orange impaled on it.

"What's that tree?" one of us says.

"Orange tree," says Ney.

"With thorns? What's that, over there. *That* looks like an orange tree."

"Thass an orange tree," says Ney.

"But the fruit are yellow."

"Yes. Grapefruit," says Ney.

"But it smells like lemon."

"Yes, lemon," says Ney.

Lots of other things happened. I had nightmares from sleeping with two captured macaws under my hammock. We went off into the interior, where I prevented (in my view) Kirven from getting lost in the jungle and he pulled me out of mud that was keeping me from crawling back to the raft. (Are we even? Well . . .) Some army ants I was trying to set fire to (at Ney's suggestion) bit me on each knee, through my rain pants, and on every knuckle of my left hand but one. Each bite felt like a blow from a small ball-peen hammer. Ney reminisced about his childhood in the rain forest:

"My father carry about five or six dynamites in his pocket, just for kicks. Sometimes he fish with it. Sometimes we fish with Indian poison: take mashed potatoes, put a little poison in them, toss them on the water, the fish hit them, pow! they jump around like crazy and you scoop 'em out before they die and cut their heads off so the poison don't get in the meat. My father was a gold prospector, a merchant, a lawyer. He came here from Spain in a small boat. He came to get the gold. He travel the whole jungle here cheating people. He left me with the Campas Indians when I was thirteen. He got into hot water with the chief of the tribe. 'If you don't trust me,' my father said, 'I'll leave my son here, and I'll be back.' I was one of forty-eight kids my father had with different women. He could care less about another son. I got scared with the Indians because this witch doctor, a lady came to him with the colic— she ate a lot of sugarcane and bar sugar. He tell that lady lie down, you got bad spirit in your stomach, and he cut a hole in her for that bad spirit to come out. With that the lady died.

"I was there six months. I escape on a two-log raft."

We caught piranhas, panfish-sized, from a dugout canoe, with cheap rods and reels, malfunctioning plastic bobbers, and hooks so flimsy the piranhas bit through them (if you held a leaf in front of its mouth, a caught piranha would take a semicircle out of it clean as a cookie cutter).

They were good fish to catch, the bigger ones fat and game as crappie, and sautéed with lemon they were oily but tasty. Ney caught a strapping piranha on a hook that had no barb or point and hardly any crook left on it. I don't know how he did it. But other than Ney, I am the only person I know who has used bits of piranha for bait, caught piranhas, eaten piranhas, and . . .

I felt a nibbling, as I say, on my upper thigh. I had been pecked at by fish before. I grew up being pecked at by fish, in waters of northern Georgia that were about the same color and temperature as this. I swam a few feet away.

I felt a sharper nibbling, in the same spot on my leg.

I thought to myself, *This is just a hysterical piranha attack. I won't give in to it.*

Then the nibbling got *fierce.*

And I hydroplaned back to the raft, yelling something that did not reflect well on me as an explorer: yelling, *"Fish! Fish!"*

Nobody else had been attacked by fish. The others were still bobbing around, and now as they bobbed, they were laughing.

I sat on the side of the raft. I pulled up the leg of my bathing suit.

And behold: ten or twelve spots of blood, growing.

"Sábalo," said Ney. A *sábalo* is not a man-eating fish. It is more or less what I would call a shiner. "This time of year, the dry season, those fish are starving," said Ney. "That is why. One hungry fish!"

Okay, I had been attacked by a charity-worthy baitfish. At least I had demonstrably been attacked. When you wiped off the blood, you could see the tooth marks. What kind of river was this, where you weren't safe from the *bait*?

At any rate, got to get back on that horse. I stood, semi-vindicated, and prepared to dive.

And something moved on my person. Went flippety flip on my thigh.

A cooler explorer would have said, "Heinz, get the camera." I said, *"Aauughhhh!"*

And it jumped out of my pocket! People witnessed this! It glistened red, blue, and voracious in the Amazonian sun! Eventually, even Ney admitted it was a small piranha.

Flip, floop, it bounced off the side of the raft and disappeared into the murk of the Great Brown God. *I had a live Amazonian piranha in my bathing suit pocket for five solid minutes and lived to tell about it!*

P.S. The piranha was not then, and is not now, a threatened species. The rain forest itself is—as more and more of it is cleared to make room for beef cattle and agriculture. The rain forest has always played an enormous role in keeping the earth sustainable by absorbing carbon from the air. Its number one enemy is the hamburger.

THE PIRATE CAPTAIN ADDRESSES THE CREW

You fo'c'sle folks'll be happy to know
The cook is now forty-six fathoms below.
That mystery stew he kept calling, risibly,
"Ratatouille" (*p'tooey!*) of his'll be

History. Has to be. As to the question
Of who among *you* might soothe our digestion—
You, you think, Louie? "I do a cold
Two-eel salad that I have been told—"

"*Boo-ooo-ooo-ooo!*"
True. Sounds too chewy. *"And too gooey, too!"*
Not you, Rousseau, 'twas you who so—
Yoo-hoo. Yes, you. 'Twas you, you know

Who jolly well made our bowels growl—
Your soup of greens and salt-pork jowl

Made *our* jowls turn aquamarine.
The sea, you'll agree, is sufficiently green,

And we sufficiently salty and swinish—
But look at the time, already nine-ish,
And who's to do dinner? Not you, Heinrich.
Was not the sea already wine-rich,

Wine-dark, however it goes, enough
Without that *Wieners mit zwei Weine* stuff
Of yours that caused us all to spew wurst
And sweet wine—what's so funny, Dewhurst?

Did those fried pies we tried, your pride
And joy, go over? Yes, over the side.
But look, an island! A bit of land which is
Sure to provide us with stuff for sandwiches!

Uh-oh. Here come some men, canoeing,
And growling and . . . it's as if they're chewing.
They've got big teeth and jutting man'ibles,
And spears, it appears. I fear they're cannibals.

Well, we'll repel 'em. They'll not dine
On pirate flesh, at least not mine.
My word, how awfully hungry they look.
Pity, we could have fed them the cook.

YOU CAN TELL A GOOD POSSUM

"This possum's got *pretty* ears," said my fellow judge Louis Moore, and I had to agree with him. Just a gut reaction. That is what you go by, mostly, on show possums, though to be sure, the Beauregard, the world's most perfectly developed possum, was sitting up there onstage for purposes of comparison. "You can just *tell* a good possum," says Basil Clark, president of the Possum Growers & Breeders Association of America Inc.

In a person show, Clark would win best of breed by default. "There isn't but one Basil," says his wife, Charlotte. He has a Coldstream Guards mustache, a bald head, a potbelly, and, usually, a doleful expression. He wears a cowboy hat, snakeskin boots, and a hand-tooled belt buckle with his name and a pair of possums on it. He says, "I was the only one who flunked subcollege English at Western Carolina College, but I am the only one from that class who ever got paid for saying anything." Talks about the possum are what he gets paid for. He says that a possum will fold the white part of its ear down in the winter to hold in the heat and stick it up in the summer to catch the sun. I don't know whether that is true or not, but I didn't need to know, to judge possums. I gave this one a full five points on "Ears."

There I was, at the annual PGBA International Possum Show at the Chilton County Fair, which takes place outside Clanton, Alabama. I was down on my hands and knees in the pine shavings on the floor of the livestock show building, trying to get a good view of a domesticated possum's feet. I wasn't even sure what a good-looking possum's foot looked like. I did know that the tail ought to look clean. A possum's tail looks bad enough without being scruffy and stained; a conscientious possum owner will not only shampoo his possum's fur before a show but also take some kind of strong cleanser to its tail. The night before,

Dr. Kent Johns, a leading owner in Clanton, had come to the back door of his house dangling a bubbly possum (shampoo was still foaming on it) by the tail and asked his wife for some Bon Ami. "Nobody uses Bon Ami anymore," she said. She gave him some Comet.

Why was I judging possums? you may wonder. Some months before, my curiosity was stirred by a story in the Nashville *Tennessean* under the headline "Eat More Possum: No Joking Matter to Some."

I had seen "Eat More Possum" bumper stickers and tags around the country, and as a boy I had often come upon a possum stretched out unconscious or dead on the sidewalk, and I knew that a possum had gotten into my mother's air conditioner in the middle of a recent Saturday night in Georgia. He made a noise like a burglar putting an aluminum ladder up against the house, she said. She had to call a policeman to coax the possum out. "I went off to teach Sunday school the next morning just knowing I was going to say 'possum' instead of 'Matthew' or 'Mark,'" she said.

But I had never heard of Basil Clark, who along with some others, *The Tennessean* reported, was developing the notion that possums were animals whose time had come. The story said the PGBA had some forty thousand members, about a hundred of them actual growers and breeders. One of the latter, Curtis V. Smith, a member of the Alabama legislature, was quoted as saying, "We're just at the beginning of this thing. If it opens up as a supply of protein, it could be very valuable." Smith and Clark were said to envision possums as the answer to the world food problem. "You can communicate with people with the possum," said Smith. "You give them something to believe in. You give them something to eat."

I wanted to know more. I called Clark and asked him when the next possum show was. In the fall, he said. He wasn't falling all over himself in response to my query. "There . . . uh, really is a show, isn't there?" I asked.

There followed the quality of pause that might follow if you were to ask the commissioner of baseball whether there really was going to be a World Series.

The greatest testament to the possum is that it has survived since before the Ice Age and spread itself wider and wider, in spite of the many natural enemies before which it falls prostrate: "playing possum" is not a stratagem; it's a fainting spell. The first Frenchman ever to meet a possum—René-Robert Cavelier, Sieur de La Salle, in 1679—killed it with a stick. Then he killed the second one he met. He hung them both from his belt and walked back to camp. They appear, pendant, in the painting *La Salle at the Portage*, by Arthur Thomas, now hanging in the courthouse of St. Joseph County, Indiana. I would like to think that after La Salle went to bed that night, the possums came to and walked off with his belt, pants, and all, but history does not tell us that.

When you consider that in 1555 the Englishman Richard Eden described the possum as a "monstrous beaste with a snowte like a foxe, a tayle lyke a marmasette, eares lyke a batte, handes lyke a man, and feete lyke an ape"; that Basil Clark has called the possum an evolutionary link one step up from the duck-billed platypus, between cold-blooded, egg-laying reptiles and higher warm-blooded, live-bearing mammals; and that "Yes I can" might be translated into Latin as *Ita possum*, it's a wonder possums aren't taken more seriously.

The first possum my then wife, Joan Ackermann, ever saw, she ate part of. As many possums as I had seen, I had never tasted one. When we walked into the back room of Barron's Restaurant, in Clanton, there on the table, surrounded by sweet potatoes, was a fresh possum. It was a former show possum of a prominent owner named Don McAfee that had lost part of its tail somehow and thus became available.

Since that night, I have often been asked what possum tastes like. The question is vexing. It is as difficult to put a taste into words as it would be to manufacture ice cream the flavor of, say, a *New York Times* editorial. Let me begin by saying what this baked possum looked like. A baked cat. I guess you could say it looked like many another baked small animal, but when I saw it, I thought, *That looks like a baked cat.*

There were two tables, set up in the shape of a T, as for a modest banquet. Joan and I sat at the head table, whose remaining seat was reserved for Basil Clark. At the other table were seated a small party of Clanton citizens. They seemed like nice folks.

So I assumed it was possum. But our hosts seemed to be holding back, as if waiting for some possibly untoward reaction. Perhaps other out-of-town guests had tasted possum in such a setting and bolted from the room. I noticed that McAfee ordered steak. But then it had been his possum.

Many people disdain the possum as food on the grounds of what it eats (just about anything), but how about the pig, the lobster, and the free-range chicken? And I am not a picky eater anyway, especially when I am sampling something proposed for the world's hungry. Maybe possum would be a little gamy. I was game. Why, then, did I feel uneasy?

I don't want to sound like a skittish person, but sometimes a situation strikes me as just slightly unsteady enough that I begin to anticipate an ontological shift. In this case, I began to wonder whether there was such a person as Basil Clark. Maybe the possum would rise up, begin to dance, and become him; or Clark, when he appeared, would be the Almighty or somebody and tell me, "You have been living a dream. In the real world, possums are Life." And then the possum would dance. You never know, on the road, what you are getting into.

Then Clark arrived. He was wearing his hat, boots, mustache, and possum belt. He was of less than medium height and stooped. Answers to several of my questions had been deferred until his arrival. In a regrettable lapse of dinner-table taste, especially in light of what was on the table, I had mentioned that my research had suggested that possums picked up a lot of parasites. "Oh, chiggers and ticks," McAfee had said. "They're not parasites; they're natives. But you better wait for Basil to give you the story on that."

Now Basil trudged across the room amid expectant silence and took his seat next to me. He sat there hunched and gave me a sidelong look. Then he looked away. "I attended Western Carolina College, where I was served a diet of green eggs and dried baloney," he said, "and it stunted my growth."

With that, McAfee began to carve his late possum, which Mrs. McAfee had parboiled for half an hour and then basted while baking it with the sweet potatoes. The possum carved easily. "This is not the little old black possum that roams the wood," said McAfee. "This is a registered possum."

"A registered possum is a better possum," said Clark. "Put that first, and everything else falls into place. Other day there was a long-distance call at the post office. They handed the phone out the window to me. It was a doctor at the University of Ohio, wants to come down and contract possums. Do embryological research on 'em. And psychological. Been using possums in the space program. The valves in their hearts are like a squirrel-cage fan.

"The fat in possum," he went on, "is polyunsaturated—clean your arteries like a Roto-Rooter. There's a husband-and-wife team working on that right now. A possum cools himself in the summer like an automobile—pumps his blood into the tail and licks it and the blood flows back into him cooled.

"Got to kicking this thing around in 1968. Incorporated in 1971. It just come time to register a possum. Had a lawyer said we couldn't do it. I said, 'They register horses, don't they?' I said, 'They register cats and dogs.' I said, 'We done put a man on the moon, you mean to tell me we can't register a possum?' Got another lawyer.

"We got to get the eagle off the national emblem and put the possum up there where it belongs. There's many a person in the United States that between '29 and '48 would've starved to death if it hadn't been for the possum. Had a dog named Katy—me and old Katy, Uncle Billy, Uncle Buck, and Uncle James would go out, and when six or eight other people were chasing the same possum, that's how you could tell that times were hard."

One more point: "You got to know when to breed a possum. You've seen a possum dead in the road, grinning like he knows something nobody else knows? When that grin turns to a smile, it's time to breed."

Possum was like dark meat of chicken, only stronger-tasting and looser on the bone, and stringy, like pork. I want to say, altogether, about like armadillo, but the only way I've had armadillo is fried.

I next saw Clark at the Clanton Drive-In Theatre, which he manages and lives next door to in a mobile home. He got out a big floppy briefcase full of PGBA materials and opened it on the counter next to the popcorn machine. "There's a bigger generation gap between me and my son Frank," he said, "than between me and Jesus Christ. Animals are dying out. People can't afford to devote two acres per animal to raising cattle. Ten years from now, when you see a cow and a calf, it's going to be in the zoo. When you eat animal protein, it's going to be possum." He produced a letter from Samuel Taylor, food for peace officer, U.S. Agency for International Development, mission in El Salvador, which said in part, "Here in El Salvador . . . possums are considered a delicacy among the rural populace. At the same time, the prevalence of protein/caloric malnutrition is estimated at over 70 percent in the age group under five. Many people still think I am joking when I try to sell the idea that possums could be an added source of protein for many rural families. What I need to get for more acceptance of the idea is scientific data. Could you send me . . ."

I felt bad about certain doubts I had still harbored about the PGBA. Clark showed a picture of himself, several possums, and a class of schoolchildren. "Possums are educational," he said. "I've had people in the association say, 'Basil, I believe you're *serious* with this thing.' He shook his head. " 'You *believe* I'm serious!' You know *vision* is what separates men from the animals. I studied to be a doctor. I could always see things other people couldn't see, even in a microscope. But I couldn't pass English. If I had, I'd be a doctor; the worst thing I coulda done. Doctors ain't got time to do anything."

Next day was show day. "You might have to judge," Basil said, so we went out to look at possums. In the first year of the PGBA, he said, people went out into the woods and rounded up the best-looking "range" possum they could and fed it for a while. "How you going to tell a good possum when you haven't got any good possums?" he said. "We just picked the best we had and named him the Beauregard and judged the others by him. I'd rather have the Beauregard than the world champion."

But then a Mrs. Wilson in Wetumpka, Alabama, was found to have produced a better possum. "She's the one bred the red on 'em," said Curtis Smith, who owns the current Beauregard and also the world champion and whose farm outside Clanton we visited. Curtis is a big old solid man who played walk-on end for Auburn in the early 1950s and looks like he might be chewing tobacco even when he isn't. "We got three from Mrs. Wilson and then started moving toward a larger, more domesticated animal."

We went out back of Smith's barn, and he started pulling possums out of homemade wood-and-chicken-wire cages. "He knows which ones you can pick up and which ones you can't," said Clark. "I don't like to mess around with another man's possums."

"When you wake them up, they're like anybody else—grouchy," said Smith.

"That's old Beauregard there. No, that's old Stonewall, I guess. See those teeth? They'll cut your finger off just like with the snips." He took out Stonewall II, the world champion, and started grooming him vigorously with a hairbrush. "That possum has been in *National Geographic* and on *To Tell the Truth*," said Basil.

"He's been breeding," said Curtis. "He looks a little poor."

"I think that's the best way to lose weight," said Basil.

I asked Curtis whether he thought possums were very intelligent. "They're intelligent if they have to be," he said. "They'd rather just mosey along."

I asked him whether his possums knew him. He seemed to muse. "I got no way of telling," he said.

"Number one rule," Basil announced at the show the next night, "any possum that bites a judge twice will be disqualified." Kent Johns, the town doctor who works himself half to death treating people with or without money, got bit by one of his possums. He said it was a considerable nip, and he should know. He takes in hurt animals—eagles, owls, skunks, woodchucks—and nurses them back to health. "I've been bit by a lot of things," he said.

Joan Ackermann was named Miss Possum International—international because she is from Cambridge, Massachusetts. She was substituting, it must be said, for the local Possum Queen, who had discovered boys and got a date. "We had a hard time getting a Possum Queen to begin with," Basil said. "Then I came up with a prize they couldn't turn down, something their mama made 'em get in for—an eight-pound bucket of pure lard. A Miss Possum is chosen on personality, looks, and poise. Poise is how they hold a possum." Joan held them by the tail. Basil said he was going to get her on the Carson show.

I found that the other two judges and I tended to come up with very nearly the same point totals from possum to possum. "See," said Basil, "you can just *tell*."

One of Dr. Johns's possums, whose name I never caught, won best boar possum, and Pat Cargile's Miss Pollyanna Possum ("We call her April around the house") repeated as best sow. Forty possums were entered, all of them from Alabama. A leading owner from Florida had been unable to appear. "They feed 'em mangoes down there," I was told. In Alabama, they tend to feed them Jim Dandy dog food.

The last International Show was criticized as not entertaining enough for fairgoers watching from bleacher seats. "We're not here to entertain," Basil snapped. "We're here to judge possums." At this show, people enjoyed coming up to talk about the possums. Somebody claimed that his "grandparents used to catch a bunch of possums, turn them loose in the mulberry tree in the backyard, and tie a dog to the trunk. We'd have a dozen or fifteen possums in the tree fattening up on berries, and when we needed one we'd go out and shake a limb or shoot one."

A lady described her emotions on seeing a possum in the Clarks' living room. "One of them came walking in there and I jumped up on Charlotte's couch, feet, shoes, and all. 'He ain't going to bother you,' they said. 'No, I ain't going to let him bother me,' I said."

None of the show possums played possum—or "sulled," as they call it in Alabama. "I've known possums the last fifty years," said a man, "and some possums sull and some won't. If he's been handled, he won't sull. He'll bite. I've had as many as six or eight in a sack at one time. I love possums."

Dorothy and Horace Goodman, from Columbus, Georgia, had driven over a hundred miles to the show for a reason. They wanted to replace their pet possum, Punky-Pooh, which had died. "He got mail at Christmas," said Mrs. Goodman. "He was a wonderful pet. He had his own little bed. He'd go to the bathroom in the bowl and wake up by an alarm clock. He ate bacon and cookies. My daughter found him in the yard, just laid out. At first she threw him in the garbage can. We didn't recognize it was a little possum till we got to looking at his feet. His tail was peeled down like a banana. A dog had got ahold of him and peeled him. But he revived."

"When I was a boy," said Clark, "the only thing in the world I'd have to look forward to was when I'd be big enough for someone else to carry the possum bag when we went on a hunt. Now look where possums have got me. You know the principle of Occam's razor: the solution to a problem is always real simple. Possum's simple."

THANKSGIVING EVE: WHAT HAPPENED IN THE WOOD

(Adapted from a dramatic reading, first performed, with musical and sound-effects accompaniment, on *A Prairie Home Companion*.)

> (*"Over the River" tune begins, fades.*)
> "Over the river and through the wood—
> Doesn't this forest make you feel good?
> This fresh-smelling air and fine autumn light
> Will help us to work up an appetite!"
> Enthuses Dad. Whereupon, he
> Skids on a slick spot, into a tree.
> (*Crash, bang, hung up.*)
> "We should have gone *around* the wood,"
> Says Mom. "I think I *said* we should."
> "The song," says Dad, "distinctly says *through*."
> "Yes," says Mom, "but I might remind you
> That songs don't give GPS, by and large.
> In the song, I recall, a horse was in charge."

Dad turns around to grumble at us,
"We'll be off in a moment, why all the fuss?"
The car is making a hung-up noise
   (*Hung-up noise.*)
And I'm in a pile with the girl and the boys—
Vera, Chuck, Dave, each one a brat.
I, by the way, am Herkey, the cat,
The family's only rational member.
This is like my ninth November
With these people. I want you to know
That every Thanksgiving, all of us go
To Grandma's house, and something goes wrong—
Which they'd never survive, if I weren't along.

When weird Uncle Bert was about to sell Dad
Some weird investment that had to be bad,
I slipped right up next to old Uncle Bert,
Purred, rubbed his pant leg, and gave him a squirt.
When a mob of cousins jumped Chuck and Dave,
For no particular reason, save
That they, understandably, just couldn't stand 'em,
I waded in slashing and made 'em unhand 'em.
When Vera poured gravy on infant Eugene,
I sprang into action and licked the boy clean.
At the moment, however, while trying to dis-
Entangle myself, I do nothing but *hissss*.
   (*Hiss sound.*)
Dad says, "What's the matter, Herkey?"
"I'll tell you what," says Mom. "A turkey!
Two turkeys! More turkeys! Up on our hood!
We should have gone around the wood."
   (*Gobbling.*)
"Well, I'll be darned," says Dad, "a flock
Of turkeys, and . . . they're trying to talk!"
"Turkeys can't talk!" the children exclaim.
Ordinarily, I'd say the same,

But as to these turkeys surrounding our car,
It does appear that, yes, they *are*.
    (*Gobbling.*)
Ten or fifteen tough-looking toms.
I'm a tom, too, but—uh-oh, now Mom's
Insisting Dad *do* something. That's never good,
Especially when we're trapped in a wood.
It's up to me, so here goes this:
I arch my back and give a *big* hiss.
    (*Hiss sound.*)
"Herkey!" Dad tells me. "That doesn't help."
But it does. One turkey responds with a yelp
    (*Turkeyish yelp sound.*)
That seems downright communicative.
Calm, reassuring. Their leader. I give
Him back a calm, reassuring meow.
    (*Meow.*)
The breed of cat he's dealing with now—
A cat whose full name is Hercules—
Won't lose his head in a bunch of trees.
I puff myself up, profoundly bouffant.
"My friend," I growl, "I don't think you want
To take on the raising of Dave, Vera, Chuck,
So be a good fellow and get us unstuck."

At that, he nods, and turkeys *abound*,
Converging upon us from all around.
"This whole thing," says Dad, "seems strange.
Is it something that turkeys somehow could *arrange*?"

"Oh gosh," whispers Mom, "what if—if they
Search the cooler? Tomorrow's entrée . . ."

But no, with the force of their presence the flock
    (*Gobbling.*)
Take hold of our car and begin to rock

And flap and jiggle us free of the snag
That had us hung up.

                      I don't mean to brag,
And the folks, of course, are oblivious that
They're saved once again by a sensitive cat,
But animals know when they are in sync,
And that alpha turkey, he gives me a wink
As tom to tom and turkey to cat.
We know what we know, essentially that
I want no part of him, and he
Ain't eating any of me.

Perhaps we've even influenced the diet
Of the folks in the car. They're awfully quiet,
As turkeys make way and Dad drives ahead
Toward Grandma's house to be well fed.
At last we see we're about to clear
The wood—when back behind us we hear
A gobbly goodbye, whose subtext I'll bet
Even my people are
    able to get:
    (*Distant, haunting,*
    faintly minatory
    gobbling.)
"No hard feelings,
    good tidings to
    you,
But next Thanksgiv-
    ing, CONSIDER
    TO-FU!
Otherwise, be it
    understood,
You'd better drive
    around our hood."

> The Gourmet Horizons specialty food cata-
> log is advertising a new freeze-wrapped
> mail-order item it calls "perky turkeys."
> Instead of slicing up one huge, bland, dry
> lunker of a gobbler for your whole Thanks-
> giving crowd, you can serve each person
> around the table one small young tender
> bird, which has been deboned, smoked over
> smoldering cranberry bushes, and marinated
> in applejack. Because these little individual
> turkettes have been kept tightly confined all
> their brief lives, like veal calves, none of their
> meat is darker than pink. PETA, the animal
> rights group, has denounced the market-
> ing of "turkey tots" who have "never had a
> chance to experience any sort of animal exis-
> tence," but Gourmet Horizons says that de-
> mand for perky turkeys, at $9.95 apiece, has
> far exceeded expectations.

The kids break our silence: "You were a-scared!"
"Was not! *You* were!" Their teeth are bared.
"For once," cries Dad, "*please* put a lid on!"
"Did you notice?" says Mom. "That stuff we slid on—
Chucky! Vera! Stop biting Davy!—
It smelled like us. And sort of like gravy."
(*Ghostly gobbling fade-out, resumption of "Over the River" tune.*)

COME BACK TO NEW ORLEANS! (2007)

Where else would I breakfast on oysters and beer and feel just fine about it? This is my eighth trip to New Orleans since Hurricane Katrina nearly killed the city. For a good while after that flood, New Orleans *smelled bad*. Can you imagine? I mean, not funky bad. Deadly bad. But as I walked over here this morning to Felix's oyster bar, which has finally reopened, I inhaled a bouquet compounded of olive salad, tropical blossoms, fresh mule manure, and just a hint of something else—rosemary? My head is pulsing slightly from last night, but it's pulsing rhythmically, because of what I would not get out of it, even if I could—the refrain a gospel group, the Dynamic Smooth Family, sang yesterday, over and over, in the gospel tent at Jazz Fest:

One morning, I woke up in a New Orleans hotel room, went into the bathroom, looked in the mirror, and saw to my astonishment that I had a big, thick gout of dried blood in the middle of my forehead. I said to myself, *I had better change my way of living.* I could remember doing several things the night before, but not, for the life of me, being shot. It was Winston Churchill, I believe, who said that the most exhilarating experience in life is to be shot at and missed. But to be shot at and hit and have no recollection? Especially if you're a writer. You need the material. If you're a writer, there's no point in getting shot if you don't remember what it was like. But then I turned on the light and looked closer. I had not been shot. I had just slept on my complimentary mint.

"There ain't no party like a Holy Ghost party, 'cause a Holy Ghost party don't stop."

Meanwhile, swirling winds were whipping heavy rain against the gospel tent, but nobody looked worried. People were where they wanted to be. "I ain't no refugee no more!" shouted the group's lead singer. "It's good to be back home! And alive! Don't you know somebody woke up this morning and didn't have the action in their limbs. But you and I, we're here!"

Yes we are. To tell the truth, it was a while after I woke up this morning before I regained the full action of my limbs. Yet I had not felt so virtuous since the last time I helped an old lady with a duck in her purse cross the street—which I did, once, many years ago, in New Orleans. The old lady wouldn't admit I was helping her, and neither would the duck, but I didn't mind, because I was delighted to be interacting in any way with that famous, ferocious character called Ruthie the Duck Lady. Ruthie isn't around anymore, but during the first post-Katrina Mardi Gras celebration in New Orleans I saw a bushy-faced fat man in a nun's habit singing "A Kiss to Build a Dream On."

In the gospel tent yesterday, a member of another gospel group asked, "Who all want to go to heaven when they die?" Maybe two hundred hands went up. "Who all *livin' like* they want to go to heaven when they die?" Only one hand went up.

The singer gave the one hand raiser a startled look. "What is *wrong* with you?" the singer said. The tent was still being buffeted by a raging thunderstorm, but that was nothing compared with what the city has survived. Leaving Jazz Fest, I had to wade through two feet of water and a big crowd wading in. Many of the sloshers looked already sloshed and pleased with themselves. Where else can you do good by misbehaving?

When I say "do good," I mean help keep a great American city alive. When I say "misbehaving," I don't mean, necessarily, pursuits that are, so to speak, nothing to write home about. Las Vegas's marketing campaign, "What happens here, stays here," wouldn't fit New Orleans.

For one thing, New Orleans is not good at mounting campaigns. "Laissez les bons temps rouler," the city's French-ish motto, relies upon the assumption that in New Orleans good times will roll if you let them.

And they will. Still. Just walk down a New Orleans street and watch out: if you're not careful, you'll be dancing.

Even now. Since Katrina, most of the hotels and restaurants and music venues have reopened. The parts of New Orleans that have always drawn out-of-towners are back in business. Take a look around the "Sliver by the River," as it's called—the French Quarter, the Garden District, the Warehouse District, the Magazine Street shops, Uptown, and the Faubourg Marigny—and you'd never know that in August 2005, the city was almost wiped out.

Except that you do know. That's another reason the Vegas campaign doesn't apply here: what goes on in New Orleans—jazz, gumbo, whoopee, disaster—doesn't stay; it gets out. The world knows that stretches of New Orleans are still mostly deserted, and that the people who live in the Big Easy still face hardship as the city's voodoo-and-corruption infrastructure slowly re-improvises itself, upon no bedrock but a beat.

The musicians, kitchen workers, oyster shuckers, buskers, bartenders, fortune-tellers, and assorted characters without whom the city would lose its savor are collectively an endangered species, because so many of them used to live in neighborhoods that were relatively inexpensive and now are gone. Where housing does survive, the shortage of it has driven up the rents.

You can do something. You can come to New Orleans and make merry and spend money.

Does that sound crass? Would you not feel right about kicking up your heels in a town where people are living in FEMA trailers, waiting for long-promised relief funds to come in, and mourning homes and family members swept away in the storm?

Consider this: you'll be indulging in what would no doubt be regarded as overeating, overdrinking, laughing too loud, and staying up too late anywhere else. In New Orleans, these activities are normal and essential. And they're a sound investment. Who can say what has become or will become of tax and charity dollars designated for New Orleans relief? But when you buy another po'boy or another Sazerac cocktail and tip the band pretty heavy at daybreak, you know (whether or not you will remember very distinctly) where that money has gone.

You don't want to be too much like Blanche DuBois in *A Streetcar Named Desire*, saying, "I don't want realism. I want magic!" So go look at the long stretches of New Orleans that were flooded out. I don't recommend one of the devastation bus tours, because some of your fellow tourists may not be as respectful as you are. Local people who come back to check on what used to be their homes are not gratified by the spectacle of people posing for pictures on what is left. For not much more than it costs to take one of those tours, a couple can get a map, rent a car, and drive to the Lower Ninth Ward and New Orleans East and St. Bernard Parish and Lakeview. It won't be as shocking as it was when houses were squashed together, cars were in trees, and the only signs of life were placards saying, "We Gut Houses," and heartbroken people picking through rubble for family photographs. In fact you'll see signs of revival here and there, notably in Lakeview, where upscale victims of the storm are rebuilding. That excursion will be sobering, though.

And when you return to the high ground that absorbed the least damage, you won't be in a bubble. New Orleanians are not shy about sharing what is on their minds. You'll be seeing defiant T-shirts—"Make Levees Not War," "It Takes More Than a Bitch Named Katrina"—and everywhere you go, you'll hear about the storm.

If the preservation of irreplaceable traditions of music and cuisine doesn't strike you as sufficient cause to frolic in that context, then do it for the penguins. You may think that coming to New Orleans for the penguins is like coming to Casablanca for the waters. If so, you have been misinformed. Check out the Aquarium of the Americas, down by the Mississippi River catty-corner to Canal Street. Other cities' aquariums surround you with just as many big flapping manta rays, swooshing hawksbill turtles, and darting fish of gaudy colors. The New Orleans aquarium is the only one I know of where the penguins are scandalous.

"Ernie and Fanny are twenty-five," says one of the penguins' keepers, when my wife and I get him going (New Orleanians love to get going, verbally) on the goings-on. "Snake is only six. Now Ernie has a nest with *each* of them. He's over four times as old as Snake—why she goes with him I don't know." Two other penguins start ramming into each other, pecking and flipper whapping. "That's Rocky and Dennis. Bunny has kicked Dennis out, for Rocky. Dennis pouts and mopes. Bunny is loving it. Come on, Dennis, you can take him."

Penguin triangles may be eternal, but New Orleans penguins are a special case: they survived the deluge. The aquarium's staff wanted to stay with their charges, but the police finally made them evacuate, and while they were gone, the generator that keeps the water aerated and temperatures correct went out. "It could have been fixed if we'd been here. Most of the fish died. When I came back into the darkness with a flashlight and counted all nineteen penguins . . ." His relief and the penguins' were mutual. "Somebody got ahold of somebody named Dan from Dallas, because he had a refrigerator truck, and he said, 'Sure, I'll come.' He was amazing, carrying dead sharks out . . . And he drove the penguins and otters to Monterey, California." Now they're back, all of them still alive except for one, Patience, who lives on (with her now widower, Tom) in the IMAX film about Katrina, *Hurricane on the Bayou*, which plays at the aquarium.

That film features scary-vivid storm footage, and it also lays out what an enormous undertaking it would be to make New Orleans secure from storms like Katrina or worse. The whole area around New Orleans, the wetlands that used to serve as natural buffers, needs to be reconstructed. You may want to devote some time to wondering how likely that is to happen, given how dysfunctional the relationships between the city, the state, and the federal governments were during the storm and have continued to be since.

A good place for reflection as you leave the aquarium is the peaceful river promenade known as the Moonwalk, after former mayor Moon Landrieu, who was popular. The incumbent mayor, Ray Nagin, cuts an elegant earthy figure. While watching him officiate in a Mardi Gras ceremony by the river here, I heard a young woman say, "I could just kiss him all day, and like it." That is by far the most wholehearted expression of enthusiasm for this mayor I have heard. This summer Nagin put the high crime rate in perspective as follows: "It's not good for us, but it also keeps the New Orleans brand out there, and it keeps people thinking about our needs."*

*Nagin himself began serving a ten-year prison sentence, for corruption, in 2014.

In fact it keeps a lot of people, who might otherwise enjoy coming to New Orleans, thinking about staying away. It is true, as the tourist bureau says, that the city's violent crime is concentrated in the underpoliced flood-blighted areas, where thugs prey on isolated resettlers and on each other. But crime has always been one aspect of New Orleans—and, okay, I guess there are others—regarding which out-of-towners should exercise prudence.

But not in broad daylight on the Moonwalk, where it's just breezy enough to make the day sultry in a good way. A man is sitting on a bench by himself, playing "Ain't She Sweet" on the trumpet. He gives his name as Alexander. He says he's been living in Morgan City, bayou country a hundred miles or so to the east, "since Katrina ran me out of town. It took my house, wife, family, everything. Picked up the foundation, I mean. I put three kids through college playing music here. Now I'm back trying to find a place to live. What used to be three hundred dollars is fifteen hundred dollars. But that Morgan City . . . I woke up one night, there's a banging on the front door. I got my twelve-gauge ready—'Who is it?' Well, it was an armadillo fighting a possum. That is too country for me. You ever watch a fourteen-foot alligator eat a raccoon? Whoo!"

Speaking of eating. From the Moonwalk, it's a short walk to Annette's* on Dauphine Street, which is the last word in untouristy. It's a

> Here's what's most distinctive about the annual Miss Outdoors pageant in Golden Hill, Maryland: in the talent portion, contestants sing, dance, twirl a baton—or some of them skin a muskrat. This rural area on the Eastern Shore is muskrat-trapping country, and there has always been a World Championship muskrat-skinning contest coincident with the beauty pageant, but in the last few years the two have begun to overlap. In 2003, wearing full makeup and sparkly earrings, seventeen-year-old Tiffany Brittingham deftly demonstrated how to separate a freshly killed muskrat's skin from its carcass with her fingers, knuckles, and a four-inch knife. In 2005, when Tiffany walked onstage with a muskrat slung over her shoulder, a man in the audience yelled above the cheers, "I want to marry you!" That year, she won the crown, and since then other local girls have followed in her footsteps. Says Samantha Phillips, whose muskrat-skinning won the talent portion this year, "It's not weird. You can be graceful and beautiful and well-poised and skin a muskrat. I can cook that big boy too."

*Now it's called Nosh, Annette having retired.

no-decor, lunchroomy sort of place where Annette Truschinger, originally of Morocco, can give you directions in French, Spanish, Italian, Portuguese, Hebrew, Arabic, or English and can whip you up grilled grape leaves and hummus or a Creole omelet. Her place has appeared in novels by James Lee Burke, and when Adam Baldwin was making a movie in town, he was a regular. "He said I made him the best scrambled eggs he ever had. I said, 'How can anybody screw up scrambled eggs?' He said, 'My wife . . .'"

As Katrina approached, Annette boarded up Annette's and evacuated. Drove around with her daughter, two grandkids, and a dog, taking a look at other towns. None of which they could stand. "The baby got New Orleans food in her soul. In Dallas, she say to me, 'Mimi, this food's nasty. When we going home?'" When they did, the restaurant was a shambles. "Looters—I'd be happy if they took food and ate it. They took food and smash it all over. Had to replace everything, all my refrigeration . . . Before Katrina, I did two hundred omelets a day on weekends. Now I hardly do anything at all." She's missing her old local customers. You can fill in for them.

But you will also want to eat more lavishly. Check out some of the finer restaurants: Cochon, Dick and Jenny's, and on Tchoupitoulas Street just out of the Quarter, August, in an old town house resplendent with chandeliers and fine linens. Try the green tomato pie with Creole tomato sorbet, grilled watermelon and heirloom tomato salad, Jim McCloud's rabbit cooked two ways over artichokes *barigoule* and squash blossoms . . .

Sound (whoever Jim McCloud is) decadent? Know ye then that August's owner and chef, John Besh, a New Orleans native, rowed a boat through the floodwaters trying to rescue all his employees, and he fed hundreds of FEMA workers with po'boys and gumbo.

Or go uptown to Casamento's. Do it for the fried oysters, the ultimate in fresh moistness enfolded in toothsome crunch. And do it for Joe Casamento, who spent his whole life living above the gleaming black-and-white-tile-covered joint founded by his father, never ate anywhere else himself, and died the night he evacuated New Orleans for Katrina.

Here's a post-Katrina banner that flew over St. Philip Street in the Quarter:

> THANK YOU VERY MUCH to all those who came and helped us in our time of need, to the volunteers who are helping us clean, recover and rebuild: to the police, fire and military personnel who rescued us and keep us safe, to EVERYONE who helped, we greatly appreciate everything everyone has been doing for us.

Maybe you have an old-dame aunt who's not like anybody else in the family; she's had severe health problems, but she's up and around again and full of zip, dresses with flair, has lots of unconventional friends, and is a great cook. Go visit her. She might not live forever.

P.S., 2016: No need to visit New Orleans for the sake of saving it anymore. Thanks to regular New Orleanians who refused to give up, and an of course crazily distributed influx of federal funds, and despite bad government, rapacious developers, and the BP oil spill, New Orleans is booming. You can walk places now that were iffy before the storm. There are more second-line street parades than before the storm. There are *lots* more restaurants. Check out Donald Link's empire: Herbsaint (house-made spaghetti with *guanciale* and fried-poached farm egg), Cochon (panéed pork cheeks with creamed corn and sugar snap peas), Pêche (the fish sticks! get the fish sticks!), Butcher (Moroccan spiced lamb!). The last three opened after Katrina. My wife and I got to New Orleans a couple of months after Katrina and kept coming back and making more friends there. We have spent the last four winters in New Orleans. Now we live there (with a hot-months outlet in western Massachusetts) more than anywhere else.

PART ELEVEN

DESSERT

PIE: THE QUEST

One afternoon, I was in the library of a small town in Mississippi, in need of some information, so I went up to the lady behind the desk there. Ahead of me were an elderly white man and a young black woman. The elderly man was saying, "Just hit me suddenly, you know, that I wanted somethin', and then . . . then it hit me what it *was*. That I wanted. It was pie."

"Well," said the lady behind the desk.

"A piece a pie. It's funny 'cause *uuu*-sually I don't want pie, this time a day. But I did, that's exactly what it was, that I wanted. A piece a pie. But I couldn't think who would *have* pie . . . this time a day."

"Uh-hmmmm," said the librarian.

"Miz Boyd a course serves extremely fine pie. But a course Miz Boyd wouldn't be open . . ."

"I was going to say," said the librarian.

". . . this time a day. So I said to myself, I said, 'Now, Wawltuh, where in town would they be liable to *know* . . . where a body could get a piece a pie."

"Mm-hm," said the librarian, looking thoughtful. "This time a day."

As a young man, Daniel Schorr invented the ice cream scoop as we know it today. Schorr spent most of 1934 hitchhiking west. In Cedar Falls, Iowa, he found work as a soda jerk at the drugstore of one Ewell Larkin. Thinking there must be some neater way of dipping ice cream, Schorr experimented in Larkin's workshop behind the store and came up with the little wiry deal that slides along the cup of the scoop to tump out the ball of ice cream when you press something with your thumb. Then he moved on westerly to another town. A reporter for *The Des Moines Register* heard this story and assumed it was an urban legend. But last week the *Register* reported that it checked out. An item in the *Cedar Falls Sentinel* actually credited young Daniel with the invention. And the patent for it is registered in the name of Ewell Larkin. "I suppose I should be a rich man," responded Schorr, "but then I would not have done the other things that I have done."

"I said, 'Well, I tell you where somebody is *liable* to know. At the li-berrry.' So I told myself that what I would do would be to just come on over here and . . ."

"I declare, Mr. Owsley . . ."

The librarian raised her voice: "IOTA?"

A faint voice replied from back in the stacks: "Uh-huuuuuuuh?"

"DO YOU KNOW WHERE MR. OWSLEY COULD GET A PIECE A PIE?"

"You mean . . . this time a *day*?"

At that point, the young black woman stepped forward and said, " 'Scuse me, but do you have anything about the army? 'Cause I got to get out of this damn town."

SONG TO HOMEMADE ICE CREAM

Homemade ice cream is utterly different,
Far more reviverant,
From that which you buy in the stores.
Homemade ice cream is something you eat enough of to feel for
   two days in your pores.

The peaches in homemade ice cream taste and chew like
   peaches,
For that is what they are.
And as for the milk and the sugar and egg whites, each is
Something Mama brought home from the grocery herself in
   the car.

And Daddy goes out and brings home some ice
And salts it down in the churn,

And each kid once
   or twice
Takes a turn at
   turning the churn,
Occasionally
   peeking in to
   learn
Whether the stuff is
   beginning to
   form,
Because the evening
   is certainly
   warm . . .

> The Lincoln, Nebraska, resident Andrew Hedridge's cat, Hattie, eats ice cream, as you can see on six different YouTube videos posted by Hedridge in the last three weeks. Not one of these videos has been clicked on by more than a handful of people. "Why don't they go viral?" demands Hedridge. "When did you ever see a cat eat ice cream so pretty! 'Myow,' she says afterward, and, again, 'myow.' I think she can *tell* nobody is clicking on her videos. But people say, 'Who *doesn't* eat ice cream? And anyway,' they say, 'ice cream isn't good for cats.' I say, tell that to Hattie."

You can't have any till after the chicken.
But considering the chicken, who's kicken?

The parents they may wrangle,
The kiddies they may roam,
But sitting round with their dishes of homemade,
They all make it home.

SONG TO PEACHES

Peaches reach us
Where we live.
Peaches teach us
To forgive
Impeachment, leeches,
Negative
Reactions, breaches,

And each es-
Cargot we have had to eat.

A peach is such a blessed thing,
However hard it tries to cling
To the pit, we cannot let it be.
It's up to us to set it free.

NO SWEETNESS IN A STONE

One summer years ago in Massachusetts, a heartily humorous friend of mine was over for lunch. I brought out dessert. She looked as if it were a slap in the face. *Watermelon?*

I was startled. Even, for a moment, dumbfounded. To be startled is a relatively unscathing gateway to learning, but I resist being found dumb. This wasn't a stereotype thing; it was actual, present, literal watermelon. Surely she knew I wouldn't serve her watermelon—or *not* serve her watermelon—*because* she was black. At her house, I had relished her fried chicken, her greens, her white beans simmered forever with ham hock. And I don't say this boastfully, but with other black people I had eaten chitlins.

Don't let me hear you all belittlin'
That ultra-down-home food, the chitlin.
You may find it infra dig,
But it worked wonders for the pig.

Watermelon, though. The moment passed, we were still friends, but she declined watermelon. I had some, but without enthusiasm, which is no way to eat watermelon. We joked freely about racial stuff, but we never talked about that.

Watermelon deserves respect. It's the closest thing in the fruit line to a pregnant belly, the most gratifying object in or out of nature to thump except a drum. Its deep red texture is almost confectionary, and yet what could be more natural? What other toothsomeness is like watermelon's melty-crisp midway between apple bite and slurp of sorbet? Do you regard it as a too-obvious, guzzly fruit, something people push their faces into and go *blblblub*, with nothing in it but sugar and water? According to the latest research, watermelon is extremely high in newly discovered nutrients, including lycopene, which is important for both heart and bone health, and citrulline, which the body converts into another amino acid that improves blood flow and "may prevent excess accumulation of fat in fat cells due to blocked activity of an enzyme called tissue-nonspecific alkaline phosphatase, or TNAP."

I am not quoting from the National Watermelon Council, if there is one; I am quoting one of the many independent health-conscious Web sites trumpeting the news that watermelon may combat cancer, Alzheimer's, and erectile dysfunction. And yes, it's sweet, but it's 92 percent water, so a cup of it is less of a glycemic load than an apple is. And water is good for us.

Furthermore, according to NationalGeographic.com, "Watermelon juice may be next 'green' fuel." Twenty percent of watermelons "have odd shapes or scarred rinds that turn off consumers," so twenty tons of watermelon may be left to rot every year in a single watermelon field. While agricultural researchers were experimenting with ugly-melon juice, extracting antioxidants from it, they got the notion that the juice could also yield biofuel. Watermelon farmers could at least produce enough home-brew ethanol to run their tractors.

What if Western culture treated the word "watermelon" with the same respect as "stone"?

Like a rolling watermelon, the Rosetta watermelon, leave no watermelon unturned, watermelon walls do not a prison make, if you live in a glass house don't throw watermelons, John Ruskin's *Watermelons of Venice*, heart made of watermelon doody-wa doody-wa, the Watermelon

Age, the Great Watermelon Face. Emma Watermelon. Oliver Watermelon. Everybody must get watermeloned.

James Dickey put out a collection of poems called *Into the Stone*. Let's move on to *Into the Watermelon*. On the cover, a sword (as in *The Sword in the Watermelon*) stuck into Watermelon Mountain, which has Melonwall Jackson carved into it on horseback. Poets think they are so hard and cool, getting down to *stone*. What's wrong with wet and sweet:

Psalms

He shall give his angels charge over thee, to keep thee in all thy
  ways,
They shall bear thee up in their hands, lest thou dash thy foot
  against a watermelon.

Edward FitzGerald

Awake! for Morning in the Bowl of Night
Has flung the Watermelon that puts the Stars to Flight.

Richard Wilbur

How should we dream of this place without us?—
The sun mere fire, the leaves untroubled about us,
A watermelon look on the watermelon's face?

John Keats

Far from the fiery noon, and eve's one star,
Sat gray-hair'd Saturn, quiet as a watermelon.

T. S. Eliot

Clear the air! clean the sky! wash the wind! take the watermelon
  from the watermelon, and wash them.

Theodore Roethke

Fear was my father, Father Fear.
His look drained the watermelons.

What other prize is associated not only with yearning but with traditionally blameless larceny?

It don't take a felon
To steal watermelon.
Ain't misdemeaning,
Just intervening
Between the rind
And what anybody's entitled to find
Inside.

I tell you, I'd
Rather hear a fat watermelon go "R-r-roach"
Than walk up to Susie with a diamond broach.
All you need's
A place to put the seeds.

I know a lady who, as a teenager, stole the *prizewinning* watermelon from the Neshoba, Mississippi, County Fair by carting it out in a baby carriage. Then, too, that lady is white.

One of Frederick Douglass's most notable speeches, writes William S. McFeely in his biography of the great black orator, "all came down to watermelons." It was in 1893 at the Chicago World's Fair. Douglass had been presiding over the Haitian exhibition, the only one under African-American control. Over at the food pavilion, the actress Nancy Green, like Douglass an ex-slave, was a big hit playing Aunt Jemima—fairgoers were sporting buttons featuring her catchphrase, "I's in town, Honey." Another exhibit presented natives of Dahomey, clad (some days shivering) in native attire and doing native things. The joyful singing of the Dahomeyan women was presumed to reflect the pleasure they must feel to be in America surrounded by technological wonders, but when the songs were translated, according to John Strausbaugh in *Black Like You: Blackface, Whiteface, Insult, and Imitation in American Popular Culture*, the lyrics were "more along the lines of, 'We have come from a far country to a land where all men are White. If you will come to our country we will take pleasure in cutting your White throats.'"

To similarly honor Douglass, and black Americans in general, the fair's organizers had declared an occasion: "Colored People's Day," with

Douglass as the featured speaker and—hey-hey, all you colored people—free watermelon.

By this time, Douglass, seventy-five, was more "antique abolitionist," as McFeely puts it, than the bold young fugitive from bondage who, in the words of Elizabeth Cady Stanton, "stood . . . like an African prince, . . . grand in his physical proportions, majestic in his wrath, as with wit, satire, and indignation he graphically described the bitterness of slavery." Once, when an audience hissed him, he had responded, "I am glad to hear these hisses. It was said by a very learned man that when the cool voice of truth falls into the burning vortex of falsehood there would always be hissing." Often in the course of an antislavery speech, he would move audiences to outbursts of laughter by taking on the voice of a white preacher explaining to enslaved people why they should be gratefully obedient.

Now, half a century later, slavery was officially gone. But in 1892 Americans had set an all-time annual record, which still stands, of 230 lynchings,* 161 of the victims being African-American. Thirty-year-old Ida B. Wells had launched an international antilynching campaign, after three of her friends in Memphis had been dragged out of jail and shot to death for defending their grocery store against people trying to drive them out of business. Wells and other up-to-date black leaders feared Colored People's Day would be a joke and Douglass the butt of it. They boycotted the occasion and urged Douglass to withdraw. Wells wrote that the fair's "horticultural department has already pledged itself to put plenty of watermelons around on the grounds with permission to the brother in black to 'appropriate' them . . . The sight of the horde that would be attracted there by the dazzling prospect of plenty of free watermelons to eat, will give our enemies all the illustration they wish as an excuse for not treating the Afro-American with the equality of other citizens."

Puck, the mainstream humor magazine of the day, ran a two-page cartoon by Frederick Opper, recognized today as a major comic artist,

*According to the most recently reported year-by-year statistics, which may be low. In 2015 the Equal Justice Initiative concluded that some hundreds more black people had been lynched since 1877 than previously recorded.

illustrating a poem titled "Darkies' Day at the Fair." Spear-carrying Africans in fancied native garb and sharply dressed black Americans with drums and tubas are shown marching together in a long procession, all of them looking big-lippedly identical except for their clothes. Then they catch sight of a watermelon stand ("The Darky's theme and dream") set up by "a Georgia coon, named Major Moon," who means to ruin the parade, "because to lead the whole affair / He had not had his way." Sure enough, all the "United Sons of Ham" swerve off to "gaily loot the luscious fruit / And lie down in the shade."

Douglass was determined to speak anyway. He began to read solemnly (as his mostly black audience was being handed leaflets titled "No Watermelon") from a paper he had prepared, "The Race Problem in America." In the crowd, young white men hooted and jeered.

Consider that at this age Douglass no longer looked like an African prince but like Jim Brown and Morgan Freeman rolled together, with a great white crop of beard and hair. Why would young white men feel free to mock him? Maybe they were readers of *Puck*—the *Saturday Night Live* or *The Daily Show* of its time. (*Puck* was published in New York City. In 1900, *Puck's* cover cartoon showed men with guns and rope passing an African-American family's house. A young black man points to them, puzzled, as an older one hustles a toddler away and a black woman holding a baby looks afraid. "Ain' this much bettah dan in de slav'ry days, Uncle Tom?" asks the young man. And old uncle answers, "I dunno, rightly. In dem times we was too valy'ble to be lynched!" This was titled, "In Georgia." In 1892, a black man was lynched in Port Jervis, New York.)

Douglass's great voice faltered. More jeering. He threw down the paper. He took off his glasses. His eyes flashed, his voice rebounded, and he held forth from the heart for over an hour. "Men talk of the Negro problem," he said. "There is no Negro problem. The problem is whether the American people have loyalty enough, honor enough, patriotism enough, to live up to their own Constitution." Thunderous applause. To listen to politicians today, you'd think "the American people" are the last word in everything. Douglass was saying, Come on, American people, show me something.

A great moment, as even Wells conceded. But why did Frederick

Douglass have to be framed by, and at odds with, watermelon? You know he liked watermelon, within reason. Everybody likes watermelon unless something spoils watermelon for them.

One of the earliest American motion pictures, *The Watermelon Patch*, shows black people who have stolen watermelons being tracked by white farmers with bloodhounds to a cabin where they're dancing the buck and wing and enjoying the melons "as only Southern 'coons' can." The farmers nail the doors and windows shut and seal off the chimney. When the merrymakers finally bust out through a window, each one is given "a kick or clout over the head to vary the monotony." But if that would put you off watermelon, then how about *The Chicken Thief* (1904), summarized by its distributor, Biograph, as follows: "From the opening of the picture, where the coon with the grinning face is seen devouring fried chicken, to the end where he hangs down from the ceiling, caught by a bear trap on his leg, the film is one continuous shout of laughter." Are you going to blame the chicken?

You know at least some of Douglass's listeners, rapt as they were by what had been described as "the magnetism and music of his wonderfully elastic voice," were also thinking, *Some of that watermelon would go good right now.* Where is the justice in people's being deprived of watermelon (not to mention: the watermelons of today are descendants of seeds brought from Africa) because others mock their appreciation of it? If anybody should be deprived of watermelon, it's the mockers.

How about those jackanapeses around the country who have made news by erecting effigies of President Obama with watermelon? In one case, the effigy consisted of just two watermelons in an empty chair— an apparently approving reference to the bizarre performance by Clint Eastwood, addressing an empty chair as if it were Obama, at the Republican National Convention. Why doesn't God turn the taste of watermelon to gall in those jackanapeses' mouths? And by the way, why did it have to be Morgan Freeman tortured to death in *Unforgiven*? I know, Clint avenged him, by shooting up the joint. How come it's never the black guy avenging a white guy who was tortured to death?

If you visit the city of Lincoln, Illinois, you will see that it honors Abraham Lincoln with a painted steel sculpture of a life-sized lengthwise slice of watermelon. Lincoln had done legal work for the founders, and though this was 1853 and Abe was just an ex-congressman, they named the town for him. According to local legend, he took it upon himself to give his namesake a christening—went to the market, bought two watermelons, carried one under each arm to the center of town, busted one open, and cast some of its juice upon the ground. Do you think Lincoln and whoever else was on hand threw away that melon, or the other one? They were white. They could relate to watermelon freely.

No watermelon was involved, but good humor was, when Frederick Douglass visited the White House for the first time in 1863. Douglass was an outspoken critic of what he saw as Lincoln's dilatory approach toward emancipation (an approach that eventually proved to be round-about). The president, he had written, "seems to have an ever increasing passion for making himself appear silly and ridiculous." Invited, Douglass found Abe seated in a low chair and immersed in books and papers. "At my approach," Douglass would recall, "he slowly drew his feet in from the different parts of the room into which they had strayed, and he began to rise, and continued to rise, until he looked down upon me, and extended his hand and gave me a welcome."

If that had been written from a white person's point of view, it would smack of paternalism—the looking-down-upon part. But Lincoln couldn't help being tall (not that he didn't *use* it), any more than watermelon can help being sweet. What if Abe had served Douglass some? Maybe someday all God's children can generate righteous cultural juice from watermelon—as from the blues, and the concept jelly roll (would white Americans, acting alone, have come up with the concept jelly roll? Have Europeans come up with it yet?), and basketball above the rim, and every new dancing trend *since* the buck and wing. And let him who is without sin cast the first whatever. Aspersion.

MARK TWAIN'S PIE DREAM

Watermelon is not cold and hard like stone. Watermelon is like pie—messy, excessive, suggestive of sex. And pie is more interesting than watermelon because it has so many different things going on at once. Ought to be right down Mark Twain's alley. Huck Finn said there was nothing wrong with the Widow Douglas's cooking except "everything was cooked by itself. In a barrel of odds and ends . . . things get mixed up, and the juice kind of swaps around, and the things go better."

In a notebook in 1897, Twain described a dream he'd had. A woman with "round black face, shiny black eyes, thick lips . . . about 22, and . . . not fleshy, not fat, merely rounded and plump; and good-natured and not at all bad-looking. She had but one garment on . . . She sold me a pie; a mushy apple pie—hot. She was eating one herself with a tin teaspoon. She made a disgusting proposition to me."

He doesn't tell us what that proposition was, just that he responded to it "a little jeeringly—and this embarrassed her." He "made a sarcastic remark." Embarrassed *her*, did it? The dream goes on, even more embarrassingly for the reader who is begging Mark's unconscious to know a good thing when he sees it. But here, in the notebook entry, is how the dream ends: "My stomach rose—there everything vanished." Stomach rose but not to the occasion.

Remember that Twain is a man who, in *A Tramp Abroad*, calls a painting by Titian, of Venus reclining nude, "the foulest, the vilest, the obscenest picture the world possesses . . . How I should like to describe her—just to see what a holy indignation I could stir up . . . [T]he world is willing to let its son and its daughter and itself look at Titian's beast, but won't stand a description of it in words."

It's a beautiful painting, and Venus looks terrific in it. She makes every other Venus you've seen look like your aunt Irene. Good head on her shoulders, too, looking right back at us with a level gaze. Let's say Twain was mocking the world's hypocrisy. He wasn't really appalled by the painting, but by the limits on what you could write for the public back then. Still, there's something more than tongue-in-cheek going on there. Titian's *beast*!

Today I am in New Orleans, a city whose quite respectable women's marching societies—jolly parade dancers promoting sisterhood in corsets of all different sizes—include the Bearded Oysters (known for wearing merkins over their tights while parading), the Pussyfooters, and the Camel Toe Lady Steppers. So I am free to tell you what Twain found so shocking about Titian's Venus. She has her hand, in a friendly sort of way, on her mound of Venus.

Today we don't see anything wrong with that. And it's hard to think of anything wrong with any imaginable combination of pie and a good-natured woman. (Not that any male notion of female good nature is the gold standard, but it ought to be worth *something*.) Still, in America today the popular expression "hot mess" comes to mind. Mark Twain's dream was head-slappingly racist, in various analyzable ways, but it's hot. It might stand in for the American dream: the union of black and white, slave and free, Yankee dry and Southern lush—deflected by guilt, fear, and shame but urged, still, by desire.

If we're still saving room for pie, we're not finished yet.

SONG TO PIE

Pie.
Oh my.
Nothing tastes sweet,
Wet, salty, and dry
All at once so well as pie.

Apple and pumpkin and mince and black bottom,
I'll come to your place every day if you've got 'em.
Pie.

ACKNOWLEDGMENTS

Thanks to Sarah Crichton, editor, and Esther Newberg, agent. And to *Garden & Gun* and *Wait Wait . . . Don't Tell Me!*, for which a good many of the items herein, in different form, were first written.

Printed in the USA
CPSIA information can be obtained
at www.ICGtesting.com
LVHW091138150724
785511LV00005B/399